Racial Fictions

Racial Fictions

Hazel V. Carby

VERSO
London • New York

First published by Verso 2025

The author and publisher extend their gratitude to all those publications in which earlier versions of these writings appeared.

The manufacturer's authorized representative in the EU for product safety (GPSR) is LOGOS EUROPE, 9 rue Nicolas Poussin, 17000, La Rochelle, France
contact@logoseurope.eu

1 3 5 7 9 10 8 6 4 2

Verso
UK: 6 Meard Street, London W1F 0EG
US: 207 East 32nd Street, New York, NY 10016
versobooks.com

Verso is the imprint of New Left Books

ISBN-13: 978-1-80429-993-7
ISBN-13: 978-1-83674-019-3 (US EBK)
ISBN-13: 978-1-83674-018-6 (UK EBK)

British Library Cataloguing in Publication Data
A catalogue record for this book is available from the British Library

Library of Congress Cataloging-in-Publication Data
A catalog record for this book is available from the Library of Congress

Typeset in Sabon LT by Hewer Text UK Ltd, Edinburgh
Printed and bound by CPI Group (UK) Ltd, Croydon, CR0 4YY

*For all my students who charted new ways of knowing
and remain constant sources of inspiration.*

Contents

Preface

Racial Fictions spans two decades of *diasporic* black intellectual life and thought from 2001 to 2021. I write as a black European of Caribbean descent and emphasize *diasporic* to signal my critical unease with and contradictory relationship to the field of knowledge in which I have been embedded for most of my career. While my academic affiliations have been tethered to universities and colleges in the United States, I walk lightly on its soil, refusing to become rooted, and my work has never been tied to the nationalist tendencies and exclusionary conceptual boundaries dominating how African American studies is organized as a field of knowledge.[1] On the contrary, my scholarly, imaginative and political commitments range across the histories, literatures and visual cultures of the multifarious black and indigenous communities of the Caribbean, Europe and the Americas.[2] It is important to me to insist on this sharp distinction between my formal affiliations and my critical imagination, though distinction is, perhaps, a word inadequate to describe what I have experienced, what I have lived, as a profound geopolitical alienation with the labels 'American' and 'British' deployed to erase or silence histories fraught with contesting geopolitical claims of boundaries, belonging and exclusion.

Written as critical interventions, these essays respond to entanglements of racialization, gendering and class formation as they were articulated in moments of political turbulence, crisis or ideological contention during these two decades. They are organized thematically into three sections: Part 1, 'Violence and

Violations'; Part 2, 'Boundaries and Circuits of Blackness'; and Part 3, 'Imperial Subjecthoods'.

The book opens with five essays addressing the forms of brutality and historical silencing that are legacies of settler colonialism, displacement, dispossession and enslavement, including the erasure of indigenous peoples and settler violence and in the preservation of the colonial history of New England; violence as spectacle in the murder of George Floyd by the police and the long history of lynching; the violations and killings of black women that take place out of sight during home invasions by increasingly militarized police forces in the US and the UK; and the racialized and gendered reconfiguration in the discourse of what constitutes home, security, self and other following 9/11.

Each of the seven essays gathered under the heading 'Boundaries and Circuits of Blackness' poses questions about what is at stake in the various scales at which blackness is circulated, consumed and performed: global, transatlantic, hemispheric, national, and as a commodity in the celebrity media marketplace. Here I interrogate how blackness becomes a historical, cultural and literary racial imaginary functioning as a medium of exchange and symbolic value for intellectuals and purveyors of culture.

In the final section, 'Imperial Subjecthoods', I seek to move beyond the dialogic critiques of traditional discursive practices, characteristic of the fields of knowledge defined as marginal, liminal or postcolonial, practices incapable of liberating our minds and bodies from the consequences of empire and contemporary Americanism: an aggressive planetary dominance ... which has unleashed forms of violence against people and the environment unprecedented in world history. I interrogate epistemologies of imperial and colonial modernity through archives and its creation of subjects and subjectivities, and engage the work of Stuart Hall and the Centre for Contemporary Cultural Studies. The final two essays, '*Imperial Intimacies*: Further Thoughts' and 'The National Archives', bring to a closure my self-critical reflection upon how researching and teaching the black diaspora have shaped me as a writer in search of the language of disruption and contradiction.

I write this preface in another historical moment when fascism in the United States has emerged from the shadows to dominate the federal government. No matter how frequently or loudly I protest, my dissent is held captive within a 'specious and dangerous imaginary' of economic, political and social life: a life in which the temporal and spatial scales which measure, sustain and rationalize what is supposed to constitute justice are heavily weighted in favour of an elite who have colonized planetary wealth and resources. This elite has garnered immense political power to govern, purging and destroying the federal government in pursuit of their rapacious and predatory forage for profit.

In 2023, the world's richest 1 per cent owned almost 48 per cent of the world's wealth while the combined wealth of the world's twenty-six richest billionaires, $2.872 trillion, was 'greater than the total goods and services' produced annually by most nations. In the United States disparities of wealth between rich and poor are vast: 'the combined wealth of US billionaires has grown by 88 percent over the past four years' and, as they continue to accumulate more wealth, 'they pay a smaller share of total US taxes.' Such extreme wealth disparities may not have been seen since the Gilded Age, but the current exploitative and extractive practices of the ultra-wealthy who govern far exceed the ruthlessness and lack of ethics of the industrialists once referred to as 'robber barons'.[3]

Whether, if, or how black history deserves to be remembered is again a contentious issue in the United States. From state legislatures to local school boards, increasing authoritarianism accompanies a steady erosion of academic freedom as restrictions are imposed upon what can be taught or discussed at every level of the educational system, from universities to elementary schools. Through increasingly vociferous and racially inflected attacks, members of the Republican Party, political operatives and activists at national, regional and local levels, with the support of right-wing 'think tanks' like the Claremont Institute, financiers and wealthy donors, have attacked the legitimacy of diversity, equity and inclusion (DEI) policies and pedagogic practices in higher education: the employment and funding of DEI offices, pledges by faculty and staff to commit to the creation of more inclusive environments, mandatory diversity training, and identity-based preferences for hiring and admissions have been banned.

A manufactured, carefully scripted, series of attacks on what is misnamed 'critical race theory' claims that teaching the history and contemporary legacies of racial injustice inflicts harm upon white students, creating political furore resulting in legislation that limits how, or whether, teachers can talk about the history of racism, and has led to the banning of literature by black authors from classrooms and libraries and to the rejection of courses in African American studies for 'lacking educational value'. In an essay published in the *Atlantic*, Lonnie Bunch III, secretary of the Smithsonian Institution and founding director of the National Museum of African American History and Culture, concluded,

> One can tell a great deal about a country by what it chooses to remember: by what graces the walls of its museums, by what monuments are venerated, and by what parts of its history are embraced. One can tell even more by what a nation chooses to forget: what memories are erased and what aspects of its past are feared.[4]

PART I.

Violence and Violations

1

We Must Burn Them

Anna Julia Cooper's collection of essays *A Voice from the South: By a Black Woman of the South*, published in 1892, identified the conflict over race as the central dilemma of her time, eleven years before W. E. B. Du Bois wrote that 'the problem of the twentieth century is the problem of the colour line'. Cooper argued that America's domestic racial formation was intimately linked with international colonialism and that the exploitation and oppression experienced by Asian, black and indigenous peoples in the US were an integral part of the imperialist ideology of racial hierarchies. She questioned why 'dominant meant righteous, and carried with it a title to inherit the earth', and identified appeals to manifest destiny as an attempt to justify consigning 'to annihilation one-third of the inhabitants of the globe'. Cooper also condemned the expansion of Western empires further into Asia and the Pacific. She believed, as Du Bois wrote, that the problem of the colour line was a matter of imperialism, 'the relation of the darker to the lighter races of men in Asia and Africa, in America and the islands of the sea'.

A different strand of black intellectual thought, focusing on racism and racist violence in the US as a product of domestic enslavement, developed almost simultaneously with the global account of imperialist and colonial exploitation proposed by Cooper and Du Bois. In 1904, Mary Church Terrell, one of the founders of the National Association of Coloured Women, published an essay which concluded that 'lynching is the aftermath of slavery.' A year later, William A. Sinclair, who was born into enslavement, published *The Aftermath of Slavery: A Study of the Condition and Environment of the American Negro*. Terrell and Sinclair used the term 'aftermath' to make the point that their own era was contiguous with the three hundred years during which people of African descent had been enslaved in America. Sinclair worked as a financial secretary at Howard University, had degrees in theology and medicine and greatly admired Queen Victoria, the British Empire and Rudyard Kipling. He believed that the 'blighting evils' of his time – 'mobs that torture human beings and roast them alive without trial; mobs who shoot down women and children; mobs who take possession of the streets of . . . cities, shooting down innocent coloured people and driving them from their homes; lynching and the reign of terror and blood perpetuated by the Ku Klux Klan' – were an affliction both to 'the white and the coloured people'. He insisted that this violence was rooted in the barbarism of US slavery, an institution which, 'bad and debasing as it was for the negro', was 'probably even worse for whites . . . for it stupefied their conscience . . . twisted and perverted their moral conceptions.' Sinclair did not mention the sufferings of indigenous peoples at the hands of white settlers and military forces; consideration of Native nations was excluded from his conceptual and historical framework.

'The afterlife of slavery' (sometimes hyphenated and sometimes plural) has become an increasingly influential way of thinking about America's domestic slavery and its consequences in the present. In *Lose Your Mother* (2006), Saidiya Hartman uses the phrase to describe the complex relation between the current inequalities and 'skewed life chances' that imperil and threaten black life, and the 'racial calculus' and 'political arithmetic' entrenched in the system of enslavement. Hartman developed the term in the sophisticated historical analysis of her subsequent work, but it has now assumed an autonomous existence, which no longer requires us to understand that the ways in which 'race' comes to acquire meaning are contingent on particular times, places, cultures and economies. The word 'afterlife' assumes an intergenerational existence, but it also grants immortality to racial logic; the term connotes a world without end, and even has a supernatural quality that stretches back to the Curse of Ham.

The 1619 Project, which contains essays as well as poetry and fiction, offers a 'new origin story' for the US, one that begins with the arrival of a ship in the British colony of Virginia with a cargo of twenty enslaved African people. The book itself is the culmination of a project by the *New York Times Magazine*, marking four hundred years since that first slave ship arrived in America. It attempted to show that 'the inheritance of 1619 reaches into every part of contemporary American society, from politics, music, diet, traffic and citizenship, to capitalism, religion and our democracy itself.' Though 1619 is an unconventional year in which to begin the national story, the project's aim – to expose 'the roots of so much of what makes the country unique' – places it firmly within the conventional narrative of American exceptionalism.

The phrase 'the afterlife of slavery' is often used in conjunction with 'antiblackness', a term that is also rarely interrogated, as if its meaning is obvious. The word has spread beyond academia in the last decade, helped by its lack of historical specificity. It can be seen everywhere on social media and in the mainstream press; it crops up in headlines in *Forbes* magazine, the *Boston Globe*, the *Los Angeles Times* and the *New York Times*. Its usefulness, however, is limited. Racialized exclusivity and national particularity ('antiblackness' nearly always pertains to African Americans) means relinquishing the possibility of forming alliances with other oppressed communities.

Academics in marginalized fields have made limited progress in establishing departments, programmes and centres for the study of ethnic, racialized and gendered histories. We have seen only modest increases in the number of black, brown and gender-non-conforming people among teaching staff. For the most part our intellectual existence remains siloed, with each field of knowledge having its own vocabulary and being organized into a discrete ontological formation. In *Silencing the Past: Power and the Production of History* (1995), Michel-Rolph Trouillot insisted that 'history is the fruit of power but power itself is never so transparent that its analysis becomes superfluous. The ultimate mark of power may be its invisibility; the ultimate challenge, the exposition of its roots.' University administrations boast of diversity, equity and inclusion, while behind the scenes they hold tightly to power, continuing to privilege the Eurocentric, settler colonial forms of knowledge that secure the marginalization of certain areas of study. Our fields are kept in constant competition for resources; as we scramble for scraps of funding, we fail to engage with, let alone expose, the roots of power. This leads me to conclude that the disciplinary borders and exclusionary concepts of contemporary academia have not only created new forms of silencing but are a betrayal of the roots of these disciplines: insurgent social movements which did not want to be incorporated into the academy as it then existed, but sought its radical transformation.

Exterminate All the Brutes, Raoul Peck's four-part film, situates the emergence of the land that would become the United States within an account of the global ambitions of European imperialism, using its ideologies and praxis of domination to organize the narrative: civilization, colonization and extermination. Peck takes his bearings from three works: Trouillot's *Silencing the Past* (1995, 2015) Sven Lindqvist's *Exterminate All the Brutes* (1996) and *An Indigenous Peoples' History of the United States* (2014) by Roxanne Dunbar-Ortiz. The film has been described as essayistic, but it would be more precise to say that it enacts these authors' historical analyses: their arguments are so deeply embedded in the film that it becomes an intellectual collaboration, an alternative to the intellectually segregated university departments that currently disseminate knowledge about race, ethnicities and indigeneity.

The film breaks with conventional documentary making in its use of scripted fictional scenes and animation, drawing on a rich visual, musical, literary and scientific vocabulary taken from a vast number of sources – everything from archival anthropological and scientific material to Hollywood films and Peck's own family archive. It bears witness to acts of brutality characteristic of Western European forms of conquest and Christian missionary zeal in Africa, the Americas and Europe, and traces the beliefs, dressed up as science, that produced and attempted to justify this brutality, right of conquest and dispossession. This means moving from the Crusades to the many genocidal wars against indigenous peoples, from atrocities committed in the name of manifest destiny and the Monroe Doctrine to the rabidly anti-migrant movements of our own times. The film does not limit its examination to extremist movements or leaders, although it features Jair Bolsonaro, Recep Tayyip Erdoğan, Boris Johnson, Marine Le Pen, Vladimir Putin and Donald Trump. The idea that US supremacy is seen as being ordained by divine providence is underlined by an episode showing American presidents speaking the words 'So help me God' when reciting the Oath of Office, immediately followed by an account of the entanglement of the US arms industry with the executive branch of government.

The *longue durée* of what Dunbar-Ortiz calls the 'inherently genocidal' impulse of settler colonialism is difficult to watch. *Exterminate All the Brutes* makes its audience witness many forms of colonial brutality: from the intimacies of bodily dismemberment to the technologies that allow death and war to happen at a distance. Peck refuses to conform to narrative linearity, rejecting the idea that the current resurgence of white supremacist and state violence can be traced back to a single origin. Instead, we move across time and place, between Europe, Africa, the Caribbean and the Americas. The film is as restless as the images of huge ocean waves that occasionally mark its transitions.

On 1 June 2020, a gathering of Black Lives Matter supporters in Lafayette Square, north of the White House, was attacked by heavily armed security forces from various federal agencies, including the US Park Police, the Bureau of Prisons Special Operations Response Teams and National Guardsmen. While dispersing the peaceful crowd to clear the way for a presidential photo opportunity, they committed human rights violations, including firing flash-bang shells, tear gas and rubber bullets. Seven months later, on 6 January 2021, television stations and social media broadcast a very different police response. Rioters carrying stun guns, knives, chemical sprays, baseball bats and flagpoles easily overwhelmed a sparse contingent of Capitol police and stormed the building. The police had been told to hold back and not to use their most powerful methods of crowd control.

Amnesty International documented 125 separate incidents of state violence against peaceful protesters in forty states, plus the District of Columbia, between 26 May and 5 June 2020. These acts were committed by members of state and local police departments, as well as by National Guard troops and security personnel from several federal agencies. Among the abuses recorded are beatings, the misuse of tear gas and pepper spray and the inappropriate and, at times, indiscriminate firing of sponge rounds and rubber bullets. In November 2016, the American Civil Liberties Union and the Leadership Conference on Civil and Human Rights called on the Justice Department to investigate the treatment by law enforcement agencies of peaceful protesters against the Dakota Access pipeline near the Standing Rock Sioux reservation (Peck includes footage of this in *Exterminate All the Brutes*). They used armoured vehicles, automatic rifles, acoustic weapons, water cannon, concussion grenades, attack dogs, pepper spray and beanbag bullets.

Other rights are also being suppressed. In 2013, the US Supreme Court ruling in *Shelby County v. Holder* removed two of the most powerful provisions in the 1965 Voting Rights Act, which addressed entrenched racial discrimination in voting: Section 5 required certain states to obtain federal clearance before changing their voting rules, and Section 4(b) determined which states had to do this. The Supreme Court ruled that the government was using an outdated process to decide which states had to get their rules approved. Since the judgment there has been a wave of voting measures aimed at limiting the rights of minority voters. The Brennan Centre for Justice reported that in 2021 alone legislators in forty-nine states drafted more than 440 restrictive voting bills, while nineteen states enacted thirty-four laws that made voting more difficult, for instance by introducing requirements for proof of citizenship or repealing the provision of postal votes.

The Spirit Lake Nation (Mni Wakan Oyate) and the Turtle Mountain Band of Chippewa recently filed a federal lawsuit challenging North Dakota's new legislative map, which, by means of redistricting, dilutes Native American voting power.

In addition to this suppression of the black and indigenous vote and of the right to protest is a national crusade to control historical knowledge. In state legislatures and on town school boards (consisting of locally elected officials), politicians and interest groups are advocating and legislating for the banning of books and of teaching that engages with racialized and gendered injustice. The advocacy group Truth in Education claims that children need to be 'protected' from the discussion of sexual and gender identities and from 'critical race theory' (CRT), a misnomer for any initiatives in state schools or state-run institutions that address past and present inequities or introduce anti-racist policies. Citizens for Renewing America offers an eight-page DIY guide to 'school board language' which promises to help those who would sanction – and potentially sack – teachers for violating these rules. No Left Turn in Education provides sample letters and petitions. This is a campaign of fear, targeted at teachers and administrators in public institutions. One group in particular is being called to arms: white parents of school-age children.

Mary Beeman, the campaign manager for the Truth in Education school board candidates in my town (all of them Republicans), summarized the threat: 'Helping kids of colour to feel they belong has a negative effect on white, Christian or conservative kids.' Our local branch of No Left Turn in Education warns parents about euphemisms for CRT that show that their children are being indoctrinated. These include 'equity, social justice initiative, systemic racism, critical race pedagogy, diversity, anti-racist, culturally responsive teaching and whiteness'. One of its goals is to 'expose CRT as an evil, divisive, Marxist, anti-American, ideology that calls for dismantling and replacing all of our cherished American institutions, including our constitution, our government, our legal system, capitalism, the nuclear family, religion, education, law enforcement, private property and individualism'. Heather MacDonald, a fellow at the Manhattan Institute, a right-wing think tank, launched a particularly vehement attack on the Art Institute of Chicago, accusing it of abandoning its mission as a guardian of Western art and deriding its director for stating that the museum's building is 'located on the traditional unceded homelands of the Council of the Three Fires: the Ojibwe, Odawa and Potawatomi Nations'.

The criticism that might be made of statements like this, which have become common in parts of the academy, including my own university, is that they are rarely written in collaboration with the elders of indigenous communities, and rarely make reference to the continued existence of these communities; instead, they relegate indigeneity to an eternal past while avoiding the pressing issue of indigenous sovereignty in the present. They obscure, rather than promote, attempts to expand our intellectual, cultural and geographical horizons, and to challenge our allegiances to home, department, academic discipline and nation.

History is written by the victors, but diligent and continual silencing is required to maintain its claims on the present and future. It is a mistake to believe that white supremacy is something nurtured and reproduced by extremist organizations and 'bad apples' in the armed forces and police. White supremacy is ubiquitous in the US. It operates in the most mundane aspects of daily life, in the economic order that decides who has what and how they get it, in the historical amnesia that makes some stories disappear, in the language we use to speak and name the past. Central here is the uncritical regurgitation of the mythologies of European settlement, the origin stories of the nation that are institutionalized at all levels of local, state and federal history and cultural memory.

In *Exterminate All the Brutes*, Peck discusses his own refusal to affect the pose of the 'restrained, moderate, balanced, judicious and neutral' film-maker. I too have broken with the conventions of intellectual neutrality in my work. His film prompted me to ask, not for the first time, how I, as a black intellectual, could think about the terms 'civilization', 'colonization' and 'extermination' and use them to confront the many layers of silence in the place from which I write.

I live on the north-eastern coast of the US in an Anglophile shoreline town. It is an excellent place from which to consider the ways in which a settlement with colonialism can reproduce the injustice and violations of white supremacy. The atmosphere in the town is one of preserved time; too content and self-satisfied with its sense of liberality, it denies the history of New England while seeming to embrace it. It seeks to draw visitors into a cocoon of English colonial history, memorializing the arrival and settlement in 1639 of a band of Puritans under the leadership of the Reverend Henry Whitfield. State and local authorities have legislated for the preservation of numerous buildings, four districts and the town green: there are five museums in historic houses, an energetic preservation alliance, and societies and foundations run by generations of residents dedicated to the stewardship of a very particular vision of the past.

In June 2014, the town installed a twenty-four-foot-long, six-foot-wide, fourteen-inch-thick pink granite slab into which is carved a replica of the covenant signed by the twenty-five male settlers on the *St John*, which was carrying them to what they thought of as a 'new world'. In stark contrast, a recent initiative by volunteers to memorialize what is known about the historical presence of enslaved people in the town has resulted in the installation of four-inch concrete cubes, each bearing a brass plate inscribed with the name given, by their owner or trader, to an enslaved person. The cubes are embedded in the sidewalks next to the few buildings where enslaved people are known to have lived and worked. Most people pass by without noticing these weathered, discoloured, dirt- encrusted and increasingly unreadable markers.

There is no town memorial to indigenous peoples, no mention of the displaced Menunkatuck, Quinnipiac, Hammonasset, Niantic, Mohegan and Wangunk who lived in the town from the mid-eighteenth century until at least the mid-nineteenth. There is no reference to the many groups of Algonquian peoples who inhabited this part of the Atlantic coast and its interior for thousands of years before the European invasion and colonization of the Kwinitekw river valley, or to their descendants who still live here. The only mark of indigenous existence in the town is a plaque on a gravestone under which lie the remains of a young male with a spinal injury, 'age 30–34 years', who lived between five hundred and a thousand years ago. The partial skeleton was uncovered on a construction site but remained in private hands until it was surrendered to the town, examined by the state archaeologist and students at Southern Connecticut State University, and reinterred in a corner of the Alder Brook cemetery in 2009.

Visitors to the town, which describes itself as 'the highlight of Connecticut tourism', can create their own itinerary, delivered to their electronic devices as they browse the town's website. The promise that they will be charmed by a 'quaint New England village' is, apparently, fulfilled. 'Charming' and 'quaint' are words I often overhear on the town green or in front of the historic houses or near the displays of colonial artefacts. The meagre paragraphs on indigenous peoples on the website make it sound as if they were essentially wiped out by disease before the arrival of English settler colonists. Only a perfunctory reference is made to the Menunkatuck, the small group of the Quinnipiac peoples whose homeland this was, and it's a reference that lends a patina of contractual legality to the English settlement: a deed, signed by Shaumpishuh, the Menunkatuck sachem, or leader, conveyed 'the use' of the land to the town's 'founding fathers'.

The website does not include any reference to the Pequot, the most influential and powerful indigenous community in the region until they were massacred by the English (a massacre so brutal that it must have influenced the decision of the Quinnipiac peoples to permit the use of their coastal territory).

The word 'quaint' suggests a comforting and comfortable relation to the past; it keeps at bay any of the anxiety or misgivings that could – that should – arise from the history of this land. What is experienced by tourists and residents as 'historic' is an assemblage of heritage for consumption, and what is meant by 'quaint' is the reassuring knowledge that there will be no confrontation with the violence and brutality of European colonization or its consequences for indigenous peoples.

As Andrew Lipman writes in *The Saltwater Frontier: Indians and the Contest for the American Coast* (2017), the 'duelling nations of foreigners did not settle [the Atlantic shore]: they unsettled it', transforming a thriving place into what Lipman calls 'a nightmarish landscape of death'. In 1637, two forces of English soldiers, one led by Captain John Mason and drawn from settlements in what is now Connecticut, and the other from the Massachusetts Bay Colony under Captain John Underhill, surrounded and fired on a stockaded Pequot village on the Mystic River, while their Narragansett and Mohegan auxiliaries stood at a distance. Each force entered through one of the two gates in a palisade protecting many closely pitched homes. Mason later claimed that his original intent was to 'destroy by the Sword and save the Plunder' – soldiers depended financially on the spoils of war – but, frustrated at meeting fierce resistance from Pequot warriors firing arrows through loopholes, decided, 'We should never kill them after that manner . . . We must burn them.' He took a log from the campfire and started to set the houses ablaze. His soldiers did the same, while Captain Underhill set a fire with a trail of powder at the other end of the village. The two fires met and became a conflagration.

On 29 December 1890, three hundred Lakota people were massacred by the US Army near Wounded Knee Creek on the Pine Ridge reservation in South Dakota. There are photographs. At first light on 26 May 1637, around seven hundred Pequot were massacred by English troops; 150 of them were warriors sent by their sachem, Sassacus, from the village of Weinshauks, to intercept the English; most of the others were women and children. Hundreds were burned alive. English troops encircled the perimeter and shot or impaled anyone who ran from the flames. Seven Pequot escaped; seven were taken prisoner. Two Englishmen were killed and twenty wounded. Mason considered the incineration and butchering of the Pequot an act mandated by God.

Underhill wrote that 'sometimes the Scripture declareth women and children must perish'. There are no photographs.

The massacre demoralized the Pequot, and sent a shock wave through all the indigenous communities in the region. The Pequot War of 1636–8 saw the English engage in total war. Their actions went beyond the murder and imprisonment of indigenous peoples to the destruction of the environment that sustained them: habitations, stores of food, fields of corn. Some of the sachems sought refuge for their people with other indigenous communities. Weinshauks was abandoned. Sassacus led the villagers west along the Mishimayagat shoreline pathway towards Quinnipiac, hoping to regroup and take a stand against the English there. Reinforced by a contingent of 120 troops from the Massachusetts Bay Colony, the Connecticut force set off in pursuit. The walk I take each day follows the route of the Mishimayagat, although there are no visible signs of the complex network of pathways used by the Algonquian peoples for centuries, routes that contemporary roads retrace. Stragglers from the group travelling with Sassacus were captured and killed as they crossed the Kwinitekw, although two sachems were spared on condition that they help the English locate the remaining Pequot.

The name of the southernmost tip of my town, Sachem's Head, should give one pause for thought. A promontory with beautiful coves and inlets jutting into Long Island Sound, it has become the exclusive preserve of wealthy families in large houses, governed by its own association and charter, with a members-only yacht club and stringent parking regulations that effectively deny public access to uninvited visitors. The association's website has nothing to say about a letter written by Captain Richard Davenport on 17 July 1637, describing his interrogation of Pequot prisoners whom 'we put to death that night and called the place Sacheme head'. Instead, any historical curiosity about the name of the area is deflected by a photograph of a very different event, the performance at a local hotel in 1915 by Buffalo Bill's Wild West Touring Company, shown smiling in full costume representing 'Indianness'.

Black and indigenous histories are closely entangled in this story. The English troops caught up with the Pequot at Sasqua, a swamp east of Quinnipiac, and surrounded them. Some escaped, but two hundred were taken prisoner. Fifty women and children were shipped to John Winthrop, governor of Massachusetts, with a note from Stoughton, the militia captain, listing the female captives he and his men wanted to enslave in their households. Those who were not domestically enslaved, including children, were taken to the West Indies under Captain Peirce on the Salem ship *Desire*. The ship left from Providence Island on its return voyage on 26 February 1638, loaded with 'cotton and tobacco and negroes'. In the Bahamas, the enslaved Pequots were fungible bodies exchanged for enslaved Africans, who were shipped to what has become known as New England.

The English declared the right to settle the land they called Connecticut 'by right of conquest'. Their pursuit of the Pequots by water and along the Mishimayagat path led directly to the colonization of Quinnipiac and the shoreline to the east. Theophilus Eaton, the Reverend John Davenport and five hundred English Puritans sailed from Boston with pigs, sheep, cattle, goats, horses and oxen, landing at Quinnipiac, later renamed New Haven, on 24 April 1638, determined to establish a settlement. Henry Whitfield's band of settler colonists arrived in Quinnipiac before exploring the coastline to its east. They declared their right to establish the Plantation of Menunkatuck in 1639, formally named Guilford in 1643. My town.

One indigenous response to the unsettling of the 'saltwater frontier' by English colonizers is recorded. The Narragansett sachem Miantonomo delivered a speech to the Montauks in 1642, arguing,

> For so are we all Indians as the English are, and say brother to one another; so must we be one as they are, otherwise we shall all be gone shortly, for you know our fathers had plenty of deer and skins, our plains were full of deer, as also our woods, and of turkies, and our coves full of fish and fowl. But these English, having

> gotten our land, they with scythes cut down the grass, and with axes fell the trees; their cows and horses eat the grass, and their hogs spoil our clam banks, and we shall be all starved. Therefore it is best for you to do as we, for we are all the Sachems from east to west, both Moquakues and Mohauks joining with us, and we are all resolved to fall on them all, at one appointed day.

Miantonomo was captured by the Mohegan leader Uncas. The Colonial Court condemned him for attempting to forge alliances against the English and asked Uncas to kill him. The Treaty of Hartford, agreed by the English, the Mohegan and the Narragansett in 1638, had declared that the Pequots could no longer speak their language, live in their former territory or even call themselves Pequots. Despite this attempt at annihilation, some Pequots survived and fought to retain their land and autonomy. Black and indigenous histories mixed together, as they did in other southern New England tribes.

The black Seminole populations of Florida and Oklahoma had a similarly mixed heritage. The Second Seminole War, conducted by the US government between 1835 and 1842 under the Indian Removal Act of 1830, attempted to return the black Seminole to enslavement and to remove the Seminole Indians from their land. *Exterminate All the Brutes* begins with a re-enactment of one of the battles in this conflict. The camera zooms in slowly on a headshot of Osceola, a male warrior of the Seminole Nation, played in the film by a woman. We are told that 'her story reaches deep into the history of this continent.' The portrait is intercut with two brief glimpses of the future, in which Osceola is shot and scalped while fighting alongside her black allies. Osceola's face dissolves into that of Peck's mother, Gisèle, as a young woman in Haiti, an intertwining of resemblance and difference that tells a global story of the greed and destruction of European imperialism and a particular story of black and indigenous solidarity.

2

Peine Forte et Dure

The city of Minneapolis, in which George Floyd lived and died, has been plagued not only by COVID-19 but also by an epidemic of police violence. As Mike Griffin, a community organizer, put it, he was 'just as likely to die from a cop as from Covid'. Major news outlets, including the *New York Times* and the *Washington Post*, seemed astonished at the scale of structural and environmental racism exposed by the pandemic. This wasn't news to black, indigenous and Hispanic Americans, who are subject to mass incarceration, who have significantly lower incomes and higher unemployment rates than the white population, and for whom the health care system and the overwhelmingly segregated education system and housing market have never provided equitable care, opportunity or provision. As a result of these inequalities, they are being infected and killed at a disproportionate rate. They are losing their jobs in unprecedented numbers. And they are over-represented in the 'essential' jobs, from transportation, cleaning and nursing to agricultural work, that are exempted from stay-at-home orders. A subway worker told the *New York Times* that he felt more sacrificial than essential.

On 25 May, at the intersection of 38th Street and Chicago Avenue, Floyd asphyxiated while being pressed into the road under the weight of law enforcement. His dying was watched by passers-by and recorded on mobile phones. Those of us who weren't present are secondary observers, accessing what was filmed and circulated on social media. The plot is all too familiar to people of colour. We know how this ends and are reluctant witnesses. Once it was told to us as stories, fragments inherited, passed down, whispered; now it is transmitted through phone footage, body cams, Twitter. The murder of George Floyd has its particularities but is also an instance in a long history of death at the hands of those sanctioned by federal, state, public, private and local authorities to enforce laws that do not protect us, to regulate inequality, to perpetuate injustice and to maintain white supremacy.

But how much do we know about the exercise of police force, despite seeing so much? The controversy and protests that followed the fatal shooting of Michael Brown, an unarmed eighteen-year-old, in Ferguson, Missouri in 2014 exposed the lack of official data on police killings. Two newspapers launched investigations. The Fatal Force, a database maintained by the *Washington Post*, records 'every fatal shooting by a police officer in the line of duty'. It began in January 2015 and continues to be updated, but doesn't track deaths in police custody, fatal shootings by off-duty officers or non-shooting deaths. *The Guardian*'s interactive database, the Counted, recorded all deaths at the hands of law enforcement between 2015 and 2016, including deaths in custody. This is where the majority of deaths that result from physical restraint occur: positional asphyxia, prone positioning with compression of torso, manual neck compression, multiple police officers on back, knees on back, feet or knees on neck, chokeholds. Such deaths are mostly out of sight – Freddie Gray died from injuries sustained during a prolonged ride in a police van while handcuffed and shackled to the floor – but in July 2015, in Montclair, California, witnesses saw between five and eight police officers sitting on top of Christian Siqueiros, who subsequently died of a heart attack.

From the early fifteenth century until the late eighteenth, *peine forte et dure*, punishment by pressing, was exercised under common law against men and women accused of capital felonies who insisted on 'standing mute', refusing to enter a plea. The legal historian Andrea McKenzie has argued that this refusal was interpreted as a show of contempt, an unacceptable challenge to the legitimacy of the court. The accused had to be coerced into submission or die. The most famous case in England was that of Margaret Clitherow, who in 1586 was charged with harbouring Catholic priests in her home. It took her fifteen minutes to die, crushed under a load of nearly eight hundred pounds. In 1721, a judge at the Old Bailey sentenced two supposed highwaymen, Thomas Cross and William Spiggot, to be pressed for refusing to submit a plea. The prisoner, he instructed, 'shall be laid upon the bare ground [and] upon his body shall be laid so much Iron and Stone as he can bear and more . . . until he die'. The mere sight of the press room was sufficient to change Cross's mind. Spiggot endured a weight of 350 pounds for half an hour, but when it was increased to four hundred pounds he agreed to plead. Later the same year, Nathaniel Haws, also accused of highway robbery, survived seven minutes under 250 lbs before submitting. Those who didn't submit were pressed to death. George Strangeways died within eight minutes in 1658. The punishment continued until 1772, when, as the lawyer Andrew Knapp wrote in 1806, it was deemed 'barbarous to Englishmen'. Silence was taken as a guilty plea for the next fifty years.

America never officially adopted *peine forte et dure*, but in 1692 Giles Corey of Salem, Massachusetts refused to plead when he was accused of witchcraft and died after two days under the press. Some consider this the only case of *peine* in US history; others argue that it may be unique to New England. This record exists, however, because Corey was a white and free person. Settler colonists inflicted many forms of brutal punishment and torture on indigenous peoples and enslaved Africans: we read of bodies in stocks wearing weighted cattle chains, labouring bodies wearing collars suspended with heavy weights, limbs pressed with sugar cane between the grinding stones of a mill, bodies tortured in the fields and barns of plantations. The words 'pressure' and 'downpresser' bear more than metaphorical weight in black diasporic culture.

George Floyd was pressed to death not as part of a judicial proceeding, nor because he was charged with a capital felony. He was accused of paying for cigarettes with a fake twenty-dollar bill. He wasn't pressed by stones or iron, but by the weight of Minneapolis police officers. In order to reconstruct his death, the *New York Times* combined recordings from bystanders and security cameras as well as audio from police scanners. At one point in the footage three officers, Derek Michael Chauvin, Alexander Kueng and Thomas Kieran Lane, can be seen kneeling on Floyd, applying pressure to his neck, torso and legs. A combined weight of around six hundred pounds pressed George Floyd into the ground while he pleaded, 'I can't breathe, man, please.'

The most widely shared recording, made by seventeen-year-old Darnella Frazier, who posted it on Facebook, shows Chauvin with one knee on Floyd's neck. On 9 June the Minneapolis Police Department amended section 5-311 of its Policy and Procedure Manual to state that 'neck restraints and chokeholds are prohibited' and that 'instructors are prohibited from teaching the use of neck restraints or chokeholds.' The tactic used by Chauvin was previously referred to as 'conscious neck restraint', a non-deadly 'force option' that 'may be used against a subject actively resisting'. Floyd wasn't resisting: he was pinned down by officers and handcuffed. But his immobility didn't satisfy the officers' desire for total subordination. At some point – it is hard to tell exactly when from the video footage – the possibility of Floyd's continuing to live is tacitly rejected. Chauvin continues to press his weight into Floyd's neck for three minutes after he appears to have stopped breathing.

Those responsible for executing *peine* wouldn't place the iron or stone directly onto the accused but onto a flat wooden surface. Using the weight of a human body or bodies to press another person to death is perversely intimate. In Frazier's recording, Chauvin, his shades pushed up, one hand in his pocket, appears detached but intent. He adjusts his knee and the angle of his foot, slightly releasing then increasing pressure as if to gain traction and make his kneeling position more comfortable. When bystanders approach shouting 'Get off,' he glances up, pulls out a container (possibly mace) and points it towards them. Then he looks back down and continues to watch Floyd asphyxiate. He shifts and adjusts his knee again, turns his foot to brace his leg, increasing pressure and crushing muscle, bone and cartilage. The killing of George Floyd is *de facto*, if not *de jure*, torture, a contemporary enactment of execution by pressing.

How and where did Chauvin learn this technique? The Minneapolis Police Department has a long history of racism, homophobia and brutality. In 2010 two of its officers, Timothy Gorman and Timothy Callahan, tackled twenty-eight-year-old David Smith, who was experiencing a mental health crisis, at the downtown YMCA. They pinned him on his stomach and applied 'prone restraint': Gorman kneeled on Smith's upper back for nearly four minutes, causing his death. Or perhaps Chauvin learnt it when he served with the 795th Military Police Battalion of the US Army between 1996 and 2000. At the time of the murder Chauvin was a training officer for the Minneapolis Police Department. Was he teaching Kueng and Lane an alternative technique to the chokehold that killed Eric Garner in New York in 2014 (and which had been banned in the NYPD since 1993)? The National Law Enforcement Training Centre and PoliceOne.com offer instruction videos for applying neck restraints. Chauvin was aware that he was being filmed and must have realized that the footage would circulate online. Although we like to imagine Chauvin's actions are universally condemned, he is performing for an audience who are not horrified but exultant at what they see.

On some days, bad days, I wonder if our survival in spite of enslavement, lynching and mass incarceration, our refusal to be annihilated, our mere presence, is perceived as a sign of contempt for and challenge to the legitimacy of the US state. To unleash venom, bullets, pain, persecution and death a black person only has to be birdwatching, whistling, walking home, riding a bike, driving a car, jogging, standing in the kitchen, sitting at home playing a video game with a nephew, lying in bed asleep; we only have to be a child playing in a city park or a teenager at a party, or be perceived as being in the wrong place at the wrong time.

Photographs of lynched and mutilated black bodies circulated throughout the nineteenth and early twentieth centuries; they were reproduced in newspapers, printed on postcards. Lynched bodies have always carried the unambiguous message that any attempt to exercise civil rights, to seek economic, political or social justice and equality, will be met with torture and death. The circulation of the Abu Ghraib photographs in 2004 similarly reproduced torture as spectacle. The vicarious pleasures and intimacies of brutality preserved in these images form an index of American racism. In addition to exposing abuse and mobilizing protest, the nine-minute murder of George Floyd is now part of this genealogy.

3

Safe? At Home?

In the past few weeks, I have been writing about black death as spectacle, focusing on the recent, very public, murders of black men by law enforcement that have been captured on mobile phones. When members of *Feminist Review* questioned how the 'household has so quickly become normalized as part of the discourse about Covid-19', I thought about how black households have been invaded with impunity by increasingly militarized police forces on both sides of the Atlantic, SWAT teams in the USA, SCO19 units in the UK. To me the blog page looked like a wall, a space on which I could post brief memorials to a few of the black women who have been killed by police officers out of sight in the space designated as home. These lives and deaths should matter and be acknowledged in the context of current protest.

Prologue to a memorial

When we were children, my mother told us that if we were ever lost, or in trouble, or felt unsafe we should find a police officer, a friendly British bobby, and 'he' would help us and bring us home. I learnt at a very young age that the police were antagonists, they did not make me feel safe then and they do not make me feel safe now. Riding my bike in my neighbourhood of Mitcham, looking out for my little brother riding alongside me on his tricycle, the police harassed us as niggers who should go home. By home they did not mean returning to the house where we lived but to the country we came from. We were both born in Britain – my brother was born a mile away in Streatham; I was born in Devon. We never could figure out what country they were telling us to go to.

Our mother was white and had grown up believing that the police offered protection. Like Amy Cooper, she took for granted that the powers of law enforcement were at her beck and call. This was a belief that was very difficult to dislodge even though the police (and most of the population) dismissed her right to protection because she was a 'nigger lover'. My mother crossed a line when she married a black man; she betrayed her 'race' and became an outcast. She discovered when she was pregnant that no one would rent rooms or a house to them, that racist common sense determined that they should not make a 'home' together. When the house they eventually purchased was vandalized by racists who left faeces as calling cards on the beds and smeared on the walls, my mother called the police, believing they would offer help and protection. But the police did not consider the bricks and mortar of the terraced building in which we lived a 'home', or inviolable: they literally did not give a shit about deposits of fascist shit. It was nothing less than she (we) deserved. But it was almost impossible to shift my mother's dogmatic belief that the police *should* offer assistance if called upon.

As a high school teacher in the London Borough of Newham in the seventies I also had to be an anti-racist organizer in and out of the classroom. The police were among the most forceful racists we faced and fought; they defended and protected the aggressive violence of the National Front. On the local council estate my black students and their families learnt that they should not feel 'at home' or safe in their flats through a variety of forms of intrusion. Missives of hatred were delivered in the form of bricks propelled through windows and faeces through letter boxes. What is it with racists and their faeces?

And then, on 17 January 1981, there was the fire in a home in New Cross in which thirteen black teenagers died. On 2 March an estimated 15,000 of us marched through London on the Black People's Day of Action protesting the indifference of the Metropolitan Police, the British press and politicians and protesting their disregard for black life and death. The action was memorialized at Goldsmiths College in the 'Thirteen Dead and Nothing Said' exhibition of photographs taken by Vron Ware accessible on the website of Goldsmith College (https://sites.gold.ac.uk).

In response, in April the police launched Operation Swamp, a ten-day invasion of Brixton which was a culmination of the stop-and-search operations and raids on black homes and meeting places that had intensified throughout the past decade. Brixton exploded in protest as St Paul's in Bristol had a year earlier.

Remembering

An important part of the current protest movements is activating an awareness that 'Black Lives Matter' in the context of a history of injury and death at the hands of those sanctioned to discipline, control and incarcerate; to enforce laws that do not protect us; to regulate inequality, perpetuate injustice and maintain white supremacy. Long before Operation Swamp British police invaded black 'households' without compunction and with little or

Banner held up at a Black Lives Matter event in the UK

Image shared by the Racial Justice Network

no redress. If the inhabitants remain unscathed, and many do not, then they usually leave behind them broken pipes and other structural damage in an attempt to render the 'home' uninhabitable. In the USA, SWAT teams invade homes on 'no-knock' warrants.

If we take account of this history, then being 'at home' and assuming that 'home' is a safe space, a sanctuary, is a privilege of those who do not live under threat, whose lives are not precarious or vulnerable to abuse by individuals or the state. Home for many is neither safe nor secure. Here are a few of them.

28 September 1985, Brixton

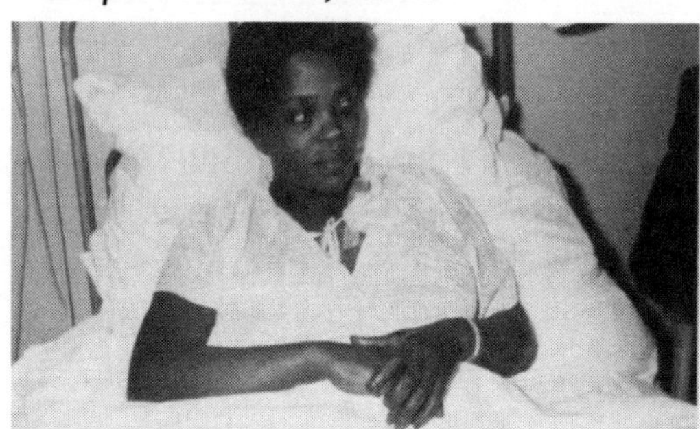

Dorothy 'Cherry' Groce.

Image credit: Wasi Daniju under CC BY- NC-ND 2.0

Dorothy (Cherry) Groce, thirty-seven years old, was shot in her chest while lying in bed, by Metropolitan police, in a raid at her home in the early hours. The bullet penetrated her lung and went through her spine. Metropolitan Police inspector Douglas Lovelock stood trial in 1987 charged with inflicting unlawful and malicious grievous bodily harm. He was acquitted.

Permanently paralysed, Groce spent two years in hospital and rehab and twenty-six years in a wheelchair. After her death in 2011 a post-mortem found metal fragments from the bullet still lodged in the base of her spine.

5 October 1985, Broadwater Farm, Tottenham

A week after the death of Dorothy Groce, **Cynthia Jarret,** forty-nine years old, collapsed and died from a heart attack when four police officers raided her home looking for her son. During the coroner's inquest into Mrs Jarret's death, her daughter, Patricia, stated that she saw one of the officers, DC Randle, push her mother, which caused her to fall.

28 July 1993, Crouch End

Joy Gardner

Five police officers from Hornsey police station and an official from the UK Immigration Service raided **Joy Gardner**'s home with orders to 'detain and remove' her and her five-year-old son for immediate deportation to Jamaica. The officers used a four-inch wide restraint belt with attached handcuffs and leather straps to restrain and shackle her around her thighs and ankles. Gagged, with thirteen feet of adhesive tape wrapped around her head and face, she suffered respiratory failure and was transported to hospital. Official records state that Joy Gardner died of cerebral hypoxia and cardiac arrest on 1 August 1993. Her family believe she was killed on July 28 at home and a post-mortem carried out on their behalf concluded that Joy Gardner was suffocated. Three police officers were charged with manslaughter and acquitted.

Home. Land. Security. USA

13 March 2020, Louisville, Kentucky

Breonna Shaquille Taylor, twenty-six years old, was a licensed emergency medical technician for the city. Narcotics detectives raided her house just after midnight on a no-knock warrant

An event marking Breonna Taylor's birthday

looking for a drug trafficker who lived miles away. Taylor and her boyfriend, Kenneth Warren, were in bed but got up when they heard the sound of a battering ram breaking down their door and people entering their apartment. Taylor and Warren did not hear any announcement by the police of their presence. Warren thought they were intruders and fired what he called a low 'warning shot'. The police blindly fired twenty-five bullets and Breonna Taylor was shot eight times. No drugs were found. Warren was initially charged with attempted murder of a police officer but this charge was dismissed.

12 October 2019, Fort Worth, Texas

Atatiana Koquice Jefferson (pictured in the banner on p. 23), twenty-eight years old, was shot and killed in her home in the early hours after a neighbour made a non-emergency call to the police saying the door to Jefferson's house was open. Body cam footage showed two police officers walking around the side of her home and one, Aaron Dean, entered her backyard. Jefferson went to the widow and when Dean saw her face he yelled, 'Put your hands up' and immediately fired through the window. Jefferson was pronounced dead at the scene. Dean was charged with murder and subsequently indicted.

18 October 2016, New York City

Deborah Danner

Image shared by Black Past

Deborah Danner, aged sixty-six, was shot twice and killed by police sergeant Hugh Barry, NYPD, in her apartment. Danner suffered from schizophrenia, about which she had written eloquently. In her essay she worried about what would happen if her medication failed her and asked, 'Is that a delusion, I ask myself, my belief that I am worthy of respect and a "normal" happy life?' Neighbours called 911 because, they said, Danner was acting erratically. According to the testimony of an emergency medical technician, Brittney Mullings, Mullings was trying to explain why they were there in her apartment when Barry arrived and Danner retreated into her bedroom. Mullings recounted that six police officers followed Danner and then there were shots. Jennifer Danner, Deborah's sister, sued and New York City agreed to a $2 million settlement. Sergeant Barry, who was eventually charged with murder, manslaughter and criminally negligent homicide, was acquitted by a judge in a non-jury trial in February 2018.

4 January 2008, Lima, Ohio

Clutching her fourteen-month-old son in her arms **Tarika Wilson**, twenty-six years old, sought shelter in her bedroom with her other children when the police raided her house, smashing down the front door apparently looking for her boyfriend. Officers shot two of their dogs and a third officer, Joseph Chavalia, fired blindly into the bedroom, killing Wilson instantly and injuring the child in her arms. Residents testified to years of abuse at the hands of the Lima Police Department. Several protest marches and a visit by Jesse Jackson followed, urging the prosecution of Officer Chavalia. Wilson's family brought a wrongful-death suit against the city of Lima which settled for $2.5 million, but in August 2008 an all-white jury acquitted Joseph Chavalia of criminal charges. The ACLU referred to the killing of Tarika Wilson in their 2014 report *War Comes Home*, an indictment of the excessive militarization of policing in the United States with no public oversight and of SWAT deployment to execute search warrants which 'revealed stark, often extreme, racial disparities'.

Image shared by Black Past

Tarika Wilson

29 October 1984, New York City

Eleanor Bumpers, elderly, disabled and mentally ill, was shot and killed in her home (pictured in the banner on p. 23). The NYPD had been called by housing authority workers who said Bumpers was resisting eviction for non-payment of rent and had a knife. An emergency service unit was unable to get her to open the door so police broke it down, Bumpers resisted restraint. Police Officer Stephen Sullivan shot her hand off with a twelve-gauge pump shotgun, then shot her again in the chest. Charged with second degree manslaughter, Sullivan was acquitted by a judge two years after Bumpers was killed. Eventually two social service workers were demoted for not obtaining an emergency rent grant for her and for failing to provide her with psychiatric aid.

4

US/UK's Special Relationship: The Culture of Torture in Abu Ghraib and Lynching Photographs

No matter where you are in the United States, since two Boeing 767 commercial jets were transformed into high-octane weapons and flown through a cerulean blue sky into the twin towers of the World Trade Center in New York, it is difficult, if not impossible, to avoid seeing evocations of the American flag. Flags are everywhere, not only in their cloth version flying from poles and windows but in paper or plastic stuck on anything that can be consumed or worn, anything that moves or grows; even gardens are not immune from being carefully cultivated in patriotic colours. I have begun to feel that I live permanently under the shadow of the flag even if streaks of red, white and blue are just in my peripheral vision or appearing in my computer screen as a ghostly reflection from the street as I sit, writing, in the corner window of my favourite coffee shop.

But at some point, maybe just before or maybe just after the invasion of Iraq, I noticed that flags were beginning to appear in pairs: the Stars and Stripes and the Union Jack were twinned on bumper stickers, benches and backsides. As restaurants deleted French fries from their menus and replaced them with 'freedom fries' it seemed as if Britain was becoming disengaged from its association with Europe in the American mind. Who knows where this will end? Maybe some senator will propose that the United Kingdom be dragged across the Atlantic, moored off Long Island and inducted as the fifty-first state.

When I saw *Love Actually* for the first time in our local multiplex theatre I laughed wholeheartedly and verbally expressed my satisfaction and approval when Hugh Grant told Billy Bob Thornton to take his obnoxious self, his national arrogance and his government's political inflexibility back across the Atlantic. (Of course, these are sentiments that I imaginatively projected into the scene.) My enthusiasm for sending the haughty Yank packing was met by surprised stares, frowns of disapproval and then angry mutterings from those around me. I slid as far down as I could go in my seat for the rest of the performance and snuck out of the nearest emergency exit as soon as the credits rolled. But, contrary to this movie experience, it has been a few good months to be a Brit, even a black Brit, in the US of A.

My accent attracts strangers who initiate conversations about their, or their family's, historic ties to the UK, or to Ireland, or they relate stories about their experiences when stationed in Britain during the Second World War, or they just reminisce about rainy holidays in London. People I have never met welcome me as a 'comrade in arms', but when they hear my intractable opposition to the war the tone of these friendly overtures changes and people walk away from me slowly as if reluctant to believe a Brit could feel this way. They glance back over their shoulders and ask with their eyes if I am just kidding. I am not kidding. They are bitterly disappointed. I dread these occasions – I feel as if I am supposed to be the local representative of the 'special relationship' between the US and the UK but, instead, I am daily reduced to the level of a traitor, who has betrayed not one but two nations. Recently, all these encounters are civil; last year my protest activities with other British women provoked direct and very aggressive threats of serious bodily harm.

The 'call for papers' for this conference stated that although 'much has been written about the "special relationship" between

Britain and the United States on the level of high politics and diplomacy . . . rather less has been written about the presumed existence of a shared common culture – a culture that has, since the American Civil War, been actively cultivated and promoted as a way of cementing that "special relationship".' The conference proposed 'a wide-ranging inquiry into the cultural manifestations of the "special relationship" and into the transatlantic traffic in cultural styles, attitudes and motifs between Britain and the United States'. Today I want to suggest that the study of the multiple and complex relationships between the UK and the US need not be confined to transatlantic exchange, that it might be fruitful to imagine how these relationships unfold in another part of the globe, like the Middle East, the Persian Gulf or Iraq.

How do you think an Iraqi civilian whose family members have been injured, killed, imprisoned or tortured distinguishes between the British and American forces? Does it matter if the bullet lodged in your body was fired from a British or US weapon, or the bombs that destroyed your neighbourhood, including the school your kids went to, and the local hospital where your daughter was born, was dropped from an American or British plane? If you have no clean water to drink, is it the fault of the Americans, or the British, or is it the fault of the invaders, the imperialists – don't they all look the same when you are standing in the gutter watching the tanks roll by? They all want the same thing, the oil that is under the tank's tread.

As the senior deputy to the director general of antiquities in Baghdad told Robert Young,

> It's the British again. They have been bombing my family for over 80 years now. Four generations have lived and died with these unwanted visitors from Britain who come to pour explosives on us from the skies. It first began in 1920. My great grandfather, Abd Al Rahman, was walking into our village for his last-born son's wedding when a two-winged plane suddenly came over the horizon and dropped a fireball amongst the celebrations . . . Since then, whenever it has suited them, the bombers come again.

> Now their big brothers from America do most of it, but you can still see the RAF planes streaking across our skies flying their familiar routes, which they first charted in the 1920s. The flights began in earnest when they were preparing to leave finally (again) after the Second World War. They mapped every metre of our territory, laboriously, meticulously, took photographs of every square centimetre of our country. My cousin who studies there told me that at Keele University in England there are millions of reconnaissance photographs on microfilm of Iraq and Iran taken by RAF 680 squadron before they left. You never know when we might need them, they said with a smile. When they look for oil or decide to bomb us . . . they want to make sure they will have more of our oil for the future. Probably they still use them today when they sit in their operation rooms in England and plan which target amongst us to hit next.[1]

US–UK 'special relationship' in the Middle East existed long before the current coalition formed for the invasion of Iraq. After 1945 US political strategists 'struggled to prevent the Soviet Union from filling the vacuum created by Britain's slow-motion withdrawal from its empire east of Suez'. Truman imagined that the UK would provide 'the military muscle and the United States bankrolling a regional security system that stretched from Turkey to Pakistan'.[2] Clearly most of the 'military muscle' is provided by the other cousin now but the US and the UK have worked in concert, if not always in harmony in the Middle East since the end of the Second World War.

Last year, courtesy of Tony Blair et al., the British rushed off to join their 'American cousins' in the most recent imperialistic, profit-driven adventure disguised as spreading the values of enlightenment and understanding and the principles of democracy. In the exportation of freedom through the medium of violence, intimidation and death, the British government are equal partners in and, I would argue, should be brought to account as equally responsible for all that has been undertaken in the name of the coalition. Yet on 25 June, when the British

Attorney General publicly condemned the military tribunals organized for the detainees held by the Americans at Guantánamo Bay, Cuba, because the tribunals do not meet the standards of international law, he did not simultaneously either condemn the torture that took place in Abu Ghraib, a prison run under the authority of the coalition forces, for breaking international law, or acknowledge the investigations into the forty-four events 'of abuse and excessive use of lethal force' perpetrated against civilians by British troops in Iraq.[3]

'Operation Iraqi Freedom', implemented through tactics of 'shock and awe', has been increasingly justified through the language of culture, as the days, weeks and months have passed and the 'weapons of mass destruction' that were presented by Bush and Blair as direct threats to the populations of the UK and US have not been found. To talk as if the invasion of Iraq delivered 'freedom' and the values and practices of social and political democracy is to use language that transforms war into an awe-inspiring gift from the Americans and British to the people of Iraq. The shock, to the American and British public, if not to the residents of Baghdad or any other ungrateful recipients of the beneficence of US and British imperial ambition, is the exposure, on global prime time, of the ground upon which such democracy and freedom rests.

In the United States, I have been reading the world press courtesy of the internet, listening to NPR and the BBC, while also reluctantly keeping an eye on what pretends to be news on American television. 'CNN the most *trusted* name in News' is an outrageous claim. Watching and listening it has been difficult to decide which has been the most obscene spectacle: media pundits, politicians and members of the Bush administration refusing to grasp the meaning of, and miserably failing to take full moral and political responsibility for, the torture of prisoners in Abu Ghraib, or the smug self-satisfaction of those same pundits, politicians and government bureaucrats as they congratulate themselves for displaying and embodying the values of American democracy, values supposedly evident in the mere fact that discussion of the 'abuses of detainees' has taken place. Of course, how open this discussion has been and how open it will be in the future remains unclear because the vast majority of the photographs, videos and statements, and all the annexes to the Taguba report, remain in the custody and control of the US Army Criminal Investigation Command, who say they are retaining these visual and written records of the torture at Abu Ghraib as evidence for possible future prosecutions, and therefore cannot make them available to the American public. But what all this evidence is evidence of, exactly, is either being avoided or profoundly misrecognized in public debate within the US. Now there is silence as everyone seems to want Abu Ghraib to just go away.

There is a profound relation between the arrogant wielding of power and the claiming of rights over land in its meticulous mapping, and the wielding of power and claiming of rights over the bodies of the people who live in that land through their systematic dehumanization through torture. What follows are my thoughts following the publication of pictures of the torturing of Iraqi prisoners in Abu Ghraib prison by American soldiers and civilian contractors. As growing evidence has shown, the behaviour of British soldiers has not been so different from that of their American counterparts. As the details of British abuse of Iraqis become clearer, we will need to ask ourselves similar questions about the cultural formations that produce not only torture but also torturers. Some questions may be the same or similar; some questions will be different. The point is, we need to ask them.

Language has created an alternate reality against which the visual evidence of tortured bodies has been read. This language reveals the extent to which the major media in the United States are no longer a fourth estate but deeply 'embedded', not only within the military but within the spin doctors of the federal government. 'News' is broadcast in the language of the Bush administration, a language invented after 9/11 to create new political realities and new categories of human being: military invasions we are to understand as 'operations'; 'enduring', as in 'enduring freedom', belies the precarious future evident in the rubble of Afghanistan or Iraqi infrastructure; daily indignities, imprisonment, injury and death constitute 'freedom'; prisoners of war, innocent civilians and military personnel have become 'detainees'; torture is renamed 'abuse' and 'humiliation'; the phrases 'enemy combatant and 'unlawful combatant' disguise and justify the withdrawal of civil and human rights. This rhetoric has formed the framework within which the photographs from Abu Ghraib have been viewed, interpreted and given meaning; it is a language which has already dehumanized the bodies of the tortured.

Writing in the *New Yorker*, Seymour Hersh reported that in the autumn of 2003 there were 'several thousand prisoners, including women and teenagers', in the recently cleaned and refurbished US military prison of Abu Ghraib. Most he describes as 'civilians, many of whom had been picked up in random military sweeps and at highway checkpoints'.[4] The front page of *Article 15-6 Investigation of the 800th Military Police Brigade*, written by Major General Antonio M. Taguba, declares that the report is 'Secret' and not for 'Foreign Dissemination'. The real problem for the US and UK governments has been not the actions of military personnel and civilian contractors within the walls of Abu Ghraib and other prisons, but that their actions have been seen by the world. As we now know, torture has been sanctioned at the highest levels of the US administration, including by Secretary of Defense Donald Rumsfeld.[5]

It is worth returning through the clouds of rhetoric that surround them to the actual accounts of the torture of Iraqi prisoners. Taguba stated that he found that the intentional 'abuse of detainees' by military police personnel included punching, slapping and kicking detainees; jumping on their naked feet; videotaping and photographing naked male and female detainees; forcibly arranging detainees in various sexually explicit positions for photographing; forcing detainees to remove their clothing and keeping them naked for several days at a time; forcing naked male detainees to wear women's underwear; forcing groups of male detainees to masturbate themselves while being photographed and videotaped; arranging naked male detainees in a pile and then jumping on them; positioning a naked detainee on a MRE box, with a sandbag on his head, and attaching wires to his fingers, toes and penis to simulate electric torture; writing 'I am a Rapest' (*sic*) on the leg of a detainee alleged to have forcibly raped a fifteen-year-old fellow detainee, and then photographing him naked; placing a dog chain or strap around a naked detainee's neck and having a female soldier pose for a picture; a male MP guard having sex with a female detainee; using military working dogs (without muzzles) to intimidate and frighten detainees, and in at least one case biting and severely injuring a detainee; taking photographs of dead Iraqi detainees. In addition, Taguba found 'credible' further reports from prisoners, including breaking chemical lights and pouring the phosphoric liquid on detainees; threatening detainees with a charged 9mm pistol; pouring cold water on naked detainees; beating detainees with a broom handle and a chair; threatening male detainees with rape; allowing a military police guard to stitch the wound of a detainee who was injured after being slammed against the wall in his cell; sodomizing a detainee with a chemical light and perhaps a broom stick.[6] This is the way the Taguba report provides a general summary of what it names 'abuse'. So in this partnership, this coalition, where should we begin to provide a historical context for understanding this?

Within the US, torture in Iraq has been presented as the acts of 'a few bad apples' in the American pie, a pie which, despite these revelations, remains wholesome. These acts, it is argued, need to be understood as outside the American character, as acts which should be placed in opposition to the beliefs and practices of American democracy. This is an exercise in historical amnesia, a denial of how integral the torture of brown bodies has been to the building of 'the land of the free' (and, I would add, to the building and maintenance of colonialism).

There is an unacknowledged but intimate interdependence between the Enlightenment principles of individual freedom, as embedded in the original Constitution of the United States, and the horrors of non-freedom, of the enslavement and dispossession of the not-fully-human who were excluded from the Constitution drawn up by the 'founding fathers'. None have known and lived the consequences of the double-sided coin of American freedom and non-freedom as the dispossessed, the descendants of those who were brutally slaughtered and driven from their lands and those who were dragged in chains by the British across the Atlantic to build the foundation of wealth upon which the modern United States of America rests. Amendments to the US Constitution, the granting of 'emancipation', of 'freedom', brought the tortured black body from the hidden domain of the plantation into public view, transformed into spectacle by the camera.

The history of the lynching of African Americans and the physical, mental and sexual abuse of prisoners perpetrated daily in federal and state penitentiaries is continually being erased from the American imagination – precisely because these brutal techniques remain central to US mechanisms of control and oppression. From where I stand, the images from Abu Ghraib are all too familiar and all too American. In 1997 in a Brooklyn station house, Abner Louima, a young Haitian immigrant, was tortured by police officers, one of whom, Justin Volpe, sodomized him with a broomstick, an act of brutality also recorded by Major General Taguba. Details of the abuse of Louima were uncovered but there was no visual evidence. Why record the acts of brutality at Abu Ghraib on film?

One of the most sensitive American responses to the photographs from Abu Ghraib has been written by Susan Sontag. She asks, 'How can someone grin at the sufferings and humiliation of another human being?'[7] This question, posed by one of America's foremost intellectuals, is stark evidence that even the most highly educated have learnt little from the history of lynching. While Sontag acknowledges that Americans torture 'when they are told or made to feel, that those over whom they have absolute power deserve to be humiliated', and 'when they are led to believe that the people they are torturing belong to an inferior race or religion', she cannot quite grasp that the practice of torture as in Abu Ghraib is not a contemporary phenomenon.

Sontag prefers to believe that torture is 'inspired by the vast repertory of pornographic imagery available on the internet' and evidence of the 'increasing acceptance of brutality in American life' like the 'video games of boys'. While reaching for something comparable to the photographs from Abu Ghraib, Sontag understands that it would be lynching photographs 'which show Americans grinning beneath the naked mutilated body of a black man or woman hanging behind them from a tree'. However, Sontag then makes a stark distinction between images of lynching and those from Abu Ghraib. She argues that lynching photographs were trophies 'taken by a photographer in order to be collected' and 'stored in albums'. The pictures taken in Abu Ghraib, Sontag argues, are different; they 'reflect a shift in the use made of pictures – less objects to be saved than messages to be disseminated, circulated'.

Spectators lynching Jesse Washington

On the contrary, the importance of spectacle, the taking of photographs and videos, the preservation and the *circulation* of the visual image of the tortured/lynched body and the participants, the erotic sexual exploitation which produced pleasure in the torturers – all these practices are continuities in the history of American racism and the unacknowledged history of American fascism.

There were almost 5,000 documented instances of lynching in the US between Reconstruction and the middle of the twentieth century. Tortured bodies were sometimes set alight and always hung for public display.[8] Contrary to what Sontag believes, the photographs of these bodies were not designed for storage but were circulating visual images and messages. The spectacle of lynching was a public warning to all black people to keep in their place, but postcards of lynched black men and women had multiple uses.

Lynching of Bennie Simmons

Front and back of a postcard

Taken March, 3, 1910.
two hours after the
lynching of the negro
rapest "Brown" He
was drug through the
street from the court
house and hanged to
the south west corner
of the arch The crowd
seen in the picture
is, nothing to be compared
with the mob, at the
time this picture was
taken the mob had
allready left scene and
was on their way to
the jail after Oats another
negro victim

Duluth lynching postcard

A postcard could be used as an advertisement for a business, as in the image of the lynching of Bennie Simmons that has the photographer's name painted in large letters in white paint on the tree from which the body hung. The postcards were also 'wish you were here' communications to friends and relatives and carried words of greeting as the gruesome image circulated.

For black Americans, lynched bodies have always carried unambiguous messages: any and all attempts to exercise civil rights, to seek economic, political, or social justice and equality, would be rewarded by torture and death. Lynching was both a tool of, and a weapon in, racialized subjection – it was sanctioned and authorized by local, state and civil authority. Lynching was a struggle over the control of bodies, about access to economic resources in the form of land, business and capital, and access to political power through the ballot.

Rather than being distinct in their circulation, pictures of the tortured bodies of Iraqis are the direct descendants of the post cards of lynched black bodies: both are images and messages to be shared with those you want to warn and those with whom you want to celebrate. Digital images of torture enclosed in attachments to emails sent home are material evidence of wielding power, they publicize conquering an enemy, they celebrate triumph, an achievement that seemed elusive outside the walls of Abu Ghraib.

Participants stand grinning beside and underneath the bodies of African Americans, exhibiting not only pleasure but pride in their participation in torture. But pleasure is not produced spontaneously. The bodies are very carefully posed. In the lynching photographs and in the photographs from Abu Ghraib we can see a very carefully staged and highly ritualized performance as if the performers were following a script.

These smiles and this pride in accomplishment are reproduced on the faces of the American torturers inside Abu Ghraib. These prisoners are not being interrogated any more than lynched victims were being interrogated. The torturers appear self-satisfied, as if justice has been dispensed at their hands. The mistreatment and torture of Iraqis is part of the process of submission to the economic and political ambition and power of the United States and Britain . . . it too is authorized and sanctioned by the financial and political ambitions of empire. The fact that the torture was photographed and filmed, that it exists as spectacle, is a crucial historical link to the practice of lynching as spectacle, and acknowledging this link is the first stage in understanding its meaning in the life and culture of the United States.

The torture in American prisons and at Abu Ghraib is also about violence perpetrated upon eroticized bodies, which also has precedent in the history of the United States. Lynchers mutilated genitals, stuffed penises in the mouths of their victims and displayed them in the windows of shops. Those who came to watch scrambled through the ashes for body parts to take home. For the last few years in the United States the military has reeled from multiple accusations that rape is pervasive throughout the ranks. Yet all this boils beneath the surface of an obsessive prudery; the exposure of Janet Jackson's right breast at the Super Bowl or oral sex in the White House occasions shock and moral outrage in the United States media.

Americans are notoriously insular and arrogant in their attitudes towards the rest of the world. Why bother to educate yourselves about other peoples and political systems when you live in the best country in the world, drive the biggest and baddest SUVs, have the best political system in the world, and when you are convinced that you are not only the leading citizens on the planet but the only ones who understand how the world should be run? When a country has a president like George W. Bush who stated in surprise on his visit to Brazil, 'Oh, you have black people here too!' one needs to ask what knowledge of Iraq and its people did American soldiers take with them on their invasion?

American popular culture is notoriously racist and anti-Arab, and in these respects has changed little since the middle of the nineteenth century. Disney's *Aladdin*, which won two Oscars, is most probably the most influential popular-cultural influence on the generation that produced the suspects that the Taguba report identified as SPC Jeremy Sivits, 372nd MP Company; SPC Sabrina Harman, 372nd MP Company; SGT Javal S. Davis, 372nd MP Company; PFC Lynndie R. England, 372nd MP Company; and Adel Nakhla, civilian translator, Titan Corp., assigned to the 205th MI Brigade.[9] The US military has drawn upon and distributed the notoriously racist book by Raphael Patai *The Arab Mind* (as if there were only one Arab mind!). Reading this text, one wonders whether here is the imaginative source or script for the staging of acts of sexual humiliation in Abu Ghraib.

Though direct testimony appears in the annexes to the Taguba report which have not been published, there is one direct description that remains within the main body of the report.

Image of Abu Ghraib pyramid of prisoners

> When **Mr. Adel L. Nakhla**, a US civilian contract translator was questioned about several detainees accused of rape. He observed [*sic*]: 'They (detainees) were all naked, a bunch of people from MI, the MP were there that night and the inmates were ordered by SGT Granier and SGT Frederick ordered the guys while questioning them to admit what they did. They made them do strange exercises by sliding on their stomach, jump up and down, throw water on them and made them some wet, called them all kinds of names such as "gays" do they like to make love to guys, then they handcuffed their hands together and their legs with shackles and started to stack them on top of each other by insuring that the bottom guys penis will touch the guy on tops butt.'[10]

When looking at the photographs one cannot help but think that these young men and women look like high school kids on their first trip abroad smiling self-consciously while announcing to the natives that they have arrived, assuring themselves of their superiority and their right to dominate while saying 'hi' to mom back home. They look like tourists from the United States in a fantasy land where exoticized bodies become the conduit for expressing and acting upon racist desires, desires that can be fully realized only in the contact zones of the 'other'. But to assume such apparent innocence would be a mistake, for the invaders have created the image of the peoples they expected to find.

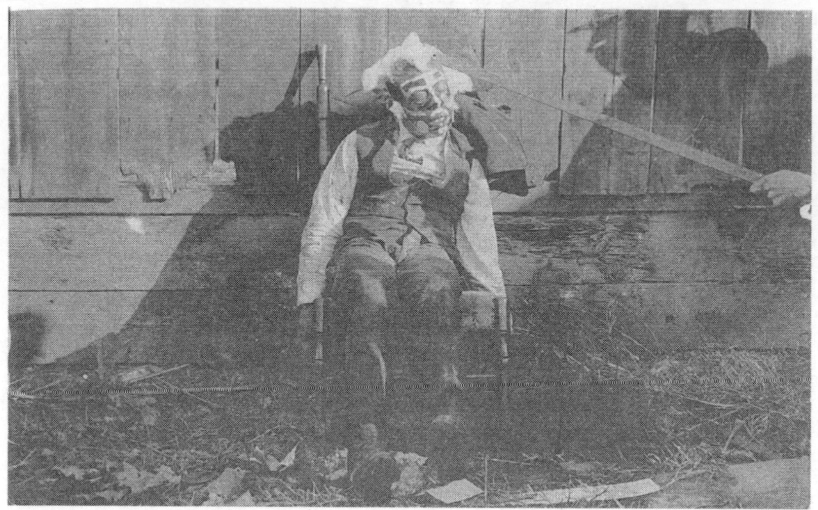

Lynching c. 1900, unknown location

How does the United States–United Kingdom partnership translate? Donald Rumsfeld is not the first to advocate 'the putting aside of international law'.[11] The combination of brutal violence, racism and desire that characterized lynching was developed and refined in the landscape of colonialism, has been taught by the US military to death squads in Latin America, and is to be found today in the jails and prisons of the homeland. For the aim is the transformation of peoples from subjects to objects, what Fanon called their decerebralization. In the shadow of the flag, underneath the layers of lies issuing like red, white and blue flowers from the White House, the Pentagon and 10 Downing Street, and corrupting the heart of democracy, is the agony of the tortured body.

5

Aftermath

While I have been writing and thinking about geographies of race and gender in the United Kingdom I find it deeply disconcerting to see how rapidly many around me have adapted to a new calendar to govern their lives, a way of measuring time and a means by which to locate the body in relation to the world that existed before and the world that existed after 11 September 2001, in the United States of America, the country in which I reside. By this new calendar, this way of measuring and locating the self, I do not mean to conjure the triggers for memory and positioning of the type which articulates itself as 'I will never forget where I was and what I was doing when President Kennedy was shot,' or 'when British troops were first sent to Northern Ireland'. Rather, what I want to name, to bring into focus, is a seismic shift in public and private discourse about the relation of the self to the other, of friend to foe, of home to foreigner, that has occurred within the borders of the United States since 11 September. As I write, bodies seem to be in suspended relation to each other while concepts of citizen and subject are renegotiated.

In this discursive crisis the United States, as a national body politic, is being reconfigured as 'home', the exact nature of that home having yet to be determined. What has been established by the Bush administration through its invention of the Department of Homeland Security and confirmed by the media, particularly the *New York Times* and CNN, is that the nation is a home that needs to be defended not only from an external but also from an internal threat: within the confines of 'home' its inhabitants are subject to a rapid surveillance of their legitimacy, a process overdetermined by the language and practices of racialization.

There is a vast disjunction between the everyday familiarity with the language of globalization and the utter incomprehension that the foreign policies of the United States, which cause death and destruction on a daily level abroad, would have any effect at 'home'. Because we have experienced these effects, we are, as President Bush initially characterized it, on a 'crusade'. To protect and preserve freedom, freedom must be curtailed; for some, perhaps for many, it will be destroyed.

The United States is also an empire. The world's most powerful nation has enormous reach: the home has a back garden, which justifies the overthrow of democratically elected presidents of foreign countries and the invasion of Grenada; the home has international interests, which justifies the maintenance of United States troops near the oil fields in Saudi Arabia; and so it goes. When Madeleine Albright was asked in an interview on *60 Minutes* in 1997 what she had to say about the deaths of 500,000 Iraqi children, deaths directly attributable to US sanctions, she responded in the august tones of a US Secretary of State that it was 'a very hard choice', but 'we think the price is worth it'. The political calculation and weighing of bodies is absolutely central to foreign policy and the defence of the homeland. Arundhati Roy has recently called this thinking 'the sophistry and fastidious algebra of infinite justice'. She asks, 'How many dead Iraqis will it take to make the world a better place? How many dead Afghans for every dead American? How many dead mojahedin for each dead investment banker?'[1]

The moment of crisis – as I write it is difficult to imagine when this historical moment will end – is riven with contradictions. 'Home' is full of multiple bodies seemingly endlessly divided, in which neighbour can be, and has been, cast as potential enemy. Although these divisions appear to be absolutely transparent, exactly whom should be blessed by God as opposed to subject to his wrath (courtesy of the US military), exactly whom is to be unified with whom, exactly whom should be embraced and comforted while others are spat upon, assaulted, even murdered, is not in fact clear. It is at this precise moment of crisis and confusion that the racialized politics of the body plays out its most deadly logic at home and abroad.

But racialization is not the only lethal weapon at work. For example, the persecution of gays and lesbians in the military has been suspended so they may go and fight for us (US) – are 'they' to be fully embraced within the confines of national domesticity permanently or merely temporarily? While the bodies of gays and lesbians are deemed suitable to be launched against the enemy, wherever it may be, their blood, which will obviously be shed in such confrontation, is not classified as suitable to be donated to the Red Cross.

We are deeply divided despite the endless sea of Stars and Stripes that hang from the porches of my neighbours, that I can see from the window of my study and out of the corner of my eye as I write in my local coffee shop. The Stars and Stripes flutter from pickup trucks, minivans and SUV's, the favoured vehicles of the small New England town in which I live, palpable evidence, supposedly, of their drivers' love for, and preparedness to defend, this homeland as they simultaneously belch their carbons into the atmosphere in complete disregard of the consequences. (In 2001 in Connecticut there have already been twice as many days of 'bad air' as there were in 2000.)[2] Bodies have to breathe but, hey, we can't put limits on freedom, even if asthma is killing our children! I guess the principle at work is that we are allowed to kill our own children in order to preserve our right to pollute as long as others don't threaten their lives. And now we march off to kill the 'others' in defence of these freedoms.

Stars and Stripes with declarations that 'We will prevail' and 'God Bless America' have been hastily but carefully drawn on blankets and draped over the bridges of I-95 under which I drive every morning. Stars and Stripes, cut from the pages of a local newspaper, are glued to the front of the desk of my administrative assistant as a wall of defiance should any terrorist enter our departmental office. Many of us, in our department, could be racially profiled at a glance as potential terrorists, with our brown skins, dark hair and eyes: we must be careful how we dress.

My flag-waving neighbours (white) are very satisfied that they live in almost total segregation from the residents of New Haven (black), leave alone New York City, a veritable Sodom and Gomorrah which very few ever visit. I do not mean that their outpouring of grief for New York is not genuine but I do mean that 'One Nation under God' cannot, must not, be taken for granted as an obvious historical entity. On the contrary, it is being ideologically constructed anew: it is being called into being every day; a homogeneity is being forged in front of our very eyes; it is being shaped by fear; it is being heralded by a blind jingoistic fantasy; and it is being fuelled by racial thinking. Our new homeland threatens to look nothing like the international, cosmopolitan, multicultural and multi-ethnic urban community that was destroyed along with the World Trade Center towers.

Meanwhile, in Britain, as gung ho Tony Blair treads the globe rallying folks to the American cause, October is Black History Month and the BBC Radio 4 ferrets me out of exile to talk about whether C. L. R. James should be regarded as an 'Uncle Tom'!

PART II.

Boundaries and Circuits of Blackness

6

What Is This 'Black' in Irish Popular Culture?

In December of 1991, in New York City, Stuart Hall challenged his audience, gathered for a conference on black popular culture, to question the terms under which we had come together. He asked, 'What is this "black" in black popular culture?'

> What sort of moment is this in which to pose the question of black popular culture? These moments are always conjunctural. They have their historical specificity; and although they always exhibit similarities and continuities with the other moments in which we pose a question like this, they are never the same moment. And the combination of what is similar and what is different defines not only the specificity of the moment, but the specificity of the question, and therefore the strategies of cultural politics with which we attempt to intervene in popular culture, and the form and style of cultural theory and criticizing that has to go along with such a mismatch.[1]

In this essay I intend to draw upon this interrogation of racial signifiers as they relate to particular historical moments, hoping both to echo and to reformulate Hall's insights. I will argue not only that we need to ask ourselves exactly what constitutes 'blackness' in what have been identified as black, and specifically African American, popular cultural forms, but also that we need to trace the ways in which these supposedly monocultural forms are now, through the processes and passages of globalization, frequently used as the means and the agents for the transnational transportation of other ethnic, national and racial signifiers. William T. Lhamon described his response to the wearing of dreadlocks by the Japanese as a realization that the black Atlantic has 'gone global'.[2]

While reaffirming that the complex patterns of black cultural and political migrations do, indeed, have their own specific histories, as Paul Gilroy has demonstrated, I also want to explore the ways which in these black routes and roots, passages and origins, are constantly interwoven with the migratory histories and cultures of other peoples whose own 'routes and roots' are sometimes carried by and sometimes expressed through political and cultural vessels marked as black.[3]

While this is a broad and sweeping conceptual brushstroke across transatlantic history, I am concerned that we collectively develop strategies that can deeply engage multiple and apparently diverse histories simultaneously. However, in this early stage of my thinking about constructing such engagements I am going to proceed with a series of juxtapositions of conjunctural moments in African American/Irish cultural exchange and transformation. In some of these moments one can see an acknowledgement of a relation between apparently discrete or autonomous elements and histories, whereas other moments may more aptly be characterized as occasions of fusion. But cultural fusion, I want to propose, may also have specific political effects melting and melding in such a way that particular histories are erased or denied, replaced instead by particular national, or racialized, or ethnic imaginings. I have organized my arguments around two historical moments: the processes of cultural exchange between Irish and African American peoples in the 1840s and the complex engagement with and fusion of African American cultural forms in the global performance of Irish popular culture in the 1990s.

I agree with Eric Lott that the self-inscription by young white men of signifiers of black masculinity onto their bodies is a dynamic which persists into adulthood and becomes a central element 'of most American white men's equipment for living'.[4] Indeed, we could also ask the extent to which the global circulation of images of black masculinity will make this more than a national phenomenon. However, I would disagree with Lott when he argues that these men remain entirely unconscious of their participation in this process. While the source of the styling of the body may be only too evident, and the consumption of circulating signifiers of black masculinity a conscious choice, the political cost of the public recognition of that source is high. Recognition contradicts both the general terms and the conditions of the segregated social formation which determines that the discrete or autonomous nature of the social relations which are supposed to exist between them are to be racially coded.

It is also important to remember that signifiers of blackness only tangentially relate to those peoples designated black. As racial signifiers and, in a complex formation of signifiers, as racial ideologies, both white and black have to negotiate their relation to blackness as it is defined in particular historical moments. This is not to ignore or negate the fact that this negotiation has to take place in a situation which is inherently unequal, structured in dominance, to use Stuart Hall's phrase, but it is to assert that what have been politically and culturally designated black peoples are also active participants in the process of signification.[5] They too have to decide to adopt, adapt, transform, ignore or deny a relation to a culturally produced and circulated blackness.

The last decade of the twentieth century was a particularly interesting conjunctural moment between the global production of blackness and Irishness. Terry Eagleton has observed, 'Modernity in Ireland means a range of precious things like feminism, pluralism, civic rights, secularization. It can also mean', he continues,

> being shamefaced and sarcastic about one's historical culture – that cultural specificity which all good postmodernists, except

> perhaps Irish ones, are supposed to celebrate ... Its admirable aim is to get out from under the dead weight of clericalism, patriarchy, patriotism, in order, rather less admirably, to leap suitably streamlined and amnesiac into a Europe ... which is characterised among other things by racism, structural unemployment, urban barbarism, the uprooting of whole communities, and the abandonment of the Irish working-class [*sic*] and small farmers to a brutal neo-liberal polity.[6]

Contradictory aspects of what Eagleton describes are embodied in the internationally successful performances of the *Riverdance* company, the Michael Flatley offshoot *Lord of the Dance* and his final extravaganza *Feet of Flames*.

In economic terms the success of these dance companies has been measured in the millions of dollars. In the first two years of its run, July 1996–1998, *Lord of the Dance* alone took in more than $200 million in ticket sales, placing it in the top five shows worldwide.[7] *Riverdance* has also been a financial blockbuster, and both dance organizations make additional profits from the sales of videotapes, compact discs and souvenir programmes.[8] The Public Broadcasting Service in the United States sought to capitalize on this popularity and endlessly recycled the shows, seeking to attract large audiences during their periods of fund-raising. Many spin-off Irish dance companies have entered the fray and all over the United States in cities and small towns classes in Irish step dancing are being offered, prompting me to ask what this international distribution and consumption of Irishness and, most disturbingly, Celticness has to do with the process of Irish modernization and incorporation into the new Europe that Eagleton defines.

At the centre of the original *Riverdance* show and film and reconfigured for the later *Riverdance Live* in New York City is a particular evocation of transatlantic migration and response to oppression.[9] In *Riverdance*, first performed at the Pointe Theatre in Dublin in 1995 and choreographed by its lead dancer, Michael Flatley, Irish migration to North America is presented as resulting in the formation of one among many other discrete diasporas. It is staged, in three parts, as a narrative of heterosexual romance. In the first section the audience is transported across the Atlantic by a solo female voice and a haunting melody entitled 'Lift the Wings'. The lyrics evoke a deep sense of the loss inherent in a migration marked as a necessity rather than a choice – 'Where will frail birds fly if their homes have been torn to the ground?' – but, visually, the narrative reduces the complex social and political history of the agonies of the famine of 1845–6 to the utterly banal. Staged as a graceful walk by a pair of young lovers, Michael Flatley and Jean Butler, who gaze longingly into each other's eyes, the passage across the Atlantic is signalled by a backdrop of the migrating birds of the song which gradually fades and re-forms as a suspension bridge.

History as matters of imperialism, colonial politics, the domination and exploitation of the English, and famine are issues that *Riverdance* avoids in relation to the Irish. Migration as a matter of material survival is replaced by a story of the heart. But upon arrival under the arch of the bridge the scene dramatically changes. The issues of history which are not carried by the young Irish dancers are articulated by and inscribed onto black bodies as an African American gospel choir (James Bignon and the Deliverance Ensemble) take their place on the stage.

In the revision of the show for a North American audience, *Riverdance Live from New York City*, the theme of migration as a matter of broken hearts is retained, although multiple couples enact the separation while the mournful strains of a violin underscore the tragic lines of a narrator: 'Dawn and the ships are leaving, /A lover's grief is lifting on the tide, / And hearts too young for sorrow torn asunder, / The cruel ocean deep and dark and wide.' The stage darkens to be gradually relit by a blue light. The music changes, a lone black male figure descends to centre stage and the narrator's voice fills the stage once more: 'Out of the night we come out of the sea, / On a new shore lights blaze in the dawn, / Motherless, fatherless torn from our homes, / We bring tears to this land we must make our own.' The rich baritone voice evokes other transatlantic crossings, 'the wounded and broken bodies' in the 'deep light from a dark space' of the enslaved as a preface to the gospel rendition of 'Lord, Where Is Our Freedom?' from the original show.

To understand this transition from Irish to black bodies, at once a cultural fusion and displacement, we need to consider the origins of the *Riverdance* phenomenon. In 1994 Ireland was host to the Eurovision Song Contest.

> The annual pop-song contest is transmitted live on European TV to an estimated 300 million viewers. While the judges debated how to allocate their votes Moya Doherty, a producer for RTV, Ireland's national television station, filled the time with a dance divertissement that she had commissioned from Flatley. The studio audience in Dublin rose to their feet at the end of the number, which celebrated Celtic myths and the River Liffey, at the heart of Ireland's capital city. The standing ovation was both a tribute to the performers and an affirmation of the Irish audience's sense of its own identity in the eyes of the watching world.[10]

Riverdance is the cultural vision of the economic narrative of the Irish as the success story of the new Europe. Just as the latter stands upon the ever-widening gap between the rich and the poor and silences the worsening material conditions of Ireland's working class which are the subjects of Roddy Doyle's novels, for example, the fiction of *Riverdance* assertively presents a newly imagined Irish nationalism as evidence of its integration into the European Union and the new world order.

As *Dance Magazine* declared, Irish dance 'stepped from obscurity to claim center stage'. While claiming to evoke tradition, Irish dance and instrumentation are refigured in *Riverdance*, shaped by the theatricalization and rhythms of the rock concert.[11] The narrative purges the material conditions from which the cultural forms emerged, creating a new, improved, authentic and purified history. The way in which *Riverdance* avoids the contradictions which lie under the surface of contemporary corporate stories of Irish success is not only by refusing to associate its new subjects with the sufferings of the past but also by disposing of the referents of victimhood and displacing it onto others. We are so used to African Americans being used as cyphers through which dominant culture can access spiritual resilience and folk wisdom that it has become common sense within popular culture that black bodies are instant referents for carrying the history of oppression.[12] In telling the story of Irish success, Irish pain is displaced onto black suffering. The Irish as those who were, historically, the racialized subjects of English oppression and exploitation are no longer racialized subjects in the present. On the contrary, their places are literally and symbolically replaced by those who still are racialized others. The gospel choir, James Bignon and the Deliverance Ensemble, articulate the struggles that the Irish faced while remaining located securely within an African American history. The performance of the new Irish heritage of *Riverdance* is the demonstrable proof of Irish belonging to the New Europe. The new nation displaces its past racialization and colonial history onto black bodies that act as icons, floating global signifiers of blackness which appear to have no limiting national belonging but are rather disparate multinational images. Irishness emerges from a spectacle of a seamless heroic tradition of Irish roots as a suitable prerequisite to, and justification of, subsequent routes which have formed the nation.

The gospel choir is followed by the Moiseyev Dance Company performing what is called, in the programme, 'The Russian Dervish'. These diasporas are presented as discrete communities, Irish, African American and Russian in this instance (also in the show is Maria Pages, an accomplished Flamenco dancer). The juxtaposition of performances of ethnicity implies that a variety of folk cultures can combine into an ensemble of interrelated parts, each folk form speaking to the experience of the other groups while maintaining a form of cultural expression, and by implication a history, that is unique to each. An African American cultural vehicle, for example, is used to express a 'hunger for liberty', 'a hatred of poverty' and a desperate search for 'freedom' that could also apply to the Irish diaspora. The effect is to establish a common reference system of human suffering while securing discrete divides between groups of peoples.

It is in this sense that the cultural and aesthetic politics of *Riverdance* imagine and present Irishness for global consumption as the story of one successful ethnic group among many, an Irishness to be understood within the frame of reference of multiculturalism. This multiculturalism is now predominantly digested within the frame of reference of corporate images like that of Benneton or Coca-Cola, a combination of numerous discrete cultures each with its own folk forms and roots. An important question to ask ourselves as cultural critics is how we interrupt the popular, comfortable and easily digestible global presentation of people's culture without history?

This global culture without history, I would argue, affirms the importance of national cultural boundaries in the face of their combination into large, corporate-controlled, political and economic international entities, like the new Europe, while at the same time denying the internationalism of its peoples and cultures whose actual histories have been messily intertwined in social, political and economic relations that consistently crossed and recrossed racial and ethnic boundaries and which are embodied in miscegenated cultural forms rather than ethnically pure folk cultures.

Metropolitan Museum of Art. Public domain

Outward-Bound (Dublin). After Erskine Nicol (British, Leith, Scotland, 1825–1904). Hand-coloured lithograph, *c.* 1860

From the point of view of African American cultural studies, attention to the black Atlantic is one stage of making the field less insular, parochial and nationally bounded, but it is only the first stage of investigation if we are to understand the complexities of multiple Atlantic crossings. Frederick Douglass, for example, when he arrived in Cork in 1845 to work with the Irish anti-slavery societies, realized that the politics of anti-slavery agitation could not be limited to black oppression alone. Douglass acknowledged the importance of cultural expression when he heard Irish workers singing. He characterized these songs as of 'a plaintive cast, [that] told a tale of grief and sorrow. In the most boisterous outbursts of rapturous sentiment, there was ever a tinge of deep melancholy. I have never heard any songs like those anywhere since I left slavery, except when in Ireland,' he concluded. Like Paul Robeson, Douglass articulated the political connection between forms of cultural expression and social conditions.[13] In a letter to William Lloyd Garrison, Douglass drew upon all his rhetorical power, hitherto directed towards evoking the condition of the enslaved in North America, and put it into service for the Irish poor. He described the Dublin streets as

> almost literally alive with beggars displaying the greatest wretchedness – some of them mere stumps of men, without feet, without legs, without hands, without arms – and others still more horribly deformed, with crooked limbs, down upon their hands and knees, their feet lapped around each other, and laid upon their backs, pressing their way through the muddy streets and merciless crowd. Women, barefooted and bareheaded, and only covered by rags which seemed to be held together by the very dirt and filth with which they were covered – many of these had infants in their arms, whose emaciated forms, sunken eyes and pallid cheeks, told too plainly that they had nursed till they had nursed in vain.

Douglass turned the attention of his *Liberator* readers temporarily away from the slave cabin towards another site of degradation:

of all places to witness human misery, ignorance, degradation, filth and wretchedness, an Irish hut is pre-eminent . . . Four mud walls about six feet high, occupying a space of ground about ten feet square, covered or thatched with straw – a mud chimney at one end, reaching about a foot above the roof – without apartments or divisions of any kind – without floor, without windows . . . In front of the door-way . . . is a hole three or four feet deep, and ten or twelve feet in circumference; into this hole all the filth and dirt of the hut are put . . . This is frequently covered with a green scum, which at times stands in bubbles, as decomposition goes on. Here you have an Irish hut or cabin, such as millions of the people of Ireland live in. And some live in worse than these. Men and women, married and single, old and young, lie down together, in much the same degradation as the American slaves . . . I confess I should be ashamed to lift up my voice against American slavery, but I know the cause of humanity is one the world over. He who really and truly feels for the American slave, cannot steel his heart to the woes of others; and he who thinks himself an abolitionist, yet cannot enter into the wrongs of others, has yet to find a true foundation for his anti-slavery faith.[14]

Metropolitan Museum of Art. Public domain

Homeward Bound (New York). After Erskine Nicol (British, Leith, Scotland, 1825–1904). Hand-coloured lithograph, *c.* 1860

Of course, this history of oppression of the Irish poor, with its dirt and filth, that Douglass so vividly and eloquently characterized, is unable to do the ideological work of summoning *Riverdance*'s nostalgia for an Irishness embodied in the lithe young white bodies of Michael Flatley and Jean Butler as they float unsullied in a sea of blue light.

Douglass would have greatly appreciated the irony of *Riverdance*'s particular contribution to the 'whitening of the Irish'. Upon his arrival in Cork, Douglass wrote to Garrison,

> no one seemed to be shocked or disturbed at my dark presence. No one seemed to feel himself contaminated by contact with me. I think it would be difficult to get the same number of persons together in any of our New England cities, without some democratic nose growing deformed at my approach. *But then you know white people in America are whiter, purer, and better than the people here. This accounts for it!*[15]

As illustrated in these lithographs, the Irish, too, were subjects of 'the alchemy of race'. It was their Celtic blood which condemned them as unfit to be equal citizens in the American republic: as one historian has described this process, 'a discernible racial chasm separated the Celt from the Anglo- Saxon . . . physical differences marked an inner, natural "difference" separating the two races undeniably.'[16] The Irish were weighed alongside the Negro in 1876, after the latter had gained the right to vote, and were found by *Harper's Weekly* to be an equal racial threat to the political future of the nation.

The Ignorant Vote – Honors Are Easy, Tomas Nast, 1876

This is the bodily image of an Irish past from which the *Riverdance* company must be forever dissociated. In its place is constructed a cartography of national type. Dance sequences are consistently introduced by traditional Irish instruments. These instruments are a key mechanism for situating the bodies of the dancers as also being traditional instruments of, or containers for, the production of Irishness. *Riverdance* opens, for example, with a single musician playing the uilleann pipes. The pipes summon the members of the chorus, who are dressed in emerald green and black. Their arms are rigidly held at their sides in the traditional pose of Irish step dancing, the females all have long hair flowing down their backs, and the visual effect is of the production of a national and ethnic uniformity. Of course, this uniformity cannot but help evoke a racialized conformity, a resurgence of Celticness which haunts *Riverdance*'s production of Irish nationalism and eventually dominates Michael Flatley's *Lord of the Dance*.

Despite the conscious attempt to present a modern and modernized Ireland, the actual performance of Irishness is traditionally patriarchal, for Michael Flatley, the lead dancer, consistently occupies a privileged position of masculinity. Only he is allowed to break and transcend the traditional conventions of form, moving his arms freely in stark contrast to the chorus of female and subordinate male dancers. The three dance sequences that precede the finale embody these contradictions. Jean Butler performs a lyrical solo in accord with the stringed instruments that introduce and accompany her. Michael Flatley is summoned onstage, as if into battle, by staggered ranks of drummers. His solo is structured as an aggressive, percussive conversation in answer to the drummers' beats. Then a series of broad sweeping movements, *à la* Fred Astaire, take Flatley up the stairs to centre stage, where he ends his solo using his taps as the percussive signal to summon the dance troupe. His arms rise as the chorus mounts from the back of the stage, making it appear as if Flatley brings them into being. Taking the role of the drums in his solo, Flatley then leads a precision chorus line. He sets the percussive rhythm; the chorus responds.

All Flatley's sequences are conscious acts of masculine prowess and become, in front of our eyes, the culminating triumph of the reconstruction of Irish dance, a reconstruction that concludes with one of Flatley's favourite moves, Michael Jackson's moonwalk. What is at the heart of the struggle to re-present authentic, at once traditional and modern, Irishness on the national and international stage is not what it pretends to be, a pure ethnicity taking its place within a field of various ethnicities. On the contrary, it is a messy miscegenation of musical and dance forms, for Michael Flatley, patriarch of Irishness gone global, is American. He grew up in Chicago, where he learnt to dance, and his repertoire style reveals a very close engagement with the work of a long history of African American tap dancers despite his assertions to the contrary.

Many journalists and dance critics have commented on what they call the Americanization of Irish dancing in *Riverdance* and subsequent derivatives. Yet what is referred to as Americanization is, more often than not, an African Americanization of dance.[17] Jacqui Malone argues that there are six definitive characteristics of black dance: 'rhythm, improvization, control, angularity, asymmetry, and dynamism'.[18] These elements are incorporated into all contemporary dance extravaganzas as the very basics with which modern dance forms engage. The first precision tap chorus line, for example, upon which so much of *Riverdance*'s choreography depends, was developed for the chorus line of *Chocolate Dandies* in 1924 by the African American choreographer Charlie Davis. Teams of black acrobatic tap dancers were a new trend on the Broadway stage in 1930. Honi Coles was the acknowledged creator of high-speed rhythm tap; along with Cholly Atkins, he blended ballet, modern dance and tap (all of which Flatley also does) in the 1930s and 1940s. In particular, Michael Flatley can be compared to James Barton, an Irish dancer from the 1920s who, after visiting the Cotton Club in Harlem, made his dancing distinctive by adding African American rhythmic complexity and making it 'swing'.[19]

While avoiding any reference to this complex dance history, a version of cultural competition is presented in *Riverdance: Live in New York City* as an encounter between the male members of the African American and Irish diasporas on the streets of New York called 'Trading Taps'. Explicitly defined by the narrator as 'battling feet on the city streets', 'Trading Taps' implicitly evokes the trading of steps that took place at the legendary Hoofers club, the 'unacknowledged headquarters of American dance', next door to the Lafayette Theater on 131st Street and Seventh Avenue in Harlem from the 1920s to the 1940s. Yet 'Trading Taps' is not performed as a cultural exchange, or even as a miscegenation of dance steps, but as a 'battle', as if staged by rival gang members, a confrontation of ethnic masculinities supported by their respective musical instruments, the fiddle versus the saxophone. Two African American and three Irish dancers do not trade, as in learn from and equally exchange, taps but compete in virtuoso performances to outdo each other. At times wittily imitating the styles of the other, at times representing a macho brawl, the number builds to a testosterone-filled climax in which one of the black dancers twice runs to a wall and up it, and into a somersault, resolving the rivalry and bringing the audience to its feet. Immediately following the gospel singers, 'Trading Taps' firmly establishes the distinction between Irish and African American cultural forms. Rather than establishing human commonalities, as the references to suffering in the previous scene implied, it is cultural difference which is reinforced as absolute in the performing of ethnicities and masculinities; each is supposed to remain distinct and apart.

Michael Flatley had already left the *Riverdance* company before they performed in New York, complaining of a lack of artistic recognition, control and financial renumeration, and he was replaced by Colin Dunne. While *Riverdance* continued to stage its separate but equal multicultural politics, Flatley forged a very different cultural vision in his *Lord of the Dance*, his consummate act of revenge against the *Riverdance* company that had fired him rather than accede to his demands. The shift, I would argue, is from the performance of discrete ethnicities, the cultural aesthetics of multiculturalism, to a cultural aesthetics of fascism.

The first stage of this shift is signalled in Flatley's description of the show as 'all new and all Irish'. Gone are the Flamenco,

Russian and African American dances in his flat rejection of the politics and aesthetics of multiculturalism. Flatley absolutely denies that the dancing and the choreography of *Lord of the Dance* owe anything to any other dance form, consequently erasing the complex forms of influence that constitute the history of modern dance. Describing the preparation of his troupe for *Lord of the Dance*, Flatley insisted,

> I don't pick and choose from other dance forms when I do this, what I do is go inside for whatever . . . I am trying to create comes from . . . inside, the trick here and probably the biggest, the hardest task is to constantly create something completely new. It's not something that you will see on television with a modern dance company, with a jazz company, with a flamenco dance company, with a tap company. You won't see this stuff anywhere else in the world because it doesn't come from anywhere else in the world. What we create here, we create on our own.[20]

CD cover of *Lord of the Dance*

In the cultural space opened by the erasure of history in *Riverdance* Flatley creates a complex web of mythologies in *Lord of the Dance*. The first is the mythology of masculine power and showmanship. The second is the replacement of Irishness with a racial mythology of Celtic origins which, I would argue, Flatley intends to be a direct counterpoint to the racialized aesthetics that he associates with black dance. These mythologies are not maintained as separate and distinct; they work apparently seamlessly together, and are mutually interdependent, each reinforcing and articulating the other.

A fantasy of masculinity, of the aggrandizement of male sexuality, power and control, *Lord of the Dance* perfectly articulates the appeal of fascist spectacle. The stage is an assemblage of monumental metallic structures woven into Celtic symbols. These symbols also adorn the dancer's bodies, forming trellises that mount legs and arms. Emblazoned on the chests of the male dancers, they also encircle the breasts and hips of the female members of the troupe. The effect is astonishing and startles in its close relation to Nazi spectacle and use of symbolism as the troupe move in tight formations around the stage.

Don Dorcha's troops, *Lord of the Dance*

Clearly, one model of showmanship that has influenced Michael Flatley is the Michael Jackson version of mass spectatorship and adoration. The elements upon which Flatley seizes goes far beyond his use of Jackson's moonwalk, his dance style, his use of the body as a percussive instrument to signal his appearance or disappearance in an explosion of fireworks, or his projection of total self-absorption. The significance of militarism as a very important factor in the presentation of symbolic masculine power forms the central iconography of an extraordinary film, 'Brace Yourself: A Kaleidoscope of Michael Jackson HIStory' which introduces the collection *Michael Jackson: Video Greatest Hits*.[21] Set to Carl Orff's *Carmina Burana*, the film is constructed as a kaleidoscope of images from Jackson's world tours. The editing emphasizes adoration of Jackson in the form of mass spectatorship and mass hysteria in a series of scenes reminiscent of the photography of Leni Riefenstahl. The power of Jackson is evoked through the intercutting of scenes of crowds of young women screaming and fainting with a sequence of juxtaposed images of Jackson in a series of militaristic costumes flanked by armies of the police or military of half a dozen different nations escorting him onto various stages throughout the globe. The effect is breathtaking in its evocation of fascist spectacle. Perhaps this sequence was specifically intended to construct an aggressive masculinity for a figure whose performances on- and offstage self-consciously undermine traditional masculine conventions, and who explicitly criticizes military might and power in such performances as 'Heal the World'. However, the unnamed filmmaker/producer of this introduction seized upon and exploited to the full the fascist aesthetics which haunt Michael Jackson's spectacular productions. While dissociating himself entirely from Jackson's sexual ambiguity, this is exactly what Flatley himself has also learnt from the production of Jackson spectacles, how the power of fascist aesthetics for militaristic masculine aggrandizement can be realized through performance. Rejecting Jackson's continual boundary crossings, Flatley works instead to reinforce and maintain sexual and boundary markers.

Lord of the Dance is about the dominance of racial fictions. It produces its own racial fiction, as Celticness, in an aggressive and utterly uncompromising representation of a racialized masculinity. Flatley's denial of influences upon his own creativity, particularly of the influence of Michael Jackson, is a denial of the hybrid nature of his own performance and a denial of the validity of the miscegenated aspects of cultural production in favour of the reinforcement of racial and sexual boundaries and the marking of racial and sexual fictions for global consumption. As such, Michael Flatley's spectacles are the perfect cultural products of the segregation of twentieth-century American urban life.

The plot of *Lord of the Dance* is too simplistic to be credible, a visual combination of *Star Wars* (with a little sprite instead of the cute robots) and *Starship Troopers*. It is the battle of unqualified good versus unqualified evil: bad men – Don Dorcha and his troops – are dressed in black uniforms, wear black masks and consort with bad women; bad women are sexual temptresses, have black hair and dress in red; the perfect female partner for our hero, the Lord of the Dance, is a blond, Irish Colleen who signals her virgin state by dressing in white; and, finally, happy peasants appear in pastels.

The racial fiction of Celticness in *Lord of the Dance* is dependent upon the production of other racial and sexual fictions. The confrontations between the massed forces of Don Dorcha and the forces of the Lord of the Dance deliberately recreate the bodily movements and style of representations of American urban (read black) masculinity. The dance movements and choreography of these scenes evoke the choreography and staging of Michael Jackson's 'Bad' video. In the performance of femininities, racial fictions are used to mark and distinguish women: the dance of the whore, for example, is introduced and accompanied by a blues saxophone – already established as the appropriate instrument for dancing black bodies by *Riverdance* – the only time this instrument is used in the show. It is specifically illicit sexuality that is marked or signalled as 'raced', though by negative implication and distinction the sexual purity of the Irish Colleen is equally racialized as authentically Celtic. Female sexuality is totally subordinated to and at the service of both good and bad masculine prowess, and the performance of sexuality is increasingly reminiscent of Nazi sexual politics as the show progresses. *Lord of the Dance*, in all aspects of its staging, choreography, movement and sculpting of bodies, explicitly reproduces a form of mythology which reduces all social relations to a black-and-white dichotomy, a dichotomy which is, at one and the same time, a racialized and patriarchal narration of the traffic in women.

But, having identified the Irish and Celtic national, ethnic and racial fictions being carried by what we have come to know as African American cultural forms, what then? We could reproduce the form of cultural analysis which argues that all this proves is that black culture continues to be appropriated and exploited and that all that is new is that now it is occurring on a global stage. But as I have already suggested in my discussion of the contradictory political aesthetics present in Michael Jackson spectacles, some of which Michael Flatley adopts and elaborates and some of which he abandons, the narratives of cultural roots and routes are not simple.

In 1842, Charles Dickens wandered the lanes and alleys of Five Points in New York. He saw, he says,

> walls bedecked with rough designs of ships and forts, and flags, and American Eagles out of number: ruined houses, open to the street, whence, through wide gaps in the walls other ruins loom upon the eye, as though the world of vice and misery had nothing else to show . . . all that is loathsome, drooping and decayed is here.

From the streets he descended into an underground chamber, 'where they dance and game', presided over by Pete Williams and 'a buxom, fat mulatto woman, with sparkling eyes'. He recorded what has now become a famous description of Juba, William Henry Lane.

> Single shuffle, double shuffle, cut and cross-cut: snapping his fingers, rolling his eyes, turning in his knees, presenting the backs of his legs in front, spinning about on his toes and heels like nothing but the man's fingers on the tambourine; dancing with two left legs, two right legs, two wooden legs, two wire legs, two spring legs – all sorts of legs and no legs – what is this to him . . . he finishes by leaping gloriously on the bar-counter.[22]

The JUBA Project

Juba dances at Vauxhall Gardens

A century and a half later, set in the scene of the equally despised streets of the post-industrial city, Michael Jackson's dance sequence that concludes the morphing sequences of 'Black or White' is choreographed to the identical script.[23] Jackson both recreates the movements of Juba and transforms and transposes them into our modern moment.

However, in addition to the reproduction of dance form, what Michael Jackson's performance and William Henry Lane have in common is that each is attempting to break through the boundaries of the available cultural grammar of its age. Five Points in the 1840s was where the migrants of the black and Irish Atlantic lived in intimate integration;[24] danced, drank and had sex together; struggled to survive working as seamen, on the docks or in the markets, running from the oppression of the English and the southern slave holders. A miscegenated and rebellious culture, it produced mulatto bodies and mulatto cultures. It was precisely its very excesses that caused it to be feared and labelled a dangerous place by the respectable classes.

George Foster, like Dickens, tried to capture this excess of the dance house in language which constantly strains against its own descriptive limitations. The orchestra in Pete Williams's establishment was sometimes 'a single black fiddler', but on Saturday nights he was joined by a trumpeter and bass drummer. Foster wrote,

> the music . . . is of no ordinary kind. You cannot, however, begin to imagine what it is. You cannot see the red-hot knitting needles spirited out by the red-faced trumpeter . . . pierce through and through your brain without remorse. Nor can you perceive the frightful mechanical contortions of the bass-drummer as he sweats and deals his blows on every side, in all violation of the laws of rhythm . . . Probably three-quarters of the women assembled here . . . are negresses, of various shades and colours . . . The 'bar' is crowded by motley and thirsty souls, refreshing themselves for the severe exercises about to commence . . . the dancers

> begin contorting their bodies and accelerating their movements ... until all observance of the figure is forgotten and everyone leaps, stamps, screams and hurrars on his or her own hook ... The black leader of the orchestra increases the momentum of his elbow and calls out the figures in convulsive efforts to be heard, until shining streams of perspiration roll in cascades down his ebony face; the dancers ... leap like howling dervishes, clasp their partners in their arms, and at length conclude the dance in hot confusion and disorder.[25]

Free blacks and Irish who are not yet white, sailors, b'hoys, and rowdies mix and mingle and produce a profound disorder. It is a disorder, as we can hear in Foster's reaching and stretching for appropriate words, that the respectable classes of the white republic did not even know how to name except through evocations of the opposite of what they recognized as providing their society with its glue by marking the boundaries and hierarchies of race and class and gender, and acceptable sexuality.[26] In this site of disorder, of contorted bodies and cacophonies of sounds, is a different moment of cultural miscegenation. Any search for the purely Africanist roots of American dance must also pay attention to this moment, a moment in which what becomes known now as a pre-eminently black dance form is developed from the black adoption, adaptation and transformation of the Irish jig. The roots and routes of black and Irish cultural migrations coalesce and re-form in these basements.

The term 'miscegenation' was invented in 1863 by the author of *Miscegenation: The Theory of the Blending of the Races, Applied to the American White Man and the Negro.*[27] The term was derived from the Latin *miscēre*, 'to mix', and *genus*, 'race'. The pamphlet was the creation of an anti-abolitionist Irish newspaper editor, David Goodman Croly, who published it anonymously in the hope that it would disrupt the election of 1864. *Miscegenation* was written as if the author was an abolitionist advocating the amalgamation of black and white in general, and the intermarriage of Negroes and the Irish in particular. The intention was to generate general antagonism among the New York electorate towards abolitionists and their cause and thus affect the presidential election of the following year. Croly states in the pamphlet,

> Whenever there is a poor community of Irish in the North they naturally herd with the poor negroes ... connubial relations are formed between the black men and white Irish women ... The white Irishwoman loves the black man and ... the negro is sure of the handsomest among the poor white females ... The fusion ... will be of infinite service to the Irish. They are a more brutal race and lower in civilization than the negro ... coarse-grained, revengeful, unintellectual ... below the level of the most degraded negro.[28]

The very nature of this political hoax indicates how much of a threat the crossing of racial and sexual boundaries was to the New York political elite, the expectation of outrage at such suggested amalgamation a measure of the perceived necessity to discipline and control the mingling of bodies and cultures.

In the organizing of our transnational cultures and their publics, we need to be sensitive to all the implications of commingling. Against the Irish/African American examples of transatlantic exchange that I have given here perhaps we should place the politics of soul against the politics of race. In Roddy Doyle's novel *The Commitments* a group of young Irish men use the music of James Brown to recognize their position as the 'niggers of Europe'. They perform blackness and through it become 'black and proud'. James Brown leads them to define soul as 'the politics of the people', as 'dignity and self-respect'. Forming a Dublin soul group called the Commitments, they tell their audience to prepare to 'put on their soul shoes because the Commitments are coming and there's going to be dancing in the street', to which they add, 'And there'll be barricades in the streets too'.[29]

Articulating the complexities of the relations between oppressions is an essential aspect of this transnational cultural exchange. What we need is an expression of black Irishness which can expose the limitations of multiculturalism as the politics of discrete, autonomous ethnic cultures as performed in *Riverdance*. In its place we need to engage the politics of soul if we are to actively oppose the aesthetics of fascism and of segregation which Michael Flatley has found so profitable.

7

Promoting Blackness

My transatlantic journeyings over the last twenty years and my reflections upon the political ambiguities of being a black European with American citizenship continue to influence my responses to black intellectual life and work in North America.

Prologue

I was born and grew up in post–Second World War Britain, the daughter of parents whose years of coming into adulthood themselves had been definitively and indelibly shaped by the events of the war which brought them together.[1] My white mother, who was born in Wales, had worked as a civil servant in the Air Ministry; my father was a black Jamaican who had served in the Bomber Command of the Royal Air Force as a navigator and wireless operator. Their experiences of the war, as related to me, were my first encounters with history.

Each parent had come from poverty, though one was from the centre of colonial power and one from its colonized periphery. Each had unquestioningly volunteered to serve and save the British Empire; each, from their distinct perspectives and places, defined themselves as British and unhesitatingly loyal to whatever Britishness meant to them. They had grown up, each in their own part of the world, feeling an unquestioned sense of belonging to British culture. They imagined that that would be my heritage too.

But, after the war, their being in the same part of the empire, its heart, presented a series of problems, not the least of which was their marriage. This, indeed, jeopardized their, as well as my, sense of cultural belonging. The history they did not pass on, and of which I only gradually became aware, was their outcast status. For example, shunned by relatives, friends and strangers and unable to find anyone willing to rent to a black and white couple with a 'half-caste' child, they had to live in separate accommodations in south London until they could afford the deposit for a house. Strapped for the mortgage payments, for years they rented a room in their house to a series of African students and, in this way, other parts of empire came home.

From being responsible, loyal, young adults serving their country in its hour of need, my parents were now relegated to the position of being irresponsible adults whose actions threatened the racialized social order and stable culture of Britain: first for their act of miscegenation, and second for bringing into the world a 'half-caste' child who by definition could never belong to British society and culture. Thus were my encounters with English racial logic shaped.

At school, the history that we were taught contradicted outright or simply ignored the history of my home. For example, no black soldiers, sailors or airmen served Britain during the war, with the exception of those on American bases, and they, as we all knew, didn't fight; they cooked. What I needed to know of history could be explained by learning about the beneficence of the English, who laboured to bring enlightenment to a third of the globe only to be paid back by boatloads of ungrateful coloured immigrants, immigrants who didn't know how to behave like decent people, landing on the shores of a kind-hearted and generous-spirited island. This generosity just had to stop; it was getting out of hand. After all, 'they' were everywhere, 'they' loved crowding together, and 'they' were so noisy. And which country did I come from anyway? If I claimed citizenship of the UK as my birthright, where, exactly, had I come from before that? After all, I couldn't be indigenous, homegrown?

What Stories?

One of the things that intellectuals do is to tell stories about themselves, about their society and about their culture. In that telling we exercise choices about how we relate to history and how we relate the history of racialization to others. Twenty years of living in North America has taught me that there are a number of different stories that describe the ways in which black intellectuals situate themselves as black Americans in the Americas. Black Canadian intellectuals, for example, participate easily in an internationalized discourse of racialization in which the racialized logics of the United States, the Caribbean and Europe form historical, cultural, economic, ideological and political reference points.[2] Black intellectuals in South America situate themselves in relation to a multiplicity of racial discourses articulating the complexity of national and international frames of reference.[3]

However, it would seem as if many of our most prominent contemporary black American intellectuals, those most celebrated by the media in the United States, act as if race and racism are transhistorical and transnational categories and processes that can be defined entirely by and through the history and experience of those of African descent in the continental US. They seem to believe that the conceptual categories of race and racism dominant in the US are *the* paradigmatic measures of processes of racial logic and histories of racialization. I regard these attitudes, wherever I find them, first as a form of intellectual imperialism, and second as a sign of the tendency, within African American studies, towards parochialism and nationalism.

Within the framework of the dominant ideologies of the racial formation of the United States, and within the ideological framework that dominates the field of African American studies, it is difficult to conceive of the cultural, political and social existence of black Europeans.[4] Within the continental United States, the history of Europe and its peoples and their influence is not only assumed but 'known' to be white: Euro-, the prefix in front of the hyphenated American identity, signifies whiteness, pure and simple.[5]

But, in fact, Europe has its own history of racialization, a context within which issues of race and racism have a different history and trajectory from the United States, a history and trajectory that cannot be understood within the dominant racial paradigms of African American studies, a field which makes unique claims to the production of an 'authentic blackness'. In the post–Second World War United Kingdom, questions of race and issues of racism were not seen as stemming from, or as embedded in, the events of Britain's past or the actions of its people. On the contrary, a concern with matters of race and racism were thought to have their origins not in British colonialism but in the migration of black peoples to Britain. Racism, in other words, was understood to be the result of black migration; it was the actions and activities of these black bodies that caused racism, and a concern with issues of race, to come into being. In this scenario, the role of English innocence played a significant role. English history, of course, expounds upon the liberal tolerance of its peoples and culture, claiming to have promoted, through colonization, a civilizing influence upon a third of the globe, liberating and enlightening wherever it went. No reference was made within the frame of this particular dominant narrative that it was the enslaved labour of African peoples which produced the wealth of British cities like Bristol, Cardiff, Liverpool and London; created the capital of British corporations like Tate and Lyle; and financed the Industrial Revolution. Race and racism infected the body politic of the British Isles only after the war when racism was carried in with black migrants as if it were the plague.[6]

English nationalism, the hegemonic form of nationalism in Britain, dominated the politics of race and nation, an arena in which being both black and British was at one and the same time an essential site of struggle for equal citizenship for minority populations and a contradiction in terms. Naming, articulating and protesting the terms and conditions of this struggle of its black populations has been the task of black intellectuals, artists and cultural workers. It constitutes, now, what Paul Gilroy has called the absolute necessity and impossibility of being a black European.[7]

The self-assured and self-promoting stance of the black intellectuals who stand as our representative and authentic black voices in the United States is a dramatic contrast to the acute sense of political, social and cultural contradiction, ambiguity and tension that characterize the stories that Paul Gilroy tells as a black European intellectual. And yet it is the latter that offers us an insurgent place from which to interrogate the extent to which African American studies has not only conformed to but is dominated by the politics of American parochialism and nationalism. This parochialism and nationalism continue to dominate our work despite the frequency and regularity of what, to my mind, have become merely rhetorical appeals to W. E. B. Du Bois's concept of double consciousness. Double consciousness is often recited like a mantra, but rarely articulated in its full political and psychological complexity.[8]

It is the early Du Bois (for example, the Du Bois of 1903 and *The Souls of Black Folk*) rather than the later Du Bois (who was an internationalist and a socialist) who is recovered and canonized as a 'founding father' of the field by Henry Louis Gates and Cornel West in a series of conservative readings of that book in which each claims his mantle at the end of the century.[9] It is *The Souls of Black Folk*, not Du Bois's far more insurgent and revolutionary *Black Reconstruction*, that is reprinted in endless numbers of editions as a founding text of the field. This is a difference of conservative versus radical reference points and a position that can also be measured in the distance between the centrality of *The Souls of Black Folk* and the marginality of C. L. R. James's *Black Jacobins* to African American studies.

While *Souls* is bounded by a concern with a national dilemma and conservative cultural politics, *Black Jacobins* is a text which argues that the first modern black subjects emerge on a world stage in the late eighteenth century from the context of revolutionary struggle. James is committed to the exposition of the ways in which black revolutionary action should be understood not just in terms of black history but as central to understanding, in particular, the course of the French Revolution and, in general, the direction in which future European colonization developed. James's work, then, is characteristic of a very different position towards history, a position which refuses to be bound by the type of racialized intellectual ghettoization that circumscribes African American studies.

I would argue that African American studies needs to renounce the perpetuation of its parochialism in the stories it tells and situate itself in reference to an internationalist and global politics and polity. To fully understand the emergence of black modernity, since 1492, a historical moment marked by the expulsion of the Jews and the Moors from Spain as well as the European invasion of the Americas, we have to be able to conceptualize and articulate both the specificities *and* the generalities of the multiple and complex racial formations established because of the Atlantic slave trade, the biggest forced migration of labour in world history.

In our contemporary moment we need to understand the relation between the international and the national reorganization of racialized and ethnicized labour forces in late capitalism. We see the 'free' but actually corporate-controlled, transnational movement of capital across the borders that people are not 'free' to cross. But can we see the relation between, on the one hand, the movement of corporations in search of ever cheaper labour forces in the Asian subcontinent, in our federal penitentiaries and in the establishment of *maquiladoras* and, on the other, the abandonment of African American labour forces in Detroit, Los Angeles or East St Louis? These labour forces were brought into being to feed the needs of industrial corporations that now have abandoned them and their children to be locked up, walled into poverty, third-rate schools, and the criminal justice system.

Likewise, we cannot begin to comprehend the current predicament of black labour, including the significant segment of which that labours, disenfranchised, within the confines of the penitentiary system, unless we can establish the relation between the nation state, acting as a prison–industrial complex, and a global restructuring of labour in late capitalism.[10]

As a black European embedded in the field of African American studies in the United States, I also feel the importance and the urgency of engaging in a dialogue across the Atlantic in order to understand the consequences of a resurgence of nationalisms and racisms in the new, corporate-controlled Europe.[11] Can we really stand apart, as black intellectuals, from, for example, the horrors perpetrated under the obscene euphemism of 'ethnic cleansing'? Do we not also need to engage the specific histories of other racial formations, whether those of Brazil, Canada or South Africa, if we are to situate the local arenas of our work within a broader perspective? To de-parochialize our work we need to dislocate and destablize fixed notions of race and cultural belonging in the stories we tell, allowing them instead to be historicized, regarded as contingent, fluid, often fractured, and hybrid.

On the backs of social movements and in the face of great antagonism we have built new fields of knowledge in American universities. The conditions under which we have built these programmes, centres, institutes or departments are ones of uneven development, and many of us frequently find ourselves in situations of competition with other programmes for scarce resources, devoting our flagging energies to our survival, or maintenance, or expansion in complete disregard of those with whom we are in competition, whether women's and gender studies or the multivalent areas that make up the fields of ethnic studies. It is time to take stock, to ask ourselves not only what we have built, but also at what cost. In our battles to establish our autonomy, to situate our distinct voices, to assert our particularity, to what extent do we promote intellectual segregation and ghettoization, characteristics which reproduce the structures of isolation of the social formation in which we live?

Too much of the work of our intellectual celebrities in African American studies, in my opinion, is about the business of producing absolutist ideas and traditions of blackness or African (US) Americanness. Far from being a radical response to both the domination and the exclusion of a racist national culture and the racial logics of academic disciplines, this sort of work is extremely conservative and just reproduces the absolutist intellectual frameworks of the culture it criticizes. African American studies should be a field which is both insurgent and interdisciplinary; instead it has been overwhelmingly popularized by the conservatives and conformists. We have been about the work of creating what are seen to be 'our own traditions' to prove that we too have a culture and we have defined the parameters of that culture in the racialized terms imposed upon us.

While the process of imagining and creating alternative traditions frequently has its origins in political resistance to domination, exploitation and exclusion, political opposition to that domination needs to go further and dismantle the mechanisms of exclusion. We do not take this second crucial step when we adopt the mechanisms of oppression for our own purposes and neglect to criticize and dismantle the processes of tradition formation and canon production, processes which act to exclude and banish that which does not fit, particularly multiplicity, dissonance and disagreement. African American studies has its origins in a social movement which was not only a struggle for liberation and social justice, but a struggle for social transformation. What should be insurgent about the field is, precisely, this commitment to transformation, not only in relation to the injustices of the status quo but also in relation to the academic order.

I do not want to pretend that insurgency is easy; tenurability within academic institutions may be measured by conformity. But as senior scholars we must be vocal in our support for the radically transformative work of our junior colleagues – work that threatens the racial logics of conventional disciplines and provides us with a constant critique of the ways in which traditional fields of knowledge are organized – rather than celebrate work that strives to conform to or, at best, reform them. Rather than be nostalgic for the lost activism of the past we could be very self-conscious and self-critical about the ways in which we are organizing African American studies as a field of knowledge for the future and consistently ask ourselves what interdisciplinarity means in our education system where single disciplines dominate the humanities and social sciences. One crucial question facing us is, should we be forming alliances with other interdisciplinary fields?

I am convinced, at this particular moment of transition into the twenty-first century, that we must consider the politics of alliance. I find myself asking, every day, to what extent do our theoretical and conceptual apparatus of cultural autonomy work to ensure our multiple parochial existences, whether in African American studies, Asian American studies, Chicano/Chicana studies, Latino/Latina studies or Native American studies, or in the fields of women's, gender and sexuality studies. As interdisciplinary fields of knowledge we have all confronted and directly challenged histories and traditions which excluded or marginalized us. But have we forged and shaped new histories and traditions which, in turn, exclude or marginalize the stories of our multiple relations to each other, stories which could convey the complex history of the commonalities between and among marginalized peoples? Indeed, I wonder whether we can effectively access our particularity without understanding the ways in which our histories are not just intertwined but interdependent, whether as gendered beings, as labour or as immigrants and migrants.

Do we need to reconceive the parameters of ethnic studies and African American studies to enable future political alliances? How many of our students can imagine a future in which our current social, political and economic relations of inequality are transformed and social justice is achieved? And how many imagine an active role for *themselves* in such a transformation? Can we teach our distinct histories in ways that also demonstrate their connections, their interrelatedness and interdependence, and thus enable our students to imagine a future in which out of these connections they can demand and determine a common humanity based upon the principles of equity and justice? Is it possible, in other words, for us to expand and cross our histories and our imaginations simultaneously?[12] Can we find new grounds for alliance in social movement, not losing our particularity, but not clinging tenaciously to it either?

I obviously have more questions than I have answers, but I feel the need to provoke us to push open the boundaries between the discrete academic distances of African American and ethnic studies. Rather than be defensive in the face of accusations that all of these areas are merely identity politics, we need to aggressively assert that the politics of identity is the work of the nation state which excludes, oppresses, exploits, interns or incarcerates on the basis of social, political and economic identities that it designates and maintains. I agree with John Hope Franklin when he says we need to be, we must be, passionate advocates. Our students need to know that they should grasp the moral, ethical and political leadership of this nation and we should teach them.

In the histories of our struggles over citizenship, the work of Lisa Lowe enables us to understand how the administration of citizenship was 'simultaneously a "technology" of racialization and gendering', and she demonstrates how, historically, Chinese men were concentrated into service sector, domesticated jobs and thus 'feminized'.[13] We can expand our understanding of African American history and black particularity if, for example, we tell this story in conjunction with the story of how African American women were locked into the same labour. In narrating our histories of agency and activism we also need to provide our students with the tools to understand why, when washerwomen in Atlanta organized against their white employers between 1877 and 1900, they also organized *against* Chinese laundry workers.[14] Do our students not need to know that this failure to define common interests worked, ultimately, to ensure the continued subordination of both?

If we wish to retain any allegiance to social movements for social justice and liberation surely we must begin by recognizing that our function contradicts our political radicalism. It may not be necessary to look far outside the walls of academia to find and support social movements for justice and equality. My own university, Yale University, is a corporation, like other corporations, with financial interests directly opposed to the welfare of its employees. In these circumstances, one social movement to be supported would be the labour organizing taking place within the university. Many of us are situated in universities with well-endowed university facilities in poor and predominantly black and latino urban areas with devastated educational systems. We do not have to summon up an abstract 'black community' with which to ally when it surrounds us and comes into our classrooms, residential buildings and dining halls every day to care for us and clean up our mess. To be nostalgic for the civil rights movement and bewail the lack of its contemporary equivalent is to turn our backs on struggles which may not be primarily articulated through or determined by a racial logic although absolutely in the interests of the black and minority working, unemployed or undocumented poor, as the protests in Seattle in 1999 against the World Trade Organization, which focused on issues including workers' rights, sustainable economies and environmental and social issues, aptly demonstrated.

Intellectuals do not build social movements but they can intervene in the social, political and economic formation to encourage their emergence. In my opinion, at the front line of future struggles is the public school system. As educators we clearly have a responsibility to be vocal advocates for its interests, to end residential and educational segregation, and to oppose the threats to the public school system from the suburban bourgeoisie.[15] As black intellectuals we should intervene in and attempt to ameliorate the crisis of our local public school systems, lobbying for increased support at the federal level and sharing our extraordinary wealth of resources and knowledge at the state and local levels. For if we are serious about our commitment to social transformation we need to recognize that it is the generation now in our high schools that are the generation that could form the backbone of the next mass social movement for equity and for social justice.

Being self-conscious of the contradictions of functioning as an intellectual could also lead us to expand the definition of the term 'intellectual' to include those activists, labour leaders, teachers, creative artists and so on who have given voice to the concerns and interests of the marginalized, oppressed and exploited. But we also need to build, in the present, institutions for intellectual exchange between and among all these people who struggle locally, not to form a Negro Academy for the twenty-first century, which I have heard promoted, but to build a movement out of an egalitarian series of forums for social, political and economic justice.

But if we are committed to equality and justice, we have to confront our failure to address, in a collective and forceful manner, issues of gender and sexuality. It frankly appalls me that the field of African American studies can be so self-satisfied and self-assured that its work is in the interests of liberation and serves the cause of equality and social justice while we maintain and perpetuate hierarchies of power that silence the voices of women, bisexuals, lesbians and gay men. Instead of accusing those of us, black feminists, lesbians, bisexuals and gay male allies, of washing dirty linen in public and threatening to destroy black unity, we need to clean house.

We must discuss the ways in which we police and discipline ourselves by institutional mechanisms that are dependent upon and conform to the patriarchal and homophobic ideologies and practices of hegemonic institutions. It seems to me, in our attempt to condemn racist abuses of power, we silence other abuses of power, particularly in our own backyard. When do we discuss systems of black patronage and structures of power, the power that black male academics exercise over younger black male and black female scholars? What are the possibilities for abuse of power in the policing and allocating of financial support, publication and tenuring of black women, bisexuals, lesbians and gay men? Do we know and do we want to know the answers to these questions? Predominantly white institutions are more than willing to have black scholars police ourselves, whether by playing active roles in the university tenure system, in the awarding of grants through the National Endowment for the Humanities or other foundations, or in establishing our own publishing series at university presses. Without a public interrogation of these relations of power and control, black feminist, lesbian, bisexual, trans and gay critiques can be very easily censored and silenced. Silence is complicity. Silence demonstrates a public lack of commitment to building more equitable, more cooperative and more communal structures of involvement.

We have a long way to go. Few black male intellectuals take seriously or engage in black feminist theoretical and political debate, most consider issues of gender apply only to women, and nearly all consider the work of deconstructing patriarchal ideologies and practices of masculinity not worthy of their attention. In the social sciences and the humanities, heterosexist assumptions, conceptual frameworks and methodologies are taken for granted as providing the norm of what is characterized as 'the black experience'.

In conclusion, I would like to address the extent to which we function, as academics and as intellectuals, as professionalized embodiments of processes of racialization and ethnicization and ask us to consider how we are defining intellectuals and intellectual practice. The conflation of black academics with black leadership has a dire effect. It severely and regressively limits our imagining of the range of intellectual life and practice. We need to create and participate in a critical debate about how we define the term 'intellectual'. I find Antonio Gramsci's argument about the grounds of distinguishing between the diverse and disparate activites of intellectuals and the activities of other social groupings very persuasive. He asks whether we can find a unitary criterion to define the activities of intellectuals and concludes,

> The most widespread error of method seems to me that of having looked for this criterion of distinction in the intrinsic nature of intellectual activities, rather than in the ensemble of the system of relations in which these activities (and therefore the intellectual groups who personify them) have their place within the general complex of social relations . . .
>
> All men are intellectuals . . . but not all men have in society the function of intellectuals.[16]

While it is true that the field of African American studies has its origins in a social movement, it is also clear that we serve a number of institutional functions for our employers. As social institutions, universities act to maintain the hierarchical nature of the status quo by excluding most of the population from their classrooms while ensuring that a small number are trained and certified to supervise others. In Gramscian terms, in the post–civil rights era black academics have functioned and continue to function as intellectuals in particular and politically contradictory ways in the 'ensemble of the system of relations in which these activities have their place within the general complex of social relations'. Are we meant to function as the black gatekeepers, ensuring the production, perpetuation and maintenance of a small, black, middle-class elite in the hope that this elite will act as a force to control the rebellious tendencies of the black oppressed?

Our current political moment (2001) is characterized by the conflation of the terms 'black intellectual', 'black academic' and 'black leader', particularly by the media.[17] Our black academic world is clearly shaped by the same market forces that produce a Michael Jordan as black icon. The media produce certain black voices as celebrity intellectuals, as voices of black leadership defined not only through the body, but through the valorization of the poverty of their ideas and praise for the clichéd generalities expressed in the form of easily digestible sound bites.

The abandonment of intellectual insurgency and critical complexity in favour of the self-promotion of celebrities and the production of formulaic and acceptable interpretations of black America for general consumption are an indication of the extent to which academic entreprenuers can function as the products and allies of corporate America. The conflation of black intellectual leadership with academic entrepreneuralism promises a dismal, if not bleak, political and intellectual future. The alliance of the media, New York Intellectuals, educational foundations and institutions, and corporate America with a small black celebrity elite influences and limits the possibilities of what can be written, filmed, published and distributed through the granting or the withholding of patronage and financial support.

There are great dangers in the attempt to retain power and influence in the hands of the few, as we should know from the history of the Tuskegee machine. It is the young scholars and creative artists who are the most vulnerable to being silenced and it is the possibility of undertaking radical, transformative work that is most at risk. Booker T. Washington sought to hold in his hands the power to approve appointments, to control and dominate access to the media, white institutions and mainstream sources of support. One hundred years later, dominant institutions and foundations, for example, are still only too eager to assign to one or two black celebrity figures the right to grant a seal of approval to black intellectual and cultural work.

Our function then, as the post–civil rights intellectuals, can be compared to that of postcolonial elites who perpetuate the interests of their former colonizers. We participate in the reduction of our sphere of knowledge production to equate with particular bodies – ethnicized and racialized bodies for ethnicized and racialized forms of knowledge. As incorporated racialized bodies, we need to talk about the extent to which we front for a society that has completely reneged on any commitment to social equality.

8

Figuring the Future in Los(t) Angeles

Los Angeles, California is a city that has a very complex symbolic relation to the rest of the US. For me, the story of the Belmont Learning Center vividly dramatizes the betrayal of minority dreams by the boosterism, corruption, ineptitude and potential for environmental disaster that characterizes the political culture of the city. Planned more than a decade ago at a projected cost of $200 million, it will be, if completed, the most expensive public high school ever built in the US.[1]

Construction of the Belmont Learning Center proceeded despite warnings issued by the State Division of Oil and Gas about the dangers of the site, an abandoned oil field. The black officials of the school board were desperate to solve the overcrowding and generally dire conditions in which so many young black, Latino and poor students do *not* get educated in the Los Angeles Unified School District. But potentially explosive methane gas and toxic hydrogen sulphide gas, known to cause neurological damage, seeped into the school structure, for which there appeared to be no remediation. Finally, after spending $170 million, the school board voted in January 2000 to abandon the project.[2] However, Superintendent Roy Romer revived the project, and, with $175 million spent so far, completion could add yet another $100 million to the costs. Oil well logs have revealed an earthquake fault underneath already existing buildings on the campus; any seismic activity would cause a rush of the gases with devastating consequences.[3] More than a metaphor for the city, this unfolding tragic narrative embodies the multilayered political, social, economic, racialized and environmental complexity of Los Angeles, from its fissures and abandoned oil fields below ground to the concrete highways soaring through, around and above its neighbourhoods.

In *Ecology of Fear*, the historian Mike Davis reminds us that the city used to be regarded as the 'Land of Endless Summer', a national symbol for a 'lifestyle against which other Americans measured the modernity of their towns and regions'. Today's metropolitan Los Angeles, however, has become 'a dystopian symbol of Dickensian inequalities and intractable racial contradictions ... with its estimated 500 gated subdivisions, 2,000 street gangs, 4,000 mini-malls, 20,000 sweat shops, and 100,000 homeless residents'. Rather than representing America's modernity, Los Angeles has come to symbolize 'the collapse of the American Century'.[4]

Davis provides us with an intriguing account of the city's fictional and filmic annihilation and claims that 'no city, in fiction or film, has been more likely to figure as the icon of a really bad future.'[5] He asks us to consider why Los Angeles is the city we love to see destroyed. Acknowledging that the city has, to a certain extent, become 'the scapegoat for the collapse of the American Century', Davis emphasizes the power and popularity of pulp fiction and film that incessantly recycles the 'ritual sacrifice of Los Angeles', and cites these texts as part of a 'malign syndrome, whose celebrants include the darkest forces in American history'.[6] While it is Robert Heinlein's novella of 1952, *The Year of the Jackpot*, that, in 'crowning Los Angeles the disaster capital of the universe ... anticipated the cornucopia of imaginary disaster to come', it is the issue of race, Davis concludes, 'which unlocks the secret meaning of Los Angeles disaster fiction'.[7]

I share Davis's distaste for much of this disaster fiction, particularly the neo-Nazi survivalist narratives with their predictions of imminent race war. But his observations prompt me to consider what motives African American writers may have for representing Los Angeles as a politically and environmentally disastrous living space for many of its residents and even, perhaps, for contemplating its destruction. Literary representations of the city in the work of black writers span many periods, take many forms and range across a variety of genres, but even when African American writers imagine its destruction, I would argue that far from being part of a 'malign syndrome', their work should be seen as an attempt to interrogate the limits and the possibilities that the city offers for imagining self, community and citizenship.

If Los Angeles is 'the most culturally heterogeneous city in the history of the world', it is also true that many of the white and wealthy are running away as fast as they can from that very heterogeneity.[8] They flee towards homogeneous gated enclaves and the suburbs to escape a declining economy, abandoning the multicoloured, multiracial and multi-ethnic residents of the metropolitan region who remain in poor neighbourhoods with declining schools. Of course, the desire of many white US citizens to live and go to school separate from citizens of colour is a wish not confined to those who live in Los Angeles. For large sectors of the white middle class, residential segregation is their American dream.

Since 11 September 2001 the racial politics of the twentieth-century US has remained securely in place: the language of democracy and justice continues to paper over a deeply segregated, poverty-ridden and unjust society, a glaring contradiction that seems to bore politicians and the media alike. At the same time, politicians and the media have fostered a blitz of public discourse about the relation of the self to the other, of friend to foe, of home to foreigner, since the destruction of the World Trade Center in New York City. Bodies seem to be in suspended relation to one another while concepts of citizen and subject are being renegotiated.

The US, as a national body politic, is publicly figured as 'home'. However, in the face of the increasing surveillance and confinement of citizens suspected of being members of terror cells or possibly planning to make 'dirty bombs', who is to be included and nourished within its walls remains ultimately unclear. For the last quarter of a century the 'have a nice day' home has been the public face which rendered invisible the home that houses the poor and the black in disproportionate numbers in the largest prison population the world has ever seen. The poor and black not within the penitentiary system are condemned to a life of segregation in devastated inner city projects and schools that do not school.

The invention of a Council and Office of Homeland Security, the pronouncements of the Bush administration and the language of the media, particularly the *New York Times*, CNN and *Time* magazine, all spoke to the need to defend 'home' from both external *and* internal threats. At 'home', residents have been subject to increasing questions about their legitimacy, a process overdetermined by the language and practices of racialization. After the first six months of apparent intensive labour, a colour-coded Homeland Security Advisory System was unveiled which represented levels of threat from red to orange, even though everyone 'knew' that it was brown bodies at home and abroad that represent potential danger.

Since the early days of President George W. Bush's 'crusade', which bodies constitute the national body has been marked by contradictions. 'Home' is multiple bodies seemingly endlessly divided, a home in which neighbour has become potential enemy. Despite the absolutist implications of 'crusading' language, exactly who is to be blessed by God, as opposed to subjected to his wrath (courtesy of the US military), exactly who is to be embraced and comforted while others are to be shunned, spat upon, assaulted, arrested and even murdered, remains ambiguous and elusive. The endless sea of Stars and Stripes that proclaims the freedom to rule the universe, and glories in the 'American way' of domination and consumption of most of the Earth's resources, waves alongside a constant stream of arrests of US citizens, people's neighbours, accused of complicity with terrorists. People disappear through the evocation of military rule of law.

My small-town American flag-waving neighbours in New England (predominantly white) are very satisfied that they live in almost total segregation from the residents of New Haven (predominantly black and Latino), let alone New York City, which many regard as a veritable Sodom and Gomorrah and very few ever visit. Although the public expression of grief from small towns and suburban America for New York City was obviously genuine, 'One Nation under God' has clearly demarcated urban/suburban borders. I doubt that most white Americans imagine their ideal homeland as international, cosmopolitan, multicultural and multi-ethnic communities of the type that was destroyed in the World Trade Center towers or that can be found in metropolitan Los Angeles.

There is clearly much more at stake for the politics of citizenship in the racialized formation of metropolis versus 'the American way' than a discussion of the literary representation of any one city can encompass. But, for a number of African American writers of the twentieth century, Los Angeles became a figure for the state of the nation. The value that black writers place upon and celebrate in the multiple and complex range of urban ethnicities is not only at odds with the class and racialized political and economic hierarchies of the city which oppresses its black residents, but contrary to contemporary dominant models of American citizenship.

Some brilliant young scholars of the black diaspora are carrying out the excavation of the earliest history of black writers from California by recovering what they wrote in British Columbia, Canada, after they left the US. As Karina Vernon states, 'more than half the black population of San Francisco migrated to British Columbia *en masse*' in 1858 when the 'California legislature passed a series of racially repressive laws, culminating in the proposal of a bill that would ban outright any further immigration of blacks' into the state. Their writing, in the form of letters, diaries, poems and autobiographies has been recently published and is, Vernon attests, a 'textual legacy . . . [of] the desires and disappointments of black subjects'.[9]

In addition to regarding Los Angeles as a significant measure of the systems of racial injustice that permeate the entire country, the work of Chester Himes, Octavia Butler and Walter Mosley offers powerful accounts of the limitations of the twentieth-century American dream and acute intellectual analyses of the future of its rampant and unrestrained capitalism. These African American writers explore the complex questions of the relation between transnational, national, regional and local geographies of self, other, community and citizenship in Los Angeles.

An unconventional history of the literary relation of African American writers to the city could begin with Chester Himes and his novel *If He Hollers Let Him Go*, written and set during the Second World War and published in 1945. *If He Hollers* presents us with a stark but convincing portrait of the particularities of the racial formation that emerged in Los Angeles during the war and shaped the city's future. For Himes, the war years marked a turning point in the development of white supremacy in the country and he imagined a Los Angeles in which the geography of its human relations prefigured and epitomized the future of the urban racial formation of the US. Himes created a particular social, political and philosophical landscape of Los Angeles that set an agenda of questions to which contemporary writers, like Butler and Mosley, continue to respond.

The forces of destruction permeate every page of *If He Hollers*, but it is not the city's infrastructure that is under siege. Rather, it is the physical, political and psychological well-being of Los Angeles's minority residents that is being attacked at each and every turn. This Los Angeles, imagined as a literal and metaphorical landscape in which the forces of oppression roam unchecked through its streets, workplaces and neighbourhoods, reappears in our contemporary moment in the work of Octavia Butler and Walter Mosley. Each interrogates Los Angeles as a site in which the struggle for economic, political and social justice is a matter of life or death. James Holston and Arjun Appadurai emphasize the importance of perceiving cities as 'challenging, diverging from, and even replacing nations as the important space of citizenship – as the lived space not only of its uncertainties but also of its emergent forms'.[10] I would argue that the fictions of Himes, Butler and Mosley explore these 'uncertainties' and 'emergent forms' of the relation between transnational, national, regional and local geographies of self, other, community and citizenship.

Chester Himes arrived in Los Angeles in 1940 on a Greyhound bus from Cleveland. What he found there, he declares in his autobiography, *The Quality of Hurt*, was a city that 'hurt [him] racially as much as any city [he] had ever known – much more than any city [he] remembered from the South'.[11] For him, the war years mark a new moment in the racial formation of the US, and he constructs a Los Angeles that both prefigures and epitomizes the new directions of American racism.

If He Hollers recreates a specific historical moment in the history of Los Angeles, the 1940s, when migrants streamed into it from all over the country to work in 'the huge industrial plants ... shipyards, refineries, oil wells, steel mills, [and] construction companies'.[12] The shipyard where the protagonist, Robert Jones, works is a microcosm of the racial formation of the US and a symbol of the shifting demographics of the state; Jones's co-workers seem to come from every state in the Union except California. The spatial organization of their work sites, categorized by racial and ethnic division, intensifies and concentrates racist hatred.

Jones lives in constant fear in both his sleeping and waking hours. He traces the source of this fear to that of the internment of Japanese Americans rather than to the Jim Crow conditions of life and work in Los Angeles, an experience with which he was all too familiar long before he moved to the city. Jones describes the nature of the racism he had to confront:

When I got here practically the only job a Negro could get was serving in the white folk's kitchens. But it wasn't that so much. It was the look on the people's faces when you asked them about a job. Most of 'em didn't say right out they wouldn't hire me. They just looked so goddam startled that I'd even asked. As if some friendly dog had come in through the door and said, 'I can talk.' It shook me.

Maybe it had started then, I'm not sure, or maybe it wasn't until I'd seen them send the Japanese away that I'd noticed it. Little Rike Oyana singing 'God Bless America' and going to Santa Anita with his parents next day. It was taking a man up by the roots and locking him up without a chance. Without a trial. Without a charge. Without even giving him a chance to say one word. It was thinking about if they ever did that to me . . . that started me to getting scared.

After that it was everything. It was the look in the white people's faces when I walked down the streets. It was that crazy, wild-eyed unleashed hatred that the first Jap bomb on Pearl Harbor let loose in a flood. All that tight, crazy feeling of race as thick in the street as gas fumes. Every time I stepped outside I saw a challenge I had to accept or ignore. Every day I had to make one decision a thousand times: *Is it now? Is now the time?*

I was the same colour as the Japanese and I couldn't tell the difference. 'A yeller-bellied Jap' coulda meant me too. I could always feel race trouble, serious trouble, never more than two feet off.[13]

I quote this passage at length to highlight the sophistication of Himes's insights into the politics and processes of racializing citizenship. He stages Jones's monologue as a gradual process of recognition. Although Jones's meditation begins with his Jim Crow experiences, he moves quickly to reflect upon the hegemonic ideological strategies of racism intended to categorize, divide and isolate groups of racial 'others', strategies which produce his experiences as a 'nigger' as distinct from those of a 'yeller-bellied Jap'. He then acknowledges the relation between these experiences and, finally, he recognizes the common threat to the rights of citizenship for all racialized peoples.

The juxtaposition within the monologue of the young Japanese American boy being taken to an internment camp with his singing of 'God Bless America' is not just a poignant evocation of an image but also a political realization, in literary form, of the contradictions between racialization, nationality and citizenship as they are articulated at this historical moment. Himes renders these contradictions visible, ambiguous and fragile. Anxiety ricochets through Jones's vision of a possible common fate for African Americans and Japanese Americans alike, but at the exact moment of realization, Himes also undermines the hegemonic spatial equation of discrete racist ideologies and distinct categories of peoples. He raises to visibility, I would argue, the possibility of renegotiating the 'geography of difference'.[14]

In an argument based upon the premise that the 'transnational flow of ideas, goods, images, and persons . . . tends to drive a deeper wedge between national space and its urban centers', Holston and Appadurai identify Los Angeles as a city which 'may sustain many aspects of a multicultural society and economy at odds with the mainstream ideologies of American identity'.[15] Though I would not disagree with this conclusion, I would question the relation of cause and effect in their premise. Rather than trying to trace a causal relation of effect from the global to the local, I would prefer to develop a way of mapping the dialectical relations between a variety of spatial scales that coalesce in one place at a specific moment.[16]

If He Hollers Let Him Go moves across and through a variety of spatial scales – the local, the national and the global – each overdetermined by ideologies of masculinity, which act *simultaneously* to reassert and reframe relations between processes of racialization and definitions of citizenship. Los Angeles enables Himes to represent how racialization and citizenship coalesce, accumulate, concentrate, intensify and, ultimately, penetrate through the skin to the body of Robert Jones, arguably the most localized site of all. The racial hurts and slurs, the slights and threats, fall like blows battering Jones, circulate throughout his system, pound in his chest and his head and, finally, seep out through his pores, drenching his body in fear. Jones wants nothing more than to kill to bring an end to this constant fear. In the end his wish is fulfilled, though not in a form he either anticipates or desires. At the end of the novel Jones is drafted into the army. His rage, arising from his recognition of the true nature of the threats to his sense of self, manhood and rights as citizen, is confined, controlled and directed by the state towards a new target. In the future Jones will kill in the interest of the nation that denies his humanity. As a writer, Chester Himes turns his back on Los Angeles and limps away. It was Los Angeles, he declares in his autobiography, which almost destroyed him:

> I had survived the humiliating last five years of the Depression in Cleveland; and still I was entire, complete, functional; my mind was sharp, my reflexes were good, and I was not bitter. But under the mental corrosion of race prejudice in Los Angeles I had become bitter and saturated with hate . . . I was thirty-one and whole when I went to Los Angeles and thirty-five and shattered when I left to go to New York.[17]

Octavia Butler was raised in Los Angeles. All her novels are concerned with the multiple forms of struggles of its population for and against domination and oppression. Unlike the uncritical masculinity of Chester Himes, Butler is particularly concerned with forms of patriarchal domination, oppression and exploitation. Patriarchal power and abuse are produced within, reproduce and maintain the destructive capitalist and repressive relations of Los Angeles and its suburbs, but patriarchs in Butler's novels are ultimately either destroyed or superseded by their female offspring and the parasitical nature of patriarchal relations transformed. Butler's work displays a 'thoroughly grounded understanding of place, space and social theory' and, alongside that of Samuel R. Delany, is among the most interesting, innovative and politically challenging contemporary science fiction being published in North America.[18]

Butler's fiction offers her readers the possibility of seeing the world from multiple perspectives, while rejecting both totalization and relativism. Because they all are set within the landscape of a decaying or destroyed Los Angeles, I will begin my discussion with the novels in her Patternist series and then turn to *Parable of the Sower* (1993). The 'pattern' of the Patternist series allows Butler to imagine a cartography of subjectivities, a cartography that in her hands becomes a tool in the fictional exploration of partial and imperfect ways of knowing, sensing and making claims upon others.[19] In two of these novels, *Patternmaster* (1976) and *Mind of My Mind* (1977), telepathy forms a primary mode of connection between and among her characters. Butler forges these connections into a web of possibilities, a web which guides the reader through an exploration of a variety of forms of knowledge. The novels are literary explorations of the use and abuse of ways of knowing structured into relations of power and subjection, control of the self and of others. The 'pattern' allows for the representation of both spatial and temporal relations between and among her characters and its manipulation produces very specific consequences for Butler's fictional geography of individual and communal politics.

Butler creates her telepathic pattern as a web of arteries, a geography and mode of communication alternative to the conventional arteries of the city and its suburbs. Literally, the pattern acts as a set of alternative lifelines to the disintegrating social and political formation of her fictional Los Angeles. Her arteries form a multiracial, interracial and multi-ethnic web of imaginary relations that replace the segregated spatial pattern of the actual city. At times, the pattern provides alternative avenues of movement to the freeways: Butler's characters are constantly physically and mentally moving between metropolis, suburb and edge city. This movement, while multilayered and multidimensional, is also structured in relations of power and control. Those who learn to control it can manipulate the web, and those who travel its threads are often drawn into movement through the will of another. However, the multiracial, interracial, and multi-ethnic mind–body relationships in the conduits of the pattern are also creative and offer the characters an opportunity to leave behind the destructive mind–body relations that characterize the city's segregation and communication systems, for which Butler appears to have utter contempt. In *Clay's Ark*, Butler describes the spatial relations of Los Angeles as follows: 'Enclaves were islands surrounded by vast, crowded, vulnerable residential areas through which ran sewers of utter lawlessness connecting cesspools – economic ghettos that regularly chewed their inhabitants up and spat the pieces into surrounding communities'.[20]

Though relations between and among members of the pattern are fraught with struggles over power and control, like that of the city and its sewers in which they are embedded, the pattern is a fictional device for theorizing the construction of social relations, communal solidarities and loyalties. It is only within the parameters of the pattern, for example, that a multiracial, interracial and multi-ethnic community is represented.

As I have said, all of Butler's novels are primarily concerned with multiple forms of struggles for and against domination and oppression. In the Patternist series and in her most recent two novels, *Parable of the Sower* and *Parable of the Talents*, Butler is particularly concerned with forms of patriarchal domination, oppression and exploitation – those produced within, reproducing and maintaining the destructive spatial–temporal relations of Los Angeles and its suburbs.[21]

Butler expresses her most elaborate, detailed and powerful condemnation of Los Angeles in *Parable of the Sower*, a deeply philosophical meditation upon the nature of our society, published in 1993. Set in the near future, the novel begins within the confines of a walled community in 2024 and closes in Humboldt County, California in 2027. Its protagonist, a young black woman only fifteen years old in the opening pages of the novel, is a most unlikely heroine for American fiction. In the racialized and gendered political discourse of the US, black female teenagers are characterized as pathological, dismissed as unworthy citizens and represented in the media predominantly as unwed mothers. In stark contrast and in direct challenge to these ideas, Octavia Butler makes her protagonist, Lauren Olamina, a symbol for the future and the force behind the building of a new society. *Parable of the Sower* opens with Lauren trying to be her father's daughter but feeling as if she is living a lie trying to please him, a Baptist minister, her middle-class community, and their God. As readers, we follow her developing analysis of the patriarchal nature of all three. In a reaction against the narrow vision of her community, Lauren embarks on a deep interrogation of the terms and conditions of her citizenship and all aspects of her belonging.

In what appears to be a revision of the opening trope of Alice Walker's novel *The Color Purple* (1982), Lauren, instead of writing to the God of her father and her community, records in her diary the invention of her own spiritual entity, which she calls God and defines as Change. Lauren dreams of escape, but in *Parable* there is no telepathic web, or pattern, to act as an alternative set of arteries through which to communicate and build alternative communities. Instead, Lauren, at eighteen, responds to the destruction of her walled community by setting out on the second stage of her journeying, a search for a new way to live. She quickly gathers around her a group of refugees from southern California and leads them north on foot along the freeways to found a community called Earthseed. In addition to surmounting her youth and her uncertainty about what she will find outside the walls of her gated community, Lauren must also learn how to transcend her own ability to enter the minds of others. This ability, called 'hyperempathy syndrome', was caused, Lauren explains, by a drug her mother took: 'Paraceto, the smart pill, the Einstein powder', which was invented to halt the deterioration of the mind associated with Alzheimer's disease but which also boosted the intellectual performance of the young and the healthy.[22] It 'became as popular as coffee among students and, if they meant to compete in any of the highly paid professions, it was as necessary as a knowledge of computers'.[23] As a consequence, Lauren is a 'sharer', one who can feel both the pain and the pleasure of others. However, because in her society there is little pleasure and much pain, the ability becomes a disability, a terrifying and frequently paralysing response to the agony of others. Yet that which disables her also brings an acute awareness and understanding of social and political conditions. While the members of her family and community put their faith in the walls of their enclaves, behind which they hide from the violence of city and suburb alike, Lauren understands that those walls will not protect them from the forces of change that will inevitably engulf them. Rather, she attempts to embrace change by adopting it as her own form of religious belief or set of doctrines. As one character tries to describe the principles of Lauren's philosophy, 'Some of the faces of her god are biological evolution, chaos theory, relativity theory, the uncertainty principle and . . . the second law of thermodynamics.'[24] It is from this rather eclectic combination of theories that Lauren shapes Earthseed, an alternative ecological, political and social philosophy and practice out of which she intends to establish an alternative community.

Whereas the pattern of telepathy in Butler's earlier novels acts as a postmodern compression of space and time analogous to cyberspace, in *Parable of the Sower* Lauren is grounded by the pain of others, though she constantly fights against paralysis, seeking always to act upon what she learns from such pain in order to allow herself and others to transcend it.[25] Her hyperempathy is at one and the same time a bizarre combination of a disabling weight and a source of vision and insight. Structuring the novel by the progress of this struggle allows Butler to create a constant fictional theoretical conversation about the processes that connect the complex relations of self, other and community, processes that are accessed through the representation of what David Harvey calls 'the militant particularism of lived lives'.[26]

Parable of the Sower, situated only twenty-four years into the future from the time of writing, is Butler's imaginative response to, and extension of, the political and social conditions which already exist in Los Angeles and its environs, conditions with which we are already too familiar but ignore: our most public secrets. The novel explicitly challenges the consequences of the conservative political agenda which has come to dominate the national body politic since the Reagan and Bush (the elder) administrations. *Maquiladoras*, renamed 'borderworks' in the novel, which currently exist along the Mexican border, have in *Parable* proliferated, flourishing along the Canadian border. The reintroduction of slavery by corporations is represented as a logical extension of current exploitative labour practices: the form of peonage under which agricultural workers labour in California at present becomes debt slavery in the novel, and industrial workers in the borderworks are similarly enslaved. In this manner, Butler deliberately crafts an interventionist role for science fiction as she disturbs and challenges the expectations of her readers, demanding that they recognize their responsibility for the shape of the future. The premise of *Parable of the Sower* rests upon a vision of an active citizenship; accepting the exploitative and oppressive economic systems of the present is an act of complicity with the state and determines the systems of re-enslavement of tomorrow.

When Lauren ventures outside her privileged, middle-class, walled community she sees the broken people who have been excluded from it and who form the residue of their exclusive existence: children with running sores, adults with missing limbs, women recently raped with blood still running down the inside of their thighs, and the dead – merely food for feral dogs. Feeling and sharing their pain is what the walls have prevented Lauren from experiencing or from knowing.

In one of Butler's earlier novels, *Mind of My Mind*, there is a vivid and horrific scene in a Los Angeles apartment which epitomizes the poverty and desperation hidden behind walls which Butler seeks to bring into view. Children lie in their own filth and a newborn baby, battered to death by its parents, lies covered in maggots. In an intertextual reference, *Parable of the Sower* extends this image to encompass the entire city and its destructive effect on processes of community formation: Los Angeles is abruptly dismissed by Lauren's father as 'a big carcass covered with too many maggots'.[27]

Lauren invents an alternative community in her imagination and records her imaginings in a diary in poetic form. Earthseed is her response to the pervasive environmental and human disaster that surrounds her and it articulates 'the need to plant ourselves far from this dying place'.[28] Earthseed is also Lauren's response to the need to escape from 'politicians and businesspeople, failing economies and tortured ecologies'.[29] Her reflections and deliberations gradually evolve into a spur to political action.

Parable of the Sower draws upon the form of nineteenth-century slave narratives while also telling a particularly Californian story and conjuring up a vision of those nineteenth-century black migrants from San Francisco moving north to Canada in the hope of finding liberty and justice. As an author, Butler abandons Los Angeles as her preferred fictional landscape. Lauren Olamina finally flees north, gathering a multiracial, interracial and multi-ethnic band of runaways and ex-slaves around her as she goes. It is interesting to note that Butler has also abandoned Los Angeles as a resident: having spent her entire life in the metropolis, she has recently moved to Seattle. Los Angeles has become the most exportable model of future metropolises, a model that has already been copied from Phoenix, Arizona, to Mexico City, to São Paolo, Brazil. But, within the terms of Butler's critique, the model of this metropolis cannot sustain a politically viable future for an inclusive vision of community, self and citizenship.

In *Parable of the Sower*, Los Angeles is disintegrating and returning to the desert it once was while the wealthy cling tenaciously to their privileged existence in their fortified outposts. Only the rich can survive intact because only they can afford that luxury. Having abandoned the poor to their fate *outside* the walls of their gated communities – except, of course, for those needed as domestic servants – the wealthy concentrate on protecting *themselve*s and *their* property in enclaves secured primarily through extensive use of advanced technology and, in case that fails, armed guards. The rich also have exclusive use of the educational system, for, while still mandatory, education is no longer free. Only those with plenty of money and resources can obtain police protection because the Los Angeles Police Department (LAPD) demands high fees for any sort of investigation. Water, being more expensive than gasoline, is sold in small amounts to the poor, those who are unhoused and those who are squatters. Consequently, trading in such a valuable commodity makes peddling water an extremely hazardous occupation. Using gasoline to fuel a car is strictly a privilege of the wealthy, but in the hands of the poor petrol becomes a weapon. Arsonists burn anything and anyone, under the influence of an easily available drug which transforms watching a fire into a source of intense sexual pleasure. This is the future in Butler's Los Angeles.

On the night the last big 'window wall' television in her neighbourhood went dark for good, Lauren records that, on its screen, 'We saw a dust-dry reservoir and three dead water peddlers with their dirty blue armbands and their heads cut halfway off. And we saw whole blocks of boarded up [*sic*] buildings burning in Los Angeles. Of course, no one would waste water trying to put such fires out.'[30]

We are already too familiar with the stark inequalities that exist in Los Angeles regarding protection from fire. Mike Davis has documented how the entire city's firefighting infrastructure, with federal support, has become focused on the protection of the wealthy in their precarious perches in canyons down which the hot, dry Santa Ana winds blow from the desert. In the centre of the city, apartment blocks that warehouse the poor are neglected by fire services already stretched to capacity: for them, inadequate or no fire inspections or protection are the norm.[31]

The wealthy, as they always have in Los Angeles, simultaneously defy its multiracial, interracial and multi-ethnic realities and environmental limitations with an arrogance that is truly breathtaking to behold. Butler deftly exposes the way in which these social contradictions and environmental disasters are inextricably interdependent, making *Parable of the Sower* a powerful political indictment of contemporary American society. It stands, I would argue, both as a stern reminder of James Baldwin's warnings in *The Fire Next Time* and as a fictional re-enactment of the street cry from Watts in 1965, and south central Los Angeles in 1992: 'let it burn, baby, burn.'

Walter Mosley, I would argue, sets up a dialogue with the fiction of Chester Himes and Octavia Butler. But while Butler's protagonist turns her back on Los Angeles and lets it burn so that we can build a more just and equable future, Mosley, in his novel *Always Outnumbered, Always Outgunned*, deliberately refuses Butler's resolution and persuades us that the ashes will produce only madness. An insane arsonist writes in his diary,

> if I could just get them to see that we got to burn down all this mess we done stacked up and hacked up and shacked up all around us. If they could see the torch of change, the burning of flames all around their eyes. We could come together in fire and steel and blood and love and make ourselves a home. Not this shit, not this TV and church world.[32]

But the response to the devastation of the world of south-central Los Angeles, Mosley suggests, is more complicated and difficult than the metaphorical and literal baptism of fire that has touched and irrevocably damaged so many lives. Mosley creates an urban hero, Socrates Fortlow, who emerges from the rejected and criminalized waste of American society and subsequently becomes a figure of compassion who offers hope for finding a way to survive in the streets of Los Angeles.[33]

The character of Socrates, like so many of Mosley's protagonists, seems to arise from the questions that Chester Himes left unresolved in *If He Hollers Let Him Go*: Easy Rawlins, Paris Minton and Socrates all struggle with the fears to which Chester Himes gave voice through Robert Jones.[34] In addition to the constant fear that haunts black manhood, Socrates is a fulfilment of Robert Jones's desire to murder and rape. When *Always Outnumbered* opens, Socrates has recently been released from jail, where he served twenty-seven years for committing both crimes. The reader must come to terms immediately with what on the surface appears to be the most unsympathetic of protagonists.

It is a testimony to Mosley's extraordinarily creative imagination that the character of Socrates Fortlow forces readers not only to live with his crimes, as Fortlow himself does on a daily level, but to transcend, while not ignoring, the fear, horror and hatred within. As Socrates emerges as a philosopher worthy of his name, out of the mouth of the murderer and the rapist come the most profound questions of justice and equality, of rights, responsibility and obligations. As Socrates stumbles, falls, picks himself and others out of the gutter and carries them with him into an uncertain future, we, the readers, cannot fail to recognize the limitless depths of his humanity in his fragile but persistent attempts to build a future for himself and others. Twenty-seven years in jail did not teach Socrates Fortlow how to survive outside it. What we learn from *Always Outnumbered* is that Socrates's constant struggle to find ways to live is irrevocably bound to his attempts to teach others how to survive, to value living in a way that improves all our chances at life. Socrates finds depths of humanity in himself by discovering the humanity in others, even though he is a product of a society that denies all of their humanity on a daily level.

If we are to find a new way of being in the world it is important that the work of African American writers, and other so-called 'minorities', break the chains with which institutions of education and publishing bind them. Within and without the borders of the US, labels like 'minority' or 'ethnic' literature ghettoize, marginalize and minimize its significance. Yet so much of this work is currently carrying the weight of the search for a more ethical and moral sense of responsibility for the state of the nation. It is carrying the weight of hope in the heart of an American empire that is skidding down the path of increasing inhumanity, injustice and disregard, not only for the majority of its own population but for the majority of the residents of this planet.

These fictions are significant acts of dissent: dissent from the perpetuation of injustice in contemporary politics, dissent from the increasing extremes of wealth and poverty and dissent from the parasitic relation of the US to the Earth and its environment. These writers should be regarded as a barometer of the American dream. Re-visioning the 'sunshine state' of California as the epitome of the twentieth-century version of that dream allows these writers to document how the condition of black existence is an important measure of who paid for and suffered in its shadows.[35]

9

The Work of Claudia Tate

When I was invited to present to this symposium I accepted with great enthusiasm, for occasions when we can gather together as feminist critics and engage with the work of black female intellectuals as the main focus of our attention, to celebrate one of our own, as it were, have been few and far between. In particular, the chance to publicly engage and celebrate the work of Claudia Tate was particularly attractive to me. Claudia's contributions to literary and cultural criticism have been important and original in so many public ways, but I also want to signal at the outset that her intellectual presence in the academy is also of personal significance to me.

The body of Claudia's work is so substantial, conceptually complex and varied, that when I sat down to write, my excitement vanished and was replaced by anxiety. If I had twenty minutes, which essays, or books, or issues, or themes, should I, or could I, select? Claudia brought an understanding of the working lives of black women writers to my desk and into my consciousness: she made me stop short and ask myself why I had avoided or neglected to discuss, in my own writing, the crucially important issues of narrative pleasure and desire, and she made me realize how careless my own readings were when I found the novels of black women in the post-Reconstruction period opaque – opaque, that is, when I was not finding them downright indigestible. I remember my first encounter with this statement: 'For a decade, black women writers of the post Reconstruction era reaffirmed in novels their belief that virtuous women like themselves could reform society by domesticating it.' Claudia's argument in *Domestic Allegories of Political Desire* was a revelation and a gift, and it helped me to read differently.

Claudia is also a nonconformist, and I have always identified with and taken great pleasure in her acts of critical rebellion, which are numerous. She breaks down barriers of critical parochialism and safety, challenges the limits of conventional paradigms, and refuses to submit to the shibboleths of the field. In fact, Claudia is a perfect fit for my favourite split infinitive, 'to boldly go where no woman has gone before'. First, she has been an intellectual leader in the detailed excavation of texts that have been too long ignored by the American critical establishment. 'Ignored' is a very polite way of putting it. While canons of African American fiction have been slowly and methodically built, Claudia's cannons have been wheeled into the arena, fused and discharged. After the dust has cleared we have all been able to see that these traditions were built by denying the validity of the texts which did not fit the paradigm being used. Claudia has been irresistibly drawn, it seems, to the texts that no one wants to talk about. A tenacious and meticulous researcher, in addition to being an innovative close reader, she is also something of a magician. We think the swords drawn through the box onstage are going to draw blood, but she inevitably shows us that there is nothing to fear from, but much to learn by, confronting post-Reconstruction fiction, W. E. B. Du Bois's *Dark Princess*, Zora Neale Hurston's *Seraph on the Suwanee* or Richard Wright's *Savage Holiday*, for example.

I have also felt from the earliest of Claudia's essays that we shared a mission, that we both were desperate to de-parochialize departments of English and to destroy, forever, the narrow ethnic definitions within which traditions of English literature have been reproduced in the academy. In this task, as in all her work, Claudia has always refused reductive visions, seeking instead to articulate the complexly different black voices that speak to a general or universal human condition. The interaction of race and gender in the work of black women is for

Claudia a site of an *increased* breadth of vision rather than a cause of narrowing our focus, as many English department critics mistakenly claim. With this breadth of vision Claudia has an acute understanding and analysis of particularity and always emphasizes and delineates location, whether that location be geographic or a state of mind. I have always admired and deeply respected Claudia's continuing insistence on this broad vision of humanity and her absolute refusal to engage in reductive or essentialized debate.

We both find the theoretical perspectives of Antonio Gramsci invaluable, and I never have to hide my Althusserian tendencies from Claudia. However, I haven't trodden the path into psychoanalysis with her, though I continue to learn from her insights and recommend it to my students, for this work is central for young scholars in the field. When loud voices condemned psychoanalysis as a 'white thang' that had absolutely nothing to say to us, Claudia ignored them and proved them wrong. For my students I find it invaluable to be able to place Claudia's work in a tradition of the psychological analysis of race and identity that includes Frantz Fanon and Richard Wright.

It turned out to be so easy, then, to identify why I am intellectually indebted to Claudia, and yet my anxiety remains, indeed deepens. I eventually came to realize during the process of writing that this anxiety did not ultimately reside in the dilemma that trying to do justice to Claudia's work in twenty minutes would be a daunting task for anyone. I knew that there would be many voices here this afternoon and that what is particularly wonderful about this occasion is precisely that this is a shared, collective endeavour. My anxiety turns out to have its origins in a contradiction, in facing what I am trying to avoid, in an intense reluctance to speak about, combined with a simultaneous sense of the absolute necessity of addressing what it has meant to be a black female critic in the academy for our generation.

Graduate students and junior faculty, when issuing invitations to their conferences, have started to address me as a 'pioneer' or 'foremother', or they have utilized a vocabulary of other similar words or phrases that place me and my work in a generation that remains at a distinct, if discrete, distance from theirs. Though I have felt deeply disconcerted by such approaches I thought that I would adopt this location, for this occasion, as a place from which to think about the question of a generation of black women scholars, a generation to which Claudia and I now belong. It seems that such positionality is now part of the field as its geography is changing and the place from which we speak needs to be considered, historically, if for no other reason than that younger women are reconstituting their relation to us and our work through space and time. Though I understand this process intellectually and theoretically, I must admit that it feels like our generation is being parked, as if on a shelf. The shelf is pretty high – it seems that we are being revered – but, speaking for myself, I am not yet ready to be dusted off and placed in the closet with the rest of the trophies.

The process of thinking about and writing this paper has meant having to grit my teeth and harness myself to what has felt like a roller coaster riding a very rocky, circuitous track of memory across the mountainous terrain in which I have located my professional self since I came to the United States more than twenty years ago. For many of us in that generation, black literature in general, and black women's literature in particular, was our subject, but I do not think it was our only, or even our ultimate, object of attainment. There are many varied routes we took to arrive at our subject, but reflecting upon Claudia's work has led me to think about how so much of what we did was part of a shared search for an intellectual history to which we could belong, a history into which we could insert our intellectual selves as black female critics, as thinking beings who could talk about many things. We were trained as literary critics in the broadest sense of the term, but for many of us we were employed in the narrowest terms possible. How Claudia's route and my route converged is, for me, a story of great personal significance, and I hope it is more generally instructive.

When I first came to Yale, as a visiting graduate student from the Center for Contemporary Cultural Studies at the University of Birmingham in England, in 1980, I was leaving behind a very supportive, closely knit intellectual and friendship community and moving to a place where I did not know anyone and with a very uncertain future before me. Professor Charles Davis, who had invited me to study with the faculty in the Afro-American Studies Program and generously offered to mentor me himself, died before I arrived. When I was introduced to his protégé, Professor Henry Louis Gates, he asked me why a nice young white woman was working on black women writers. Looking back on those early days, in what I came to understand was the Ivy League, I wish I had had Adrian Piper's artistic and political vision and ability and had designed and handed out discrete cards as aids in the negotiation of the minefields of North American racialized readings of the body and, in particular, to help me counter the national tendency to reduce spheres of knowledge to particular bodies.

It was very difficult trying to persuade professors on both sides of the Atlantic that the work of black women writers constituted a field that was intellectually substantial enough to warrant a dissertation, but then Professor Gates gave me Barbara Christian's *Black Women Writers* for my thirty-second birthday and the next thing that I knew was that I was being invited to teach the first course on African American Women at Yale. But while black women writers were becoming 'hot commodities', as critics our entry into the field of African American studies was simultaneously being located within a distinct hierarchy. Susan Willis, Abena Busia, Mae Henderson and I sloshed around with the water beetles in our shared basement offices and women's bathroom while the men walked the hallowed halls above ground and literally over our heads.

I moved to my first real job at Wesleyan but found myself very, very isolated from those I imagined to be my peers in our emerging field. I was told in person and in print that I could not know anything about my chosen field of knowledge, or that I should not speak about black women writers in the USA because I was from Britain and/or because I wasn't dark enough; either way I didn't have the right to do what I was doing. And as for the male critics . . . well, we all know they felt that our feminism was washing dirty laundry in public and betraying black men. I may have been on an intellectual search for a history of sisterhood but sisterhood was not found in and did not support my daily intellectual existence.

And this is where Claudia enters, not only because of what she wrote and what I read, but because Claudia was the first black woman critic in the academy after I had been here many years who took my work seriously enough to offer to read and comment on drafts of my work. Claudia didn't just open up my mind through her publications; she opened up a pair of supportive arms and through this gesture I felt for the first time that I was being welcomed into a community that had shunned me, and remembering that she did this still has the power to make me want to cry.

One way to tell the story of how we all got here from there is to structure it as a progressive narrative, like a narrative of emergence into modernity, of increasing commercial success and recognition for the black women writers that we wrote about, a success that for many culminated in the award of a Nobel Prize for Literature to Toni Morrison. While celebrating Toni's tremendous and very well-deserved recognition, a friend said to me, 'doesn't it feel like we are all, as black women, walking up there with her?' I knew exactly what she meant, but no, as a literary and cultural critic I didn't actually feel that I was walking in Toni's shadow.

Our story isn't the same as the story of those novelists and poets who have gained national and international fame and recognition; our story is a story of black women critics who have been driven to give our all to build and maintain a field of knowledge, who have trained the next generation of young scholars, but who remain deep in the shadows of academe. It is trying to come to terms with, and think about how to tell, this latter story that makes me anxious because it is a story full of pain and frustration, a story which I believe is, to a large extent, still being told not only from the basements of African American studies, but also from the basements of English departments and literary studies in general. It is a story of a continuous and to-be-continued struggle, a battle that has wounded and permanently scarred many, and left others exhausted and weary.

Yet it is a story that I think needs to be told, and in conclusion I offer a suggestion about how we might think about telling it. If we return for a moment to Claudia's first book, *Black Women Writers at Work*, does this offer us a model for how we might tell the story of the conditions of our own work? For as I look around me and I see how we work it seems that we are overwhelmingly responsible for the domestic labour of our profession, spending our lives in the academic kitchens, and having more than our fair share of responsibility for keeping house and training and nurturing the next generation, even though we are so few. Could we take the questions that Claudia asks about writing as work, about how our work shapes our life, about the distinctions between male and female critics, about being black and female in the academy? Would we be willing and brave enough to pose these important questions to ourselves?

10

The New Auction Block: Blackness and the Marketplace

In an essay entitled 'Reification and Utopia in Mass Culture', published in 1979, Fredric Jameson observed,

> The only authentic cultural production today has seemed to be that which can draw on the collective experience of marginal pockets of the social life of the world system: black literature and the blues, British working-class rock, women's literature, gay literature, the *roman québécois*, the literature of the Third World: and this production is possible only to the degree to which these forms of collective life or collective solidarity have not yet been fully penetrated by the market and by the commodity system.[1]

I would like to tell a story that begins with this observation but takes as its subject 'authentic cultural production' not as an object but as a process, the authentication of black cultural production and black intellectuals. I also want to acknowledge and probe the intellectual hesitation about appearance and qualification of authenticity implicit in Jameson's phrase 'has seemed to be', as I focus on the issue of public presence, appearance and image. I will trace what I argue is a transition from the utopian moment in which it was possible to imagine black literature as an example of 'authentic cultural production ... not yet penetrated by the market and by the commodity system', to what Pierre Bourdieu has called 'the utopia of unlimited exploitation', a tyranny of the market most effectively embodied in Salman Rushdie's novel *Fury*, a vitriolic condemnation of the commodification of black intellectual production.[2]

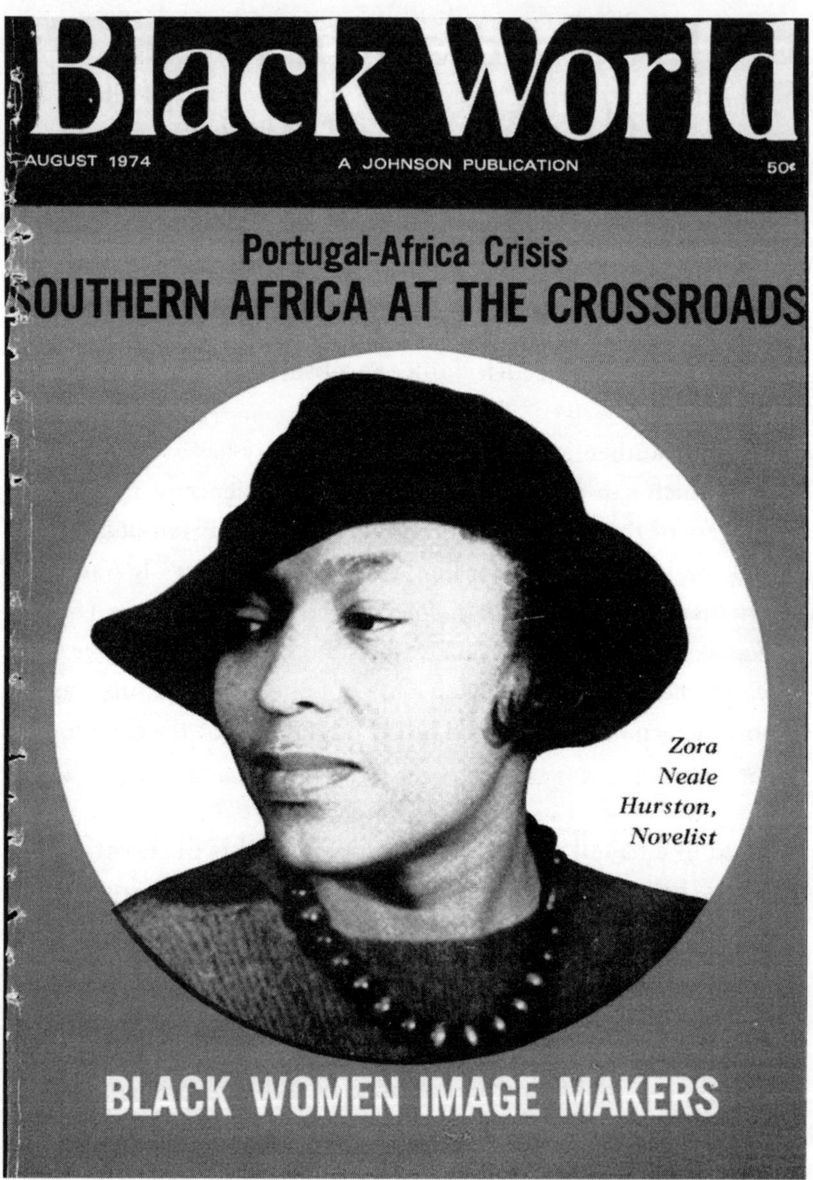

In the summer of 1974 a picture of Zora Neale Hurston, then a relatively unknown writer, appeared on the cover of one of the last issues of *Black World* above the caption 'Black Women Image Makers'.[3] In the spring of 1990 a picture of Henry Louis Gates Jr appeared on the cover of the *New York Times Magazine*, with the heading 'Black Studies' New Star'. These two moments signal the first stage of a shift in interest in the literary, cultural and political imagining of the possibilities of black intellectual endeavour from a black magazine to the press of the white establishment. They also frame the gendered nature of the public face of African American studies.

Barbara Christian wrote about the significance of the 1974 issue of *Black World*, a significance which she felt lay neither with the black female writer on the cover, for Gwendolyn Brooks had been featured on the cover of the previous issue, nor with the inclusion of literary analyses of black women's fiction, which was not new. Rather, Christian argued, the configuration of this particular issue of *Black World* marked

> the growing visibility of Afro-American women and the significant impact they were having on contemporary black culture. The articulation of that impact had been the basis for Toni Cade's edition of *The Black Woman* in 1970. But that collection had not dealt specifically with literature/creativity. Coupled with the publication of Alice Walker's 'In Search of Our Mother's Gardens', only a few months before in the May issue of *Ms.*, the August 1974 *Black World* signaled a shift in position among those interested in Afro-American literature about women's creativity. Perhaps because I had experienced a decade of the intense literary activity of the 1960s, but also much antifemale black cultural nationalist rhetoric, these two publications had a lightning effect on me. Afro-American women were making public, were able to make public, their search for themselves in literary culture.[4]

This essay mapped Christian's own personal trajectory as a literary critic, but it also created a genealogy of black feminist literary criticism while providing a trenchant assessment of its debates and the state of the field from her fiercely claimed feminist perspective. What Christian celebrates is her sense of a utopian moment, the transformative effect, what she calls 'the impact' of a growing public awareness of the collective presence of black female creativity and intellectual life, experience drawn from the 'marginal pockets of the social life of the world system', and presented as a force against 'antifemale black cultural nationalist rhetoric'.

Christian's essay appeared in a collection, *Changing Our Own Words*, edited by Cheryl Wall, in 1989.[5] *Changing Our Own Words* grew from papers presented at a symposium hosted by Wall at Rutgers University a few years earlier. Wall's introduction makes clear that its publication is intended to contribute to this transformation, consolidating the public presence of a black female literary culture and confirming that 'the community of black women writing in the United States now can be regarded as a vivid new fact of national life'.[6] Wall states, 'Over the last two decades, Afro-American women have written themselves into the national consciousness. Their work is widely read, frequently taught, and increasingly the object of critical inquiry.'[7] The publication of the symposium was tangible evidence of a substantial critical community and of the collective nature of the project. However, Wall could also see that curricular transformation was not accompanied by a transformation in the constitution of the faculty in educational institutions. She acknowledged that while the work of a number of black women writers had and would continue to maintain this public presence in the culture of the United States and be written about by a wide and diverse body of literary critics, black female critics wrote from a position or place 'assigned on the margins of the academy'. While not wanting 'to claim a "privileged" status' for black female critics, she did hope that their 'words will have resonance beyond the community of black women writing'.[8] The aim of black feminists and their allies in the project of the promotion of black female intellectual and creative endeavour was the expansion of the possibilities of critical and analytic engagement, not exclusivity, and retained the utopian hope that broadcasting the words of both creative and critical black women intellectuals would enable the community of black women to become equal citizens of the world. But, of course, voice cannot substitute for the lack of political power that men hold.[9]

But, just as Barbara Christian had been haunted by the anti-female black nationalist rhetoric of the recent past, Deborah McDowell, in the same anthology, reminded us that an expansion of consciousness, justice and toleration did not always flow from an encounter with powerful black female voices whose vision of the world had been fiercely opposed by male critics.[10] McDowell demonstrated what was at stake in the frequently contentious debate over the work of Toni Morrison, Gayl Jones, Ntozake Shange and Alice Walker, writers who were accused of portraying black men in an 'unflichingly candid and often negative manner' as 'thieves, sadists, rapists, and ne'er-do-wells'.[11] She argued that while accusations and arguments of these types were easy to discredit and the reputations of the writers were unaffected by such rantings, it was important to consider them because,

> for all their questionable arguments, from the perspective of readers more informed, these are men whose judgments help to influence the masses of readers largely untutored in Afro-American literature, who take their cues of what and how to read from the *New York Times Book Review*, *New York Review of Books* and other organs of the literary establishment.

And, as McDowell shows, this debate was waged primarily in the pages of the very influential journals and newspapers of the New York literary establishment who tended 'mainly to employ black men to review and comment on the literature of black women'.[12] What was apparently a debate over the portrayal of black men by black women writers was not, in fact, about that issue at all: McDowell concludes that 'what lies behind this smoke screen is an unacknowledged jostling for space in the literary marketplace ... which brings to mind Hawthorne's famous complaint about the "damn'd mob of scribbling women" of the 1850s'.[13]

My interest lies in this issue of public presence, the public face of the relation between black intellectuals, their work and the field of African American studies.[14] I want to follow McDowell's suggestive comment about 'jostling' in the marketplace and examine some of the publications of the New York literary and cultural establishment, the *New York Times*, the *New York Times Book Review*, the *New Yorker*, and the *Atlantic Monthly*, because although their discussions of black intellectuals are parochial and paternalistic, their sphere of influence extends far beyond Amtrak's north-east corridor and many regard them as national publications.

Because the United States is still such a deeply segregated nation, universities have become an important site on which battles over the future racial formation of the country are being fought. The outrageous fact is that for many undergraduates their first experience of integration, of living and working in a racially and ethnically diverse community, occurs on university campuses. I recognize that these campuses are only minimally, unevenly or patchily integrated, but they have the potential for enabling their students to imagine the possibility of a diverse society. The significance of this has been recognized by the right as well as by liberals, as confirmed by the timing of President George W. Bush's direct intervention in support of the white plaintiffs in the University of Michigan's affirmative action case on 15 January 2003, Martin Luther King's birthday. I would argue that this case is not really about the white students who claim that their admission to the university was unfairly rejected, but is actually about halting in its tracks any potential for imagining the radical transformation of the racial formation of the United States. The recognition of the importance of university campuses as sites of (limited) diversity by the liberal press may be of a different order than the Bush administration's fundamentalist vision, but it is ambiguous about racialized social transformation. I would argue that while the fascination of the liberal press with black intellectuals is, seemingly, more sympathetic to increased diversity, their interest lies in the management and containment of any potential for imagining a profound transformation in the racial or ethnic order. Beneath the appearance of attention paid to African American studies and/or the work of black intellectuals, the liberal press deliberately turn their gaze away from intellectual production and consistently reduce and displace ideas in favour of the promotion of celebrity, a reflection of their desire for and fascination with issues of style, not substance.

As C. Wright Mills insisted in his 1959 essay 'The Cultural Apparatus', interpretation does not take place in a vacuum: 'Every man *interprets* what he observes ... but his terms of interpretation are not his own.'[15] The elaborate and complex system of institutions that Mills describes as constituting the 'cultural apparatus', 'composed of all the organizations and *milieux* in which artistic, intellectual and scientific work goes on, and of the means by which such work is made available to circles, publics, and masses',[16] stands as a very accurate portrait of the Eastern Seaboard literary and cultural journals, magazines, publishing houses and foundations, most based in New York, that have played a crucial role in shaping the public representation of the field of black cultural politics and the designation of its major players. An important facet of the national establishment for the public at large, this cultural apparatus has, in its own terms, authenticated and legitimated certain black intellectuals and particular aspects of the field of black studies while it also delegitimated the insurgency of radical and feminist politics.

In hindsight, to imagine that the collective nature of the feminist project undertaken by marginalized but deeply committed black women intellectuals in the academy in the 1980s would gain a strong public presence appears a naive utopian dream. For in spite of pioneering studies like *The Black Woman*, edited by Toni Cade Bambara in 1970; groundbreaking work from critics Mary Helen Washington, June Jordan and Ellease Southerland in the 1974 issue of *Black World*; from Frances Smith Foster, Barbara Smith, Audre Lorde and Claudia Tate and from Cheryl Wall, Abena Busia, Barbara Christian, Mae Henderson, Gloria Hull, Deborah McDowell, Valerie Smith, Hortense Spillers, Claudia Tate and Susan Willis in *Changing Our Own Words*; and many others, many women who undertook the excavation and critical evaluation of black women's writing, the ultimate management of black women's public presence, when it became a commodity, would be placed, securely, in the hands of a male establishment. Indeed, the deaths of Barbara Christian, Audre Lorde, June Jordan and Claudia Tate made barely a ripple in the press of the New York establishment.

Writing in the early 1990s, Ann duCille analysed how, 'Within the modern academy, racial and gender alterity has become a hot commodity that has claimed black women as its principal signifier ... the peasants under glass of intellectual inquiry in the 1990s.'[17] She asks why this interest – 'which seems to me to have reached occult status – increasingly marginalizes both the black women critics and scholars who excavated the fields in question and their black feminist "daughters" who would further develop those fields'.[18] DuCille then asked a series of questions about the politics of the discipline and the inequities of the cultural apparatus, among which were:

> What does it mean, for instance, that many prestigious university presses and influential literary publications regularly rely not on these seasoned black women scholars but on male intellectuals – black and white – to review the manuscripts and books of young black women just entering the profession ... What does it mean for the field in general and for junior African Americanists in particular that senior scholars, who are not trained in African American studies and whose career-building work often has excluded black women, are now teaching courses in and publishing texts about African American literature and generating 'new scholarship' on black women writers? What does it mean for the future of black feminist studies that a large portion of the growing body of scholarship on black women is now being written by white feminists and by men whose work frequently achieves

> greater critical and commercial success than that of the black female scholars who carved out the field?[19]

DuCille has no interest in what she calls 'territoriality', the essentialist reduction of particular fields of knowledge to 'raced' bodies, but she does demonstrate the inequities inherent in how the field was being valued, judged and taught, in relation to the paradoxes of market forces.

In my experience, academic institutions daily reduce bodies to fields of knowledge when black or ethnic scholars are thought suitable only for, and appointed only in, programmes of black or ethnic studies. The majority of African Americanists have argued that their field should be open to all who have a rigorous training in the discipline, like any other academic discipline would demand, and yet the common sense attitude that dominates the academy assumes that while black scholars are fit only for black studies, anyone else can 'just do it', without any previous training or expertise required. At my home institution, African American studies is the most integrated department in the university.

Adam Begley, in the *New York Times Magazine*, named Henry Louis Gates Jr 'Black Studies' New Star' at the end of the decade, and listed 'literary archaeology', particularly the discovery of Harriet E. Wilson's *Our Nig*, and the editorship of the Schomberg Library of Nineteenth-Century Black Women Writers and the Perennial Library's Zora Neale Hurston series among his many other accomplishments.[20] In this move the *New York Times* rendered invisible the substantial community of critics and their work that had made ventures like the Schomberg Library of Nineteenth-Century Black Woman Writers possible. Black women's expressivity, argues duCille, 'is not merely discourse; it has become lucre in the intellectual marketplace, cultural commerce. What for many began as a search for our mother's gardens, to appropriate Alice Walker's metaphor, has become for some a Random House harvest worth millions in book sales and university professorships'.[21] The eastern literary establishment anointed its own midwife of black women's writing, a production manager of black women's texts and authentic interpreter of the field, ignoring and effectively erasing the collective work of generations of scholars, men and women, black and white, who were the actual labourers in the critical process. While one black male scholar could be legitimated as the production manager of profitable black women's texts for the marketplace, there was no profit in engaging the work of multiple black women critics. Ignoring the multiplicity of critical presences also produced value through the invention of scarcity.

Marketing the field has led to a preoccupation with the 'newness' of African American studies, an arena in which scholars constantly make 'discoveries' erasing the history of any previous critical engagement with these texts. Just as successful corporations realized in the mid-1980s that they should produce brands as opposed to products, African American studies was marketed as a series of brand name individuals. The field was presented as producing black stars, or celebrities, not insurgent knowledge. Instead of presenting the field as a collectivity of multiple critical presences, the *New York Times* created an easily recognizable brand name for the literary field in Henry Louis Gates Jr. Prominent in the article are references to entertainment, to the success of Professor Gates's 'entrepreneurial P. T. Barnumism'. Being characterized not only as an entrepreneur but as a circus manager works simultaneously to discredit him as an intellectual and to increase his value as celebrity.[22] Adam Begley made claims to the uniqueness of his subject, and thereby increased not only

the value of his discovery but also his own value as pioneering journalist in previously unknown territory by emphasizing the supposed scarcity of black scholars in his opening paragraphs, which described how universities had to enter bidding wars to obtain one of these valuable commodities.[23]

In the next few years the media would become obsessed with the newness, or novelty value, of African American studies and the originality and rarity of their 'discovery' of black intellectuals. In 1995 blackness arrived packaged on the cover of the *New Yorker*. The double April and May issue was titled *Black in America* (at least it wasn't a February publication); its red, white, blue and black cover was the head of a black statute of liberty by Michael Roberts, presumably after the style of Aaron Douglas.[24]

As C. Wright Mills observed, 'the essential feature of any establishment is a traffic between culture and authority, a tacit co-operation of cultural workmen and authorities of ruling institutions. This means of exchange between them includes money, career, privilege; but above all, it includes *prestige*.'[25] With prestige, I would add, was granted the authority to define and exclude. The 'traffic between culture and authority' would be apparent in the decade of the 1990s when contemporary black intellectuals were 'discovered', and in the process authenticated, by the New York literary establishment. Media investigations into African American studies and the role of black intellectuals read like journalistic sorties into the colonial wilderness of the academic outback. But, although they note their existence, these accounts do not stray so far into the outback as to confront the ideas of its indigenous, feminist women.

In a paternalistic fashion, black intellectuals were presented as 'coming of age' in a debate that fashioned itself as a response to Russell Jacoby. In *The Last Intellectuals*, published in 1987, Jacoby had declared that Philip Rahv, Edmund Wilson, Lionel Trilling, Alfred Kazin, Irving Howe and Daniel Bell, all associated with *Partisan Review* in the 1930s, 1940s and 1950s and known as the New York Intellectuals, were in fact the last public intellectuals in the United States.[26] In January 1995, in what appeared to be a review of books by Derrick Bell, Michael Eric Dyson, bell hooks and Cornel West, in the *New Yorker*, Michael Bérubé announced that 'a new African-American intelligentsia has become part of this country's cultural landscape'. First, both groups of intellectuals, Bérubé argued, 'seek to redefine what it means to be an intellectual in the United States';[27] second, both Cornel West and Lionel Trilling wrote bestsellers, *Race Matters* and *The Liberal Imagination*; and third, 'though bell hooks (neé Gloria Watkins) looks and sounds nothing like the later Irving Howe, she now has the same title that he once held at CUNY; namely distinguished professor'.[28] In this bizarre series of analogies the marketplace and academic prestige are the most important signifiers of authentic intellectual practice: for Bérubé, 'what's distinctive about this generation of African American intellectuals is that their work has become a fixture of mall bookstores, talk shows, élite universities, and black popular culture'.[29] But Bérubé's review, instead of being a review of this work, of books and ideas, turns out to be a review of the authors; they are paraded as if models on the catwalk of the latest academic fashion show.

In March 1995, Robert S. Boynton, in the *Atlantic Monthly*, without acknowledging Bérubé's previous discovery, countered Jacoby's thesis with his own 'discovery' of a new group of post–Cold War public intellectuals that differed from the New York Intellectuals in what he calls 'striking ways':

> Whereas Jacoby's intellectuals were freelance writers based in New York, most of this group is ensconced in elite universities across the country. Whereas the New Yorkers were predominantly male and Jewish, this group includes women and is entirely gentile. In contrast to the New Yorkers, who were formed by their encounters with socialism and European culture, these intellectuals work solidly within the American grain, and are products of the political upheaval of the 1950s and 1960s. And, most significant, they are black.[30]

A POLITICAL PORTRAIT OF PHIL GRAMM / FICTION BY JOHN BARTH

The Atlantic Monthly

MARCH 1995

THE NEW INTELLECTUALS

Sophisticated, political, morally aware, at times fiercely contentious— the breed known as "public intellectuals" has seemed close to extinction. Suddenly they're back. And they're black.

BY ROBERT S. BOYNTON

$2.95
Can. $3.50

The symbol of this newly discovered group of public intellectuals, emblazoned on the cover of the *Atlantic Monthly*, was a dark brown fist and arm raised in a black power salute clutching a pen.

Boynton's observations are more elaborate than Bérubé's, though they clearly articulate many of the same premises. Boynton argues that the 'core elements of a definition of the public intellectual' were in place by the late nineteenth century:

'a writer, informed by a strong moral impulse, who addressed a general, educated audience in accessible language about the most important issues of the day'.[31] Because they address 'a large and attentive audience about today's most pressing issues', Boynton concludes that the contemporary black intellectuals he names are the direct inheritors of 'the mantle of the New York Intellectuals'. Whereas Bérubé argues that what had been lacking for earlier generations of black intellectuals was 'a black public sphere of commensurate size', Boynton insists that black intellectuals have become popular for four reasons:[32] first, because of their 'unprecedented access to the mass-circulation print media'; second, because 'they have been sought out by the electronic media, and shows like *Nightline*, *Today*, and *The Oprah Winfrey Show* give them extraordinary visibility'; third, because they have 'used their prestigious university positions to extend their influence beyond the academy'; and, finally, because 'they have benefited from America's current concern about race'.[33]

For Bérubé, politics are also a ground of comparison between the New York Intellectuals and contemporary black intellectuals:

> What Marxism was to Lionel Trilling, Clement Greenberg, Philip Rahv, and company, black nationalism is to West, Gates, Hooks et al.: the inspiration, the springboard, the template, but also the antagonist and the goad. Just as the postwar Jewish intelligentsia largely abandoned radical politics but remained committed to rethinking American's progressive traditions . . . the black intelligentsia of our fin de siècle has largely abandoned cultural nationalism while remaining committed to rethinking forms of African American collectivity.[34]

But it is the issue of race, not politics, that Boynton utilizes as the ground for his comparison, in his attempt to give coherence to an otherwise totally absurd thesis. Whereas Bérubé thought that both the New York Intellectuals and black intellectuals 'redefined what it meant to be an intellectual in the United

States',[35] Boynton argues that it is 'the particular burden of the American intellectual . . . to reflect on what it means to be an "American." '

> The New Yorkers devoted much of their careers to grappling with the demands of being both American and intellectuals, as well as to pondering the significance of their Jewish identities in their work. The current focus by many black thinkers on the significance of their American citizenship is further proof that they are reviving America's rich public-intellectual tradition. Like so many stories these days, this one is about blacks and Jews – or, more precisely, about how one ethnically marginalized group of public intellectuals has followed in the footsteps of another.[36]

Later in the article Boynton is forced to admit, just as Bérubé conceded in his review, that contemporary black intellectuals are not, of course the first generation of black public intellectuals and that issues of race and ethnicity were not the core focus of the work of the New York Intellectuals during the 1930s. The latter, he states, only confronted their Jewish heritage in their work after learning of the horrors of the holocaust at the end of the Second World War.

So if Boynton admits that an earlier generation of black intellectuals that included W. E. B. Du Bois (and Ida B. Wells, I and Bérubé would add) were by his own definition public intellectuals 'informed by a strong moral impulse, who addressed a general, educated audience in accessible language about the most important issues of the day', and confronted what it meant to be American, why doesn't he create an alternative genealogy, a genealogy in which the New York Intellectuals inherit the mantle of the previous generation of black intellectuals? This earlier generation of black public intellectuals interrogated the relation between Americanness and blackness in their confrontation with the legacy of enslavement and the continuing horror of lynching, and, by Boynton's own definition, they pre-date by half a century what he describes as the turn of the New York Intellectuals to ethnicity in the 1940s.

But, of course, it is not intellectual history that is at stake in this story, it is marketing.

The point is to erase history and to deny an organic relation between contemporary black intellectuals and a past of collective struggle. Whereas Boynton claims that the New York Intellectuals were first concerned with broad issues of Americanness and American politics and only later focused on ethnicity, he reverses this paradigm for contemporary black intellectuals. Described as the generation to emerge 'between the civil-rights movement and the Reagan backlash', Boynton insists that they were initially concerned with 'a race-based identity politics' but have redirected their attention to 'the importance of American citizenship for race relations'.[37] Of course it can be argued that Du Bois's *The Souls of Black Folk*, published in 1903, among many other works by black intellectuals, was concerned with 'the importance of American citizenship for race relations', but Boynton insists, in the most paternalistic manner, that black intellectuals are maturing and becoming more sophisticated in their thought and he invents a paradigm to prove it.

Bérubé's and Boynton's 'discovery' of black public intellectuals in 1995 was a fraudulent journalistic invention that ranks with the historical recording of the 'discovery' of America by Europeans as if the peoples already in residence were incapable of conceptualizing their own material existence. Their claims of discovery, the assertions of the newness of black, public, intellectual life, are the occasion which allows them to tell and sell their stories. Boynton wonders how substantial the legacy of his group of black public intellectuals will be, as if he did not already know that two centuries of substantial work by black thinkers in the Americas already exists, and then he questions whether this legacy 'will be compromised' by their media popularity: 'As public intellectuals gain greater access to mainstream culture,' Boynton asks, 'do they become more important thinkers or only better known?'[38] But while Boynton speculates about the ways in which the work of black public intellectuals could be compromised by the culture industry, he and Bérubé remain totally unselfconscious of the ways in which they are trading in 'blackness' in the journalistic marketplace with their newly 'discovered', designer-brand black intellectuals.

Deborah McDowell's observation about an 'unacknowledged jostling in the literary marketplace' could be extended to apply to the black intellectual marketplace as resentments between and among black intellectuals surfaced. In 1992, in Boston, the Reverend Eugene Rivers, in a letter to the *Boston Review*, issued a direct challenge to 'black intellectuals at elite universities', naming Cornel West, Henry Louis Gates, bell hooks, Orlando Patterson, Jerry Watts, K. Anthony Appiah and Martin Kilson, to discuss their relationship with the black urban poor in open debate.[39] As a model of accountability, Rev. Rivers used Noam Chomsky's 1967 essay published in the *New York Review of Books* on 'The Responsibility of Intellectuals'. Chomsky had asked, 'What are the special moral responsibilities of intellectuals, "given the unique privileges that intellectuals enjoy" in Western capitalist democracies?' and answered 'that intellectuals have a "responsibility ... to speak the truth and to expose lies" and a duty "to see events in their historical perspective." '[40] Rivers called his letter to black academics 'On the Responsibility of Intellectuals in the Age of Crack'. What followed were two public forums.

The first was held at the Arco Forum at Harvard University's Kennedy School of Government on 30 November 1992 and the second a year later at MIT.[41] Accused of abandoning the black poor in their pursuit of large salaries, honoraria and academic success, for many it seemed as if resentment had brought black academic celebrities to trial and many of them were on the defensive. Rivers issued yet another challenge to them in 1995.[42] But, as Robin Kelley asked, 'Do we need yet another call for annual conferences of high-profile academics to examine the crisis in black America?'[43] Targeting black celebrity academics was going to get Rivers publicity, but it would not tell him anything about the social and political commitments and achievements of black public intellectuals.

Today there are many vibrant, dynamic collaborative projects that already bring together scholars and activists, but stories about these efforts don't sell as many papers as *ad hominem* attacks on black intellectuals. We might acknowledge, for example, the wonderful work being done by the Children's Defense Fund, particularly it's Black Student Leadership Network and its Black Community Crusade for Children, where young activist–intellectuals – including Lisa Sullivan, Matthew Countryman, Greg Hodge, Keith Jennings and Stacey Shears – work with such faculty and community organizers as James Jennings (whom Rivers mentions), Geoffrey Canada, Carl Taylor, Farah Griffin and others. We might point to Walter Davis and the Southern Empowerment Project, or the important work being done by Elizabeth Higginbotham of the Center for Research on Women at the University of Memphis. There is the Washington, DC, group that produces Black Political Agenda – Clarence Lusane, James Steele and CDF activists Lisa Sullivan and Keith Jennings. On drug and alcohol policy, we might point to Makani Themba of the Marin Institute and public health scholar Denise Herd at Berkeley.

Eugene Rivers sacrificed a chance to actually debate and gain a wide audience for the work that non-celebrity black intellectuals were undertaking to improve the lives of the poor outside of the glare of the media, in favour of targeting black celebrities.[44] The mass-marketing of blackness, via the branding of black intellectuals as media stars and as logos for the field, has been an overwhelmingly masculine project. In Boynton's broadest list of thirty contemporary black public intellectuals, six are women but he has a subgroup of six key people from the list, those he describes as getting the most attention, of whom only one is a woman: Cornel West, Stanley Crouch, Henry Louis Gates Jr, Stephen Carter, Shelby Steele and Toni Morrison. In Boynton's supposedly in-depth discussion of black thinkers only the ideas of men (the former plus Ralph Ellison, James

Baldwin, Albert Murray, Randolph Kennedy and Glenn Loury) are engaged, while there is only one reference to anything Morrison wrote, plus a one-sentence quote from Patricia Williams. Though Boynton is at great pains to assert that his new intellectuals are not of one mind and inhabit different points on the US political spectrum, in the shift that he tracks from concerns with blackness to citizenship, issues of gender or feminist politics are not included as one aspect of the range or diversity of political thought about which the new black public intellectuals concern themselves, even though all the black female intellectuals in his list have made major national and international contributions to a feminist and gendered understanding of the world, among their other intellectual accomplishments.

But of course, Boynton is not alone in his masculine focus on and definition of black intellectual activity. In July of 1994 Don Terry in the 'Ideas and Trends' section of the *New York Times* examined the contemporary role of the NAACP. The article was headed by six portraits of black male intellectual and political leaders: Rev. Benjamin Chavis, Louis Farrakhan, Prof. Cornel West, Rev. Jesse Jackson, Robert Woodson and Rev. Al Sharpton. The point of the story was the number and range of differing opinions about the future role of the NAACP. As Adolph Reed Jr characterized it, 'It's not just a diversity of opinion . . . It's a diversity of interests. There used to be at least a common denominator. There isn't any more.'[45] For Don Terry and the *New York Times*, diversity in a civil rights organization was constituted in, by and through the interests of an all-male body.

In 1994 in a very thoughtful analysis of the contemporary situation of the black creative intellectual, Hortense Spillers marked the years that had passed since the publication of Harold Cruse's *The Crisis of the Negro Intellectual* in 1967:[46]

> yielding apparently little resistance to the sound intrusion of market imperatives on the entire intellectual object, including

> that of African American studies, today's black creative intellectual lends herself/himself – like candy being taken from a child – to the mighty seductions of publicity and the 'pinup', rather like what an editor of *Lingua Franca* only half-jokingly dubbed, once upon a time, the 'African American du jour'.[47]

The media production of and fascination with the antics of black celebrity intellectuals is not only a displacement of a lack of concern for the general condition of black existence in the United States, but an effective erasure of concern with poverty, lack of education and imprisonment as a form of racialized social control.

In Salman Rushdie's novel *Fury*, the spectacle of the self-indulgence, overindulgence and aggressive and insatiable appetites of wealthy Americans evokes a bloated and parasitic empire devouring the globe to satisfy and sustain its desires and ways of life:

> Professor Malik Solanka ... in his silvered years found himself living in a golden age. Outside his window a long, humid summer, the first hot season of the third millennium, baked and perspired. The city boiled with money. Rents and property values had never been higher, and in the garment industry it was widely held that fashion had never been so fashionable. New restaurants opened every hour. Stores, dealerships, galleries struggled to satisfy the skyrocketing demand for ever more recherché produce: limited-edition olive oils, three-hundred-dollar corkscrews, customised Humvees, the latest anti-virus software, escort services featuring contortionists and twins, video installations, outsider art, featherlight shawls made from the chin-fluff of extinct mountain goats.[48]

During the novel its protagonist, Malik Solanka, confronts and attempts to resolve the contradictions that arise from his move from Britain to New York City despite the fact he hates American political, economic and cultural claims to world domination.[49]

Solanka is a professor, 'a retired historian of ideas', a Cambridge don who, in despair about academic life, resigns as an act of protest against its 'narrowness, infighting, and ultimate provincialism'.[50] In lieu of an academic income, Professor Solanka lives on the wealth created by his invention, a series of 'Great Minds' dolls including Bertrand Russell, Kierkegaard, Machiavelli, Socrates and Galileo, figures for whom he has created complex, imaginary, historical and philosophical lives. When Solanka quits the academy, his dolls, originally a hobby, go to work for him as the protagonists of a popular history-of-philosophy television show. With the addition of 'Little Brain', a female 'time-travelling interrogator', a 'questing knowledge-seeker created to be an audience surrogate', these dolls become media stars and *The Adventures of Little Brain* a prime-time hit.[51] Once famous, the dolls remain Professor Solanka's creatures for only a very short time; he is replaced by a cultural industry which emerges to sustain and reproduce their imaginary lives. Solanka vehemently despises the product, but it makes him rich.

Solanka's rage grows to potentially murderous proportions, and fearing that he will vent his rage on those he loves, he runs away from his family and friends and towards that which epitomizes all that he despises: the USA. As Solanka has long been a diehard critic of 'the immense goddam *power* . . . [and] immense fucking *seduction* of America', his friends are amused by the irony of his decision 'to relocate . . . in the bosom of the Great Satan'. But Solanka is unable to explain this act of self-abnegation. He ponders, 'how to say, America is the great devourer, and so I have come to America to be devoured?'[52]

Salman Rushdie's *Fury* is extraordinarily prescient of events that would only intrude on the consciousness of most American citizens on 11 September 2001. One night while standing in Washington Square Solanka feels his own internal demons shrink in significance when confronted by the commitment of revolutionaries and the solidarities formed in the cauldron of American injustice and resistance to American might:

> He looked at the bloodstains drying on the darkened square, evidence here in New York City of the force of a gathering fury on the far side of the world: a group fury, born of long injustice, beside which his own unpredictable temper was a thing of pathetic insignificance, the indulgence, perhaps, of a privileged individual with too much self-interest.[53]

The novel strains to make incremental connections between Solanka's individual rage and what remains as a rather amorphous and vague gesture to a global order in which 'everyone was an American now, or at least Americanized.' Solanka fears 'his terrorist anger that kept taking him hostage', and he recognizes that he too has succumbed to America's vast potency and its brilliance; that he is compromised, desiring what America promises but constantly withholds. Solanka concludes that what he opposed in America he must attack in himself. Though *Fury* does not and, one could argue, cannot resolve this tension, Rushdie's dissection of intellectual anxiety is powerful.[54]

Rushdie writes with intense passion and tempestuousness. A powerful satire and virulent condemnation of the politics and culture of the American empire, *Fury* analyses both the process of attraction and the consequences of its seductions for intellectuals. A close friend and colleague of Solanka, Jack Reinhart, is seduced into the imaginary and material world of intellectual celebrity in the United States. Once a radical black journalist 'with a distinguished record of investigating American racism and a consequent stirring of powerful enemies', Reinhart becomes a chronicler of the rich and famous, of 'today's Caesars in their Palaces', and, in the process of recording their lives, becomes part of the 'guilded milieu'. Solanka realizes that Reinhart is only apparently a critic of the superficiality of the world about which he writes and with which he has fallen in love and concludes that it suits the elite to keep him around as 'a sort of pet', the 'house nigger' of the rich and famous. Rushdie's critical eye, however, is focused on the individual and social cost of being seduced by American wealth and power:

> Behind the infinite layers of Reinhart's cool was this ignoble fact: he had been seduced, and his desire to be accepted into this white man's club was the dark secret he could not confess to anyone, perhaps not even to himself. And these are the secrets from which the anger comes. In this dark bed the seeds of fury grow. And though Jack's act was armor-plated, although his mask never slipped, Solanka was sure he could see, in his friend's blazing eyes, the self-loathing fire of his rage. It took him a long while to concede that Jack's suppressed fury was the mirror of his own.[55]

Much of the power and persuasiveness of *Fury* lies in Rushdie's fierce but subtle presentation of the particularities of the processes of this seduction: of the contradictions that shape intellectual critiques of capitalism and American dominance of the world, contradictions that are simultaneously located in and implicated by those same structures of power and domination; of the necessity of recognizing, naming and condemning collaboration; and of the self-hatred and intellectual paralysis that seduction produces. *Fury* raises, though it cannot resolve, contradictions pertinent to any discussion of intellectual life in America, from a broad condemnation of the anti-intellectual nature of late capitalism to the complex satirical portraits of the seduction of Professors Solanka and Reinhart courted and celebrated by the media on both sides of the Atlantic.

I admire and empathize with Rushdie's portrait of the dilemma of the displaced transatlantic intellectual striving for a location from which to launch a global critique of Anglo/American power while sitting securely, if with some discomfort, within its borders. Within the Anglo/North American transatlantic world that Rushdie portrays, intellectuals are either uncritical tools of powerful elites or rendered inarticulate and impotent by their own inner rage. In an era in which ideas are of little value, the only possible 'public' role for intellectuals is circumscribed by the extent to which they can perform for the market. The contemporary penchant for the intellectual 'sound bite' is represented by Rushdie as the antics of 'little brains' disseminated by the cultural conglomerates. *Fury* is an ambitious attempt to construct a narrative of consistent contradiction between the internal discontent of its displaced protagonist, the poverty of whose intellectual life is signalled by the mass-marketing of the fruits of his imagination, and a global discontent, the result of rampant capitalist exploitation, inequality and injustice.

While it is true that the field of African American studies has its origins in a social movement, it is also clear that we serve several institutional functions for our employers. As social institutions, universities act to maintain the hierarchical nature of the status quo by excluding most of the population from its classrooms while ensuring that a small number are trained and certified to supervise others. In Gramscian terms in the post–civil rights era, black academics have functioned and continue to function as intellectuals in particular and politically contradictory ways in the 'ensemble of the system of relations in which these activities have their place within the general complex of social relations'.[56] Are we meant to function as the black gatekeepers, ensuring the production, perpetuation and maintenance of a small, black, middle-class elite in the hope that this elite will act as a force to control the rebellious tendencies of the black oppressed? If, in 1979, Jameson could argue that 'the only authentic cultural production today *has seemed to be* that which can draw on the collective experience of marginal pockets of social life' in which he had included black literature, now Slavoj Žižek sees a very different reality:

> the problematic of multiculturalism – the hybrid coexistence of diverse cultural life worlds – which imposes itself today is the form of appearance of its opposite, of the massive presence of capitalism as *universal* world system: it bears witness to the unprecedented homogenization of the contemporary world. It is effectively as if, since the horizon of social imagination no longer allows us to entertain the idea of an eventual demise of

> capitalism – since, as we might put it, everybody accepts that *capitalism is here to stay* – critical energy has found a substitute outlet in fighting for cultural differences which leave the basic homogeneity of the capitalist world system intact.[57]

We need to ask ourselves what role we play in the 'unprecedented homogenization' and unprecedented corporatization of the contemporary world.

Roland Barthes recounted that he was in the barbers when someone offered him a copy of *Paris Match*. On the cover a young black soldier 'in French uniform is saluting, with his eyes uplifted, probably fixed on a fold of the tricolour'. What this cover signifies, Barthes continues, is 'that France is a great Empire, that all her sons, without any colour discrimination, faithfully serve under her flag, and that there is no better answer to the detractors of an alleged colonialism than the zeal shown by this Negro in serving his so-called oppressors'.[58]

I was in my kitchen when I opened my copy of the *New Yorker* and saw Professor Henry Louis Gates paying homage to the IBM Thinkpad, or IBM paying homage to Professor Gates, and thought immediately of Barthes's black soldier.[59] It is a beautiful picture, rich colours, the warm tones of wood, the window looking out onto Harvard Yard, and the scholar, frowning in concentration as he writes on his laptop. The advert brings to a culmination my argument about the process of authentication of the black intellectual and his integration into the utopia of unlimited exploitation. Two logos exist in perfect harmony, and to mutual benefit: the figure of Professor Gates, the brand name of African American literature and the field of African American studies, attests to the presence of capitalism as a universal world system, through multiculturalism. IBM becomes the conduit to the black past. As Barthes claimed, 'history evaporates' and, I would conclude, the corporate world is past, present and future and authenticates our being through the market.[60]

Our current political moment is characterized by the public conflation of the terms 'black intellectual', 'black academic' and 'black leader' and the black academic world is reduced to the chin-fluff of extinct mountain goats, fulfilling desires and unspoken needs like yellow Hummers. The authentication of blackness has become celebrated and defined through the body and through the valorization of the impoverishment of ideas. Critical complexity is replaced by clichéd generalities and easily digestible sound bites. The abandonment of intellectual insurgency in favour of the self-promotion of celebrities and the production of formulaic and acceptable interpretations of black America for general consumption is an indication of the extent to which academic entrepreneurs can function as the products and allies of corporate America.

The conflation of black intellectual leadership with academic entrepreneurialism is one sign of the 'tyranny of the market' and promises a dismal, if not bleak, political and intellectual future. The alliance of the media, New York intellectuals, educational foundations and institutions, and corporate America with a small black celebrity elite influences and limits the possibilities of what can be written, filmed, published and distributed through the granting, or the withholding, of patronage and financial support. There are great dangers in the attempt to retain power and influence in the hands of the few, as we should know from the history of the Tuskegee machine. It is the young scholars and creative artists who are the most vulnerable to being silenced and it is the possibility of radical, transformative work that is most at risk. Booker T. Washington sought to hold in his hands the power to approve appointments, to control and dominate access to the media, white institutions and mainstream sources of support. One hundred years later, dominant institutions and foundations, for example, are still only too eager to assign to one or two black celebrity figures the right to grant a seal of approval to black intellectual and cultural work.

Our function then, as the generation of post–civil rights intellectuals, should be compared to that of postcolonial elites who perpetuate the interests of their former colonizers. We participate in the reduction of a sphere of knowledge to equate with particular bodies – ethnicized and racialized bodies for ethnicized and racialized forms of knowledge. As incorporated, if not corporate, racialized bodies, we need to talk about the extent to which a multiculturalism, 'which is the form of appearance of its opposite', is the product of an unrepentantly capitalist world order that has completely reneged on any commitment to social equality and justice. Perhaps that is why the media is most comfortable with black intellectuals who function as an extension of black entertainment, as professionally racialized bodies reduced to perform spectacular acts of blackness in intellectual face.

11

Black Feminism

I wish to sketch the trajectory of black feminism as it emerged in the UK and the USA to consider what it can teach us about the present and organizing for a feminist future. Black feminism has its roots in movements for emancipation and liberation: anti-slavery and anti-colonial. I speak here in broad generalities and from my experience as a black British woman who is involved in the black feminist movement on both sides of the Atlantic, but I do not pretend to represent all black feminists who speak in multiple voices.

Black feminism in the USA has its roots in the struggle against enslavement, articulated, in its written form, primarily through documents of the anti-slavery movement, but it existed also in the everyday practices of resistance to the brutal exploitation of the black female body in the reproduction of property.

After the Civil War, black feminist critique develops from the contentious debate that split apart the alliance formed in the anti-slavery movement as white female leaders of the emerging women's movement organized against granting the vote to black men in favour of their gaining the franchise themselves. By the turn of the century, black feminist liberation politics had produced a sophisticated theorization of the racialized sex–gender system of the US in an anti-lynching campaign and in opposition to the brutal suppression of the black vote.[1]

In the first half of the twentieth century, black women's feminism was dominated by the middle-class politics of uplift, though a small group of black feminists who joined the Communist Party were active in a variety of labour, cultural and organizing struggles in urban and rural areas, North and South. Younger generations of black women articulated their opposition to being told that their position in the civil rights movement was subordinate to men's through a radical black feminist politics that in turn influenced the flowering of creative writers and black women who enter the academy as historians, literary critics and theorists. It is this generation of women who recover the history of the black feminists who preceded them.

Black British feminism was by necessity transnational: a political struggle to survive in the North, it was informed by the politics of Empire and of the South. Its 'blackness' was structured by a firm commitment to the politics of alliance, a politics which sought to establish a fragile balance between acknowledging the importance of the particularities of the life histories of women of African, Asian and Caribbean descent, while forging links of solidarity out of their common experiences of oppression in Britain. The politics of alliance grew from shared conditions and oppressions – colonialism, migration and racism – and was a feminism of the workplace and the streets.

Contemporary black women writers seeking to establish the multiple origins of black British feminism have rediscovered and documented the political, grass-roots and labour activism of women like Una Marson Claudia Jones, Olive Morris and Jayaben Desai, migrants to the UK from various parts of the British Empire in the first half of the twentieth century.[2] Establishing this history is important but it has underestimated the significance of the various knowledges that these women brought with them to the UK and that contributed to their international perspective on the British political and social formation.

The Organization of Women of African and Asian Descent (OWAAD) was the first national black women's organization and held its first annual conference in 1979. OWAAD's members included both migrant women and their first- and second-generation daughters born in the UK; anti-colonial and anti-imperialist movements in South Asia, East and West Africa and the English-speaking Caribbean informed its political agenda. Many of us were aware of those who had preceded us, but at the time we were focused on a series of very immediate struggles against, and confrontations with, a racist state: black women were fighting vigorous battles against the sexist racialization of the workplace and the exploitative terms and conditions of employment, against racist educational practices which streamed black kids into classes for the educationally subnormal, against the racism we faced in housing and social services, against the sterilization of young black women; and we were involved in a series of protests against a deeply racist police force that was arresting and jailing our children and siblings. Women in OWAAD also aggressively challenged the refusal of the Women's Liberation Movement (WLM) to engage or even acknowledge that colonialism and imperialism were feminist issues, and OWAAD condemned its total failure to address the oppression of black women within its ranks. But it would be untrue to say that there were no coalitions with white women; one of the most fruitful venues for alliance was the Rock against Racism movement.

Informed and inspired by this alliance, intellectuals developed black feminist political and cultural theory and artistic practice. Black feminism posed multiple challenges – political, social, cultural and intellectual – to the critique of patriarchy as articulated by the British WLM. Black feminist and anti-racist discourse contested the WLM's narrow definitions of class and gender and articulated a powerful analysis of the ways in which processes of racialization overdetermined class and gender oppression. Though OWAAD as a national movement had fragmented by the mid-1980s, split over a debate about the autonomous organizing of black lesbians, alliances of Asian and African Caribbean women can still be seen in local organizations that focus on particular issues, like Southall Black Sisters, who work to empower black women experiencing gender and domestic violence.[3]

'Black' in black feminism or 'womanism' in the United States is limited in its application to African American women. I have been dismayed to find black feminism in the US to be far more narrowly class-bounded and nationally parochial than in the UK.[4] (It has also not escaped the narrow-minded, uncritical and unreflective patriotism which has dominated American politics since 11 September 2001.)

An exception to the narrow frame of reference among African American feminist activists would be Angela Davis, who has for many years called for a feminist politics of alliance and solidarity between and among women of colour, and organizations like INCITE! Women of Colour against Violence, which was 'formed to continue efforts to develop strategies to end violence that addressed community and state violence simultaneously', focus on grass-roots organizing. It has a broader social, political and economic framework against violence than Southall Black Sisters.[5]

Currently, the US academy is dominated by a feminism that appears to concern itself with transnational issues but, as is the case at my own institution, consists of a cadre of middle-class women who organize only with other universities in the North and for whom women of the South are abject subjects.

I would argue that a transnational and international politics of alliance with the South is what we need to build for the future to counter an insidious turn to the politics of cultural identity which uses cultural difference as the ground for drawing absolute distinctions between and among human beings, producing and supporting ideologies of cultural normativity, cultural pathology and a politics of the body. The model for a world feminist forum would be complex and draw its strength from its numerous local bases. Perhaps the model could be similar to that of the World Social Forum, and we could benefit from the example of its weaknesses.[6]

If our first encounter with the forces of globalization was the transatlantic trade in enslaved bodies, we now live and die under a system of global governance led by institutions such as the

World Bank and the IMF that are the direct inheritors of that trade and manage all our bodies through the negotiations of capital. Only with a transnational and multinational feminist alliance can we hope to emancipate ourselves from such biopolitical governmentality.

12

Between Black and White

In one of the glass cabinets in the central rotunda of the fourth floor of the National Museum of African American History and Culture (NMAAHC) in Washington, DC, is a wooden canoe seat on which is carved a spider sitting in the middle of a web. Anansi, a spider of boundless ingenuity, is celebrated in the folklore of African-descended communities across the Americas for his ability to outwit his oppressors. The canoe seat is probably one of the most modest items in the museum's collection: it is only five and a half inches tall and just under thirteen inches wide, easily passed by and passed over. There is no acknowledgement that it was an inaugural gift to the museum and no particular attention is drawn to its country of origin, Ecuador. But it attests to the existence of a wider black Atlantic world – a world that is barely registered in the rest of the museum.

The NMAAHC is the newest Smithsonian museum and had been open for less than six months when I first visited three years ago. I arrived early, joining an excited crowd, and as we waited, I studied the African and African-diasporic design elements incorporated into the exterior of the building. The queue dissolved into a tide, washing across Heritage Hall and down to the subterranean galleries. For hundreds of years Atlantic trade was dominated by Britain, Portugal, Spain and the Netherlands. These nations forced some 12.5 million enslaved people from the African continent onto their ships, about 10.7 million of whom survived the crossing. Yet as I walked around the museum, I was unable to find any evidence of the descendants of the Africans who were transported to Central and South America and to the Caribbean, those who became Afro-Brazilian, Afro-Ecuadorian, Afro-Mexican, Afro-Peruvian or West Indian. Recently 'Latinx' and 'Latin America' have been added to the collection's categories, but holdings are sparse – mainly photographs or artworks created by American artists. There are more items associated with the history of the black community on Martha's Vineyard than with the whole of Latin America, including the Caribbean.

The museum sets out to challenge the marginalization of African Americans; that is, the descendants of the 388,746 enslaved people who disembarked in the region of North America that would become the United States. It represents their histories and culture as not only central to but exemplary of a singular national narrative – 'a people's journey, a nation's story' – the culmination of which is the establishment of a wealthy black middle class: tangible evidence of triumph over adversity. The trade in commodified human beings was, however, integral to a global, not national, project of colonial modernity. As African and indigenous peoples were dispossessed and subjugated, a multiplicity of complex, entangled racial formations were created across the Americas. The black national narrative has come to dominate the popular and academic imagination in the US, mirroring the theory of American exceptionalism and separating the history of African Americans from the histories of the descendants of other survivors of the crossing. The plural geopolitical concept of 'the Americas' is rendered meaningless when the US is seen *as* America rather than a region *within* America, and the history of its black population treated as definitive of a black experience separate from the histories of the peoples oppressed, displaced and eradicated by settler colonialism and its aftermath.

Isabel Wilkerson's bestselling books – *The Warmth of Other Suns: The Epic Story of America's Great Migration* (2010) and *Caste: The Origins of Our Discontents* (2020) – are, like the NMAAHC, situated within a gated community of knowledge.

The Warmth of Other Suns is a paean to the generations of people, including her parents, who left the southern states in huge numbers (around 6 million in total) to move north and west between 1915 and 1970. The book's title suggests a comprehensive, definitive account of black migration, but Wilkerson neglects the massive concurrent black migration from the Caribbean, a movement of people which was technically voluntary but, like the migration within the borders of the US, was in reality a matter of survival.

At the start of the twentieth century, a British Foreign Office memo noted, 'Her Majesty's black and coloured subjects in the West Indies have had to choose between a death from starvation in their native islands and suffering ill-treatment as immigrants ... because their native islands are merely Islands of Death.'* Hundreds of thousands migrated to Central America, where they laboured on the construction of the Panama Canal and the vast banana plantations that were being established by the United Fruit Company in Costa Rica, Guatemala, Honduras and elsewhere. Black migrants from the Caribbean also entered the US, arriving first in the north-eastern cities, then in Florida. The majority settled in Brooklyn and Manhattan. By 1930, a quarter of the black population of Harlem and a third of the black professional class of New York City were from the Caribbean. Black foreign migration ebbed and flowed with the tightening and easing of immigration restrictions, dramatically increasing during the Second World War and again in the 1960s.

The Warmth of Other Suns conveys a vivid sense of place and time in its descriptions of the journeys undertaken by people determined to carve out a better future for themselves. Wilkerson interweaves archival research with accounts of the everyday survival strategies of the interviewees who became her three major characters – their humiliations, large and small; the harsh conditions under which they laboured; the pleasures and problems of mounting resistance and plotting escape. By contrast,

* FO 23/96, 1899, National Archives, Kew.

her latest book, *Caste*, is haunted by the material and symbolic anxieties of the present. It begins in the dystopian landscape of 2016. A sense of emergency, of imminent threat, is palpable. The temperature of the planet continues its inexorable rise, the Arctic is melting, wildfires burn, pathogen spores rise from thawing permafrost and people across the world recoil from the vitriol of the television celebrity campaigning to be the next occupant of the White House. Published a few months before the 2020 election, after four years of increasing authoritarianism and the rampant spread of white supremacist hatred and violence, *Caste* is an attempt to reckon with the roots of America's racial formation.

In *The Warmth of Other Suns*, Wilkerson deployed 'caste' as a concept and a practice, replacing both structural racism and class. The 'thick walls of the caste system kept everyone in prison', white and black alike. Caste supremacy was maintained by the 'pressure . . . to stay within the narrow confines of acceptability', by drawing 'appropriate lines between oneself and those of lower rank of either race in that world' and by pitting the 'lowliest people' against one another. While it might appear to account for barriers to employment and housing restrictions in the cities of the North and West, a theory of racial inequity predicated on caste can't account for the resentment and antagonism that new arrivals experienced when they encountered black residents determined to protect their own tenuous position – members of the aspiring black middle class. In *Caste* the anecdotal sits uneasily alongside information from secondary sources. Wilkerson draws on the work of anthropologists of the 1930s and 1940s who used the word 'caste' to describe the racialized hierarchies of the Deep South, those states most dependent on a plantation economy and enslaved labour before the Civil War. The caste system associated with enslavement, they argued, was resurrected by Jim Crow laws after the ratification of the Thirteenth Amendment and policed through arbitrary violence, terror and the spectacle of lynching. She doesn't examine similar policies and practices instituted beyond the US, though they governed the lives of migrants from the Caribbean who laboured on the Panama Canal and elsewhere.

Wilkerson is intent on portraying the protracted power of caste oppression as an invisible rot within American society. Although racism might be its everyday expression, it is only by recognizing the 'subconscious code' of caste that we can start on the path to its eradication. At times her analogies struggle under the burden of this responsibility: our appearance is the 'visible cue' to caste, while race is a 'visible decoy'; caste is the bones, race the skin; we are trained in the language of race, but caste is the grammar that structures the language; the United States is a house, caste its supporting framework, the architecture of human hierarchy, and so on. In this analysis, race and caste are not synonymous: race is the visible agent of the unseen force that is caste. But Wilkerson also creates exceptions. A surfeit of anecdotes about highly accomplished, well-educated and wealthy black people who are unable to escape the draconian effects of caste discrimination stand in contrast to her references to black migrants working to distance themselves from the caste system by adopting strategies such as speaking 'with British diction' to make sure people know they are Jamaican or Grenadian or Ghanaian.

Where the NMAAHC celebrates the establishment of a black middle class as a pinnacle of the national success story, Wilkerson is concerned for the plight of those (among whom she places herself) who have excelled in their professions but nonetheless suffer from the prejudice and hostility inherent in the caste system. Health inequities between white people and people of colour in the US are stark, but her focus is not those who are currently dying of COVID-19 at three times the rate of the white population: the black, indigenous and Latinx populations who are overrepresented in the carceral system; who rely on underfunded, understaffed schools and hospitals; who live in the poorest neighbourhoods; have the highest exposure to environmental pollution and toxins; and who experience food insecurity on a regular basis. Rather, she chooses to write about those black people whose higher socio-economic status and privilege offer them no protection against the stress and heart disease associated with high levels of discrimination. The studies on which Wilkerson draws claim that 'the caste system takes years off the lives of subordinate-caste people who find themselves in contention with it': these people are highly educated, 'compete in fields where they are not expected to be' and 'experience a lower life expectancy as a result'.

Wilkerson recounts the biography of W. Allison Davis (1902–83), who faced discrimination despite being an accomplished and 'impeccably tailored' academic, with two degrees from Harvard and a year spent studying at the London School of Economics. In 1942, he completed his PhD in anthropology at the University of Chicago and was appointed to the faculty, the first black scholar to hold a full-time position at a predominantly white university. Five years later he became the first black faculty member at an elite university to be appointed to a tenured position. His colleagues, meanwhile, debated whether or not Davis should be teaching white students at all, the university wouldn't allow him to eat in its Quadrangle Club, and he was denied housing in the white neighbourhood surrounding the university.

Davis was the lead researcher on W. Lloyd Warner's project, which applied the concept of caste to race relations in the US and was published as *Deep South: A Social Anthropological Study of Caste and Class* (1941). Wilkerson cites the book as an influence on her own thinking, although its conceptualization of 'caste' doesn't exhibit the rigidity she favours (the authors of *Deep South* insist on its malleability). In her chapter on Davis, Wilkerson describes him as being 'on the early front lines of caste', but Davis's own work emphasized the importance of social and economic class. He also believed that knowledge about race 'can make little further progress until scientific studies of the range and variation of Negro societies outside of the United States have been completed'. An account of the great diversity among African diasporic peoples across the world could, he thought, be used as ammunition in the fight against racism at home. Unable to find funding for such a project, Davis encouraged his student St Clair Drake to pursue a diasporic research agenda. Drake completed his dissertation on 'Value Systems, Social Structure and Race Relations in the British Isles' in 1954.

In May 1948, the Trinidadian American sociologist Oliver Cromwell Cox published *Caste, Class and Race: A Study in Social Dynamics*, a critique of the use of 'caste' by white academics, particularly Lloyd Warner and Gunnar Myrdal, whose study of race relations, *An American Dilemma*, was published in 1944. In contrast to Wilkerson's national perspective, Cox saw a world system in which race prejudice and racial antagonism had originated from the commercialization of human labour in the Americas and the East Indies and the capitalist exploitation of these regions. Racism, Cox believed, was distinct from caste and reached 'full maturation in the second half of the 19th century with the second wave of British imperialism and the emergence of scientific racism'. Race relations were 'definitely not caste relations but relationships of labour, capital and profits . . . and hence political-class relations'.

Caste, Class and Race was a major study, but Wilkerson dismisses 'the Caribbean-born Oliver Cromwell Cox' as a 'contrarian' for having mounted such a 'cantankerous' critique. Racism, she insists, is 'one of the most contentious and misunderstood' words in the US. Since the Civil Rights Act of 1964, it has been 'reduced to a feeling, a character flaw'. The label 'racist' is wielded 'as an either/or accusation' against individuals – a label that even extremists refuse to take up. Because 'racism' is easily denied, lacks a 'universally agreed on definition' and cloaks the 'invisible structure that created and maintains hierarchy and inequality' in the US, Wilkerson adopts 'caste' as a superordinate concept to describe the mechanisms of this invisible structure and account for its rigidity and longevity. Race, she claims, is 'a recent phenomenon in human history', deriving from the Spanish word *raza* (in the context of the Atlantic slave trade), and 'caste' the much older term.

She is thinking here of India, but 'caste' is neither more rigid nor much older than the concept of 'race'. Caste is the anglicized form of the Spanish and Portuguese *casta*, which encompassed race, lineage, blood descent and breeding. The term was introduced to Asia by the Portuguese in the sixteenth century, and then to the Iberian empires of the Americas. Scholars of the Indian caste system describe it as a complex system of heritable hierarchy that has changed over time and isn't as rigid as is often assumed. As the work of Anupama Rao demonstrates, what outsiders think they see is in fact a modern form of caste, which was produced and codified 'as a social identity and a political mechanism of control' under British colonial rule.

Wilkerson could more profitably have considered caste (*casta*) in the history of the colonization of the Americas. The residue of Portuguese, as opposed to Anglo-Dutch, colonial domination is evident in the language used to differentiate bodies, and in the social and political practices which either forced their separation, for fear of 'mixture', or acknowledged intermingling and its results: the twenty-eight categories of skin colour and descent used in Brazil can't easily be mapped onto the definitions of 'black', 'coloured' and 'white' subjects in the *de jure* segregation of South African apartheid or the *de facto* 'black' and 'white' segregation of the US. Neither of these systems corresponds to the complex linguistic and visual vocabularies used to catalogue the African, European and Amerindian heterogeneity of Spain's American empire. In the course of individual and communal daily life in eighteenth-century Mexico, for example, corporeal identities and racial categories were mutable, but the elite art form of *casta* paintings attempted to place limits on this, showing pairings of differently racialized bodies while constraining the potential for greater fluidity by means of genealogical captions, which superimposed a taxonomic language based on rigid lines of descent.

These racial imaginaries rooted in colonization are not only historical but also geopolitical in character. After the Abolition Act of 1833, the British repurposed slave ships to transport more than a million indentured labourers from India to work on plantations in their colonies around the globe, resulting in the complex entanglements of caste and race in British Guiana, Jamaica and Trinidad. Wilkerson sees caste as both cause and symptom of a Manichaean division between black and white in the early days of North American colonization, but this division tells us little about the effects of gender and class, and can't account for indigeneity. If we broaden our understanding to include the history of racial geographies across the Americas, rather than uncritically accepting national boundaries established long after the European invasions, encounters with indigenous inhabitants become central to any attempt at making sense of the classification and division of humanity.

In the final pages of *Caste*, Wilkerson says she wants her book to help change minds and increase empathy, encouraging 'the work to educate one's self and to listen with a humble heart, to understand another's experience from their perspective'. Yet she tells stories of migration without revealing any empathy for the history of foreign black migrants or for the contemporary migrants from other parts of the Americas who have been confined in camps and cages in the US or deported in violation of international law. Instead of thinking in exclusionary national units, our work and our institutions should acknowledge these interconnected histories and forge links between black, indigenous and Latinx communities. It is time for a reckoning, but hoping to change minds isn't enough when we are faced with a larger system of racial capitalism that perpetuates inequality and injustice.

The Anansi canoe seat was donated to the NMAAHC by Juan García Salazar, a celebrated Afro-Ecuadorian activist and master storyteller, who spent many years travelling the rivers of Ecuador to collect and document oral histories as part of a fifty-year project of black cultural revitalization. The seat belonged to his grandmother, Déborah Nazareno Quitero: she used it as a storytelling stool, reciting folk tales to her young grandson as she cooked, or when paddling the rivers of Esmeraldas Province in her dugout canoe. Salazar clearly believed that this precious family heirloom and artefact of black Ecuadorian culture belonged in a museum of African American history at the heart of Washington, DC, to serve as a portal to the Americas.

PART III.

Imperial Subjecthoods

13

Making Race Matter

In the autumn of 2003 a prominent British historian, with all the requisite degrees earned from Oxbridge and the Ivy League, was extremely distressed by a lecture of mine, a lecture which argued that British subjects were racialized in very particular ways in the years immediately following the Second World War. With a slight tremor in his voice, a tremor which betrayed the existence of strong emotions simmering beneath a surface of intellectual detachment, this historian forcefully declared that 'race' was a concept that was absolutely irrelevant to understanding British history, for 'we British' were never motivated to act upon beliefs about race. On the contrary, he concluded, 'history demonstrates that the British just don't like strangers.' Claire Alexander and Caroline Knowles have assembled an impressive collection of essays which expose and counter precisely this type of historical amnesia and denial. They show just how much race does matter, how race is constantly being made to matter and made into matter, given a material reality, an identity, an embodiment. Racialization, they argue, is a constant process of becoming: it is matter which adheres to all aspects of everyday life.

The publication of *Making Race Matter* is an important intervention in this particular moment, a moment when so many intellectuals are responding to what they perceive as a crisis of nationhood and national identity. The call to defend Britain and Britishness is characterized not only by expressions of fear for the fragmentation of a national identity but also by a deep melancholy for the loss of empire. Meanings and interpretations of time, space, place and bodies are fiercely contested and rhetorical claims are being made over the shape and sites of memory, over subjecthood and subjectivity. In particular, many notable historians are wielding their pens against the past and future implications of a multicultural Britain: they write to re-establish exclusive and authentic national roots, to reclaim 'their' heritage and disentangle it from that of the multicultural hordes whose presence threatens British national identity and whose voices speak heresy to the greatness of its imperial past. History has become the domain for the establishment of British 'difference' and singularity.

Claire Alexander and Caroline Knowles argue that 'our understandings of what "race" means' have been transformed since W. E. B. Du Bois declared that 'the problem of the 20th century is the problem of the colour line', evoking the time when '"race" was traced on the skin or in the blood and could be mapped onto geographical space.' The essays included in *Making Race Matter* provide rich analytic evidence of this transformation and demonstrate how '"race" and racial attitudes' are not only 'changing and complex', but also 'a product of culture rather than nature'. But reading them can also help us critique recent work that evokes culture with the intention of demonstrating the existence of absolute differences between peoples. In many of these accounts, evocations of affiliation and allegiance based on blood and spatial belonging remain.

Simon Schama's *Landscape and Memory* (1995) is a good example of a regressive return to the use of the body, to the 'bone of my bone and flesh of my flesh' analogies that W. E. B Du Bois inherited from nineteenth-century racial discourse and repurposed in 1903 in *The Souls of Black Folk* .[1] Schama, in his introduction to *Landscape and Memory*, places his authorial self as emerging in intimate relation to a very particular space, time and place:

> the low, gull-swept estuary, the marriage bed of salt and fresh water, stretching as far as I could see from my northern Essex bank, toward a thin black horizon on the other side . . . Kent, the sinister enemy who always seemed to beat us in the County Cricket Championship . . . When the tide went out, exposing an expanse of rusty mud, I could walk for what seemed miles from the shore, testing the depth of the ooze, paddling my feet among the scuttling crabs and the winkles, and staring intensely at the exact point where, I imagined, the river met the sea.[2]

The place where the river meets the sea is claimed by Schama as the source of national and imperial greatness and pride, evoking, as he does later in the passage, the navy that gathered there on so many occasions; it provides Schama with an occasion to reflect upon Joseph Conrad's use of the estuary as a site from which to tell the story of empire. *Landscape and Memory* also returns to nineteenth-century ideas of race, identity and land through the words of Henry David Thoreau which frame the book:

> It is vain to dream of a wildness distant from ourselves. There is none such. It is the bog in our brains and bowels, the primitive vigor of Nature in us, that inspires that dream.[3]

Thoreau's bog becomes Schama's estuary, and the ooze is moulded and sculpted into the primeval matter of a national identity through space and place, a landscape of apparently shared cultural memory, English county cricket matches. Schama aims to create an autochthonous relation between his youth, his self emerging as historian, and the soil of the land from which he sprang: the mud which oozes up between the young boy's toes forms the location from which the adult historian gains the authority to speak. His premise is that

> inherited landscape myths and memories share two common characteristics: their surprising endurance through the centuries

> and their power to shape institutions that we still live with. National identity, to take just the most obvious example, would lose much of its ferocious enchantment without the mystique of a particular landscape tradition: its topography mapped, elaborated, and enriched as a homeland.[4]

This authentic homeland has its authentic English bards who have sung praises and its authentic English heroes whose blood has fed and invigorates its soil. But Schama rebels against what he feels is the negation of this past and its values. He recovers the Rudyard Kipling of his youth, a celebrant of empire, whom Schama discovers many years later he isn't 'supposed to like'. The tone of injury in which this 'discovery' is expressed is elaborated in the introduction to the book into a regret for a loss of a heritage Schama is now 'supposed to deny'. *Landscape and Memory* works to retrieve and cement the relation between national identity, blood, soil and English heroes. The most vivid of these occasions is a description of the beheading of Walter Raleigh, whose blood, 'running over the block . . . formed little ponds and streams between the cobbles, before draining finally into the moist, Thames-side earth'. This blood circulates in the earth, preserving a nationhood that Schama can access between his toes four centuries later.[5]

Linda Colley, in *Britons: Forging the Nation 1707–1837*, wonders whether Britishness will survive. In Colley's terms, Britons emerge at a very particular time and place in history:

> between the Act of Union joining Scotland to England and Wales in 1707 and the formal beginning of the Victorian Age in 1837 . . . it was during this period that a sense of British national identity was forged, and that the manner in which it was forged has shaped the quality of this particular sense of nationhood and belonging ever since, both in terms of its remarkable strengths and resilience, and in terms of its considerable and increasingly evident weaknesses.[6]

What a startlingly static understanding of history this is! Like Schama, Colley refuses the possibility that Britishness is a complex and contradictory formation, constantly shaped and reshaped through and by a multicultural and multi-ethnic array of affiliations and allegiances. In *Britons*, ethnic and cultural diversity is present only as the English, Welsh and Scots who forge their Britishness out of the confrontation with the absolute difference of the country's enemies and its colonized others. National identity, Colley argues, is initially forged by war, 'And, increasingly as the wars went on, they defined themselves in contrast to the colonial peoples they conquered, peoples who were manifestly alien in terms of culture, religion and colour.'[7]

In stark contrast to Colley's thesis, contributors to *Making Race Matter* present the formation of subjecthood and citizenship in all its multiplicity and complexity and show us how historically constructed and contested racialized identities are embedded in relations of power in a whole range of localities: from the UK, in which African, Asian, Caribbean, European and North American histories converge and coalesce in particular cities and neighbourhoods, to the routes of diasporic and global relations.

Niall Ferguson, in *Empire: How Britain Made the Modern World* (2003), an unapologetic defence of the 'good' that Britain's imperial ventures brought to peoples across the world, claims a national identity which is global in its reach. I realized, when reading the book, that Niall Ferguson and I are not only both children of empire but distinctly different products of the 1948 British Nationality Act. I was born in Britain, the daughter of a Jamaican father who had served in the RAF and a Welsh mother who worked in the Air Ministry. After the war, British politicians realized that it was the United States of America and the Soviet Union that had emerged as the pre-eminent powers on the global stage. It was emigration from Britain that established its international presence and the ties of those emigrants to Britain that maintained it. The aim of the British Nationality Act was to secure Britain at the centre of empire, in the face of

American and Soviet hegemony, as a great power among great powers, and it tried to accomplish this by 'balancing several different, competing communities of Britishness within a single empire'.[8] These competing and contradictory articulations and definitions of Britishness embodied in the Nationality Act can be found inscribed in and through both my and Niall Ferguson's lives and work.

The British Nationality Act created a type of global citizenship, extending British subjecthood to all members of the empire. In practice, however, a multiplicity of definitions of Britishness emerged. Emigrants from Britain that secured its imperial presence were regarded as 'British stock'. Although all 'British stock' were British subjects, the political elites of the United Kingdom and the 'old' dominions did not consider all British subjects to be British stock. Rather, policymakers conceived of separate spheres of nationality: residents of the empire with a white skin and European cultural descent were British stock; residents of the empire with a skin of colour and African or Asian heritage were British subjects only. 'British stock' described 'a familial community defined by blood and culture'.[9] It was a restrictive term that contradicted the universal language of the Act.

Within the notion of imperial subjecthood were incompatible ideas of belonging which constituted a minefield that I, as a young black girl, would have to negotiate. I grew as the contradictions between and among conflicting communities of Britishness increased, culminating in the passing of the Commonwealth Immigrants Act of 1962, which eradicated any remnant of equality of subjecthood, policed the borders of the nation against black migrants and heralded my adolescence. Throughout the 1950s, government reports and working parties debated ways to limit the migration of black British subjects while not threatening the stability or unity of the Commonwealth upon which Britain's 'greatness' depended. The racial hostility towards black citizens on the national stage had its counterpart in my local universe. I was born a few months before the Nationality Act was passed, but because all domestic Britons were considered to be of pure European descent my being was consistently referenced through the paradigm of immigrant. While totally unaware of the machinations of Anthony Eden's and Harold Macmillan's cabinet-level discussions of the 'immigrant problem', I was aware of the fact that my belonging was daily in question.

In *Empire*, Niall Ferguson, who spent his childhood years in Kenya, has no doubts about his right to 'belong' and speak with the authority of 'British stock'. For him, to reassert the 'good' of empire is synonymous with the recovery of a national identity which has a simultaneous global existence through kith and kin:

> Thanks to the British Empire, I have relatives scattered all over the world – in Alberta, Ontario, Philadelphia and Perth, Australia. Because of Empire my paternal grandfather John spent his early twenties selling hardware and hooch to Indians in Ecuador . . . my other grandfather . . . spent more than three years as an RAF officer fighting the Japanese in India and Burma . . . Thanks to the Empire, my Uncle Ian Ferguson's first job after he qualified as an architect was with the Calcutta firm of McIntosh Burn . . . Ian had started his working life in the Royal Navy; he spent the rest of his life abroad, first in Africa, then in the Gulf states . . . His brother – my father . . . defied the advice of friends and relatives by taking his wife and two infant children to Kenya . . . Thus, thanks to the British Empire, my earliest childhood memories are of colonial Africa . . . We had our bungalow, our maid, our smattering of Swahili – and our sense of unshakeable security. It was a magical time, which indelibly impressed on my consciousness the sight of the hunting cheetah, the sound of Kikuyu women singing, the smell of the first rains and the taste of ripe mango.[10]

Here is an extraordinary, unquestioned sense of entitlement to walk the globe, to settle at will and to have your domestic needs taken care of by a Kenyan maid; this is the embodiment of racial privilege and racial power. The romance of memory fills the senses of the white British subject; eyes, ears, nose and tongue transmit empire as a sensuous lingering pleasure, the loss of which is occasion for deep regret. Niall Ferguson's allegiance to this 'magical time' is what Schama calls a 'ferocious enchantment' with 'the mystique of a particular landscape tradition'. In this landscape the subject is master over all he surveys, all that surrounds and services his needs is absorbed into the production and maintenance of the white male British subject.

As Claire Alexander and Caroline Knowles state, unequivocally, in the introduction to their book *Making Race Matter*, 'race still matters . . . it is an ongoing issue for academic concern and for study, and . . . it carries consequence'.[11] In the British academy, perhaps, race has never mattered more.

14

Lost (and Found?) in Translation

[H]istorical authenticity resides not in the fidelity to an alleged past but in an honesty vis-á-vis the present as it re-presents that past.

Michel-Rolph Trouillot, *Silencing the Past*

I am continually modifying my understanding of what it means to be a child of empire as I discover, rediscover and rewrite the intersecting and interdependent worlds of empire that produced my parents. Whatever volcanic fault lines, or fissures, eventually divided them when they were living together in the imperial homeland as adults, in the places and spaces before they met they were each schooled into understandings of imperial British subjecthood: understandings that they shared despite the geographical distance between Britain and Jamaica. The Britishness of my parents was realized as a structure of ethics and values with particular ideas about empire at its centre.

It was very important to my mother that she was born in Wales, even though she grew up in Somerset in the south-west of England. The daughter of an agricultural labourer, my mother chose to be Welsh rather than English. Living in London, as we all did throughout my childhood, she would often assert this allegiance to Wales, regaling my brother and me with tales of the heroic Owain Glyndwr, born in 1359, declared Prince of Wales in 1400 and crowned Owain IV king of Wales in 1404.[1] Glyndwr raised a Welsh army in revolt against English domination and for years successfully fought the armies of the English king, Henry IV, but he was destined to be the last native Prince of Wales. I never knew when Glyndwr and the Welsh suffered their final indignity at the hands of their English oppressors, for their defeat was never acknowledged within the walls of our home, but I did grow up with the distinct sense that my brother and I were being raised on the wrong side of the border between England and Wales. In 1969, when I was an undergraduate, the entire nation was glued to its television sets to watch the spectacular ceremony of the formal investiture of Prince Charles, son of Queen Elizabeth II, as Prince of Wales within the medieval walls of Caernarfon Castle.[2] It occurred to me then, as it occurs to me now, that although my mother expressed the requisite respect for the royal family, particularly the Queen Mother, I never heard her refer to Prince Charles as the Prince of Wales, though he had carried the title since he was born.

Refusing to be English did not prevent my mother from being British. She had vivid memories of everyone in her school and community participating in the annual celebrations of Empire Day in her youth: occasions when even the most marginal members of small rural communities felt themselves connected to, and part of, a much larger world. When I remember now what my mother told me when I was young about Empire Day celebrations, I recognize them as significant sites for producing multiple meanings of Britishness. Whatever she learnt about Britishness through this schooling formed the core of an ethical code and basis of judgement, which, although never explicitly articulated as a coherent whole, punctuated her attempts to provide her offspring with guidelines for living. My mother deeply regretted the fact that Empire Day had disappeared by the time my brother and I were of school age; she mined her memories to reproduce in our lives the sense of inclusion, communal ethics and values she thought we obviously lacked. Her descriptions of Empire Day concluded with recitations from Rudyard Kipling's poem 'If–'. She would purse her lips, in an effort of recall, tilt her head until she found the words she wanted and begin,

> If you can keep your head while all about you
> Are losing theirs and blaming it on you . . .

The recitations became so familiar and so predictable that my mind would wander. I have no memory of the middle part of the poem; maybe she skipped large chunks of it. Anyway, a quick turn of my mother's head and a sharp glance was all it took to have my full attention back for the last lines delivered slowly and with great deliberation:

> Yours is the earth and everything that's in it
> And – which is more – you'll be a Man, my son!

These words, learnt by rote in my mother's elementary school classroom, were transmitted as a valued and valuable legacy, knowledge that could help her son and daughter negotiate the present and prepare them for the future. They were words offered, but not received, as gifts.

The childhood of those in my mother's generation – she was born in 1920 – was saturated by the imperialism and class divisions of the Edwardian age. Empire Day was instituted in schools in 1902, when 'textbooks focused increasingly on the benefits of spreading trade and civilization'.[3] Imperialism, as it was experienced 'at home', worked to glue together a society otherwise sharply divided by class. As Bill Woods, a working-class labourer from Bristol, described his childhood,

> They used to encourage us to be proud of the flag, salute the flag when we was at school. Yes, I was proud of being British. We was always taught to be proud of the Queen and King. We was the people of the world wasn't us?[4]

My mother's immediate and extended working-class family migrated from the city of Bristol to Wales and the south-west, and they all expressed this pride and worldly sense. They never spoke of the fact (did they even know?) that Bristol became a wealthy and international city because of the transatlantic trade in enslaved black bodies.

I am a great fan of the novels, if not the politics, of P. D. James, who, like my mother, was born in 1920, but, unlike her, was a child of the middle classes. James's father, a middle-level civil servant, had served as an officer in the First World War. My grandfather also served in the First World War but as a private in the infantry, and when he left the military he returned to the life of an agricultural labourer. P. D. James may have been raised within the same national borders as my mother, but the material conditions of her life separated and insulated her from the poverty that characterized the rural world of my mother, or the urban England of Bill Woods's Bristol working class. Nevertheless, James, looking back on her childhood from her eighties, also describes the shared imaginary of a British community, as, 'people of the world', an imaginary visually realized on the walls of her Ludlow school:

> A map, permanently displayed in the largest double classroom, with its splurges of red – Canada, India, Australia, New Zealand – its small islands like splashes of blood in all the oceans of the world, enabled our teacher to point out that this was, in truth as well as legend, an empire on which the sun never set. Empire Day was a notable event celebrated with a march round the playground and a salute to the flag.[5]

For P. D. James, in a twenty-first-century act of recall, the British-owned territories of the West Indies remain unnamed, and unrecognized, just some 'small islands like splashes of blood in . . . the oceans of the world'. This reference to 'blood' appropriately, if unconsciously, colours the 'islands' of the empire, islands where blood-soaked cane fields and factories were the source of her family's supply of sugar. But, neither P. D. James, Bill Woods nor my mother would ever have been reminded of blood when they stirred a spoonful of the granules into their cups of tea.

Celebrations of Empire Day during the month of May predominate in memories of schooling in oral histories of the 1920s: the wearing of 'rosettes of red, white and blue'; the singing of 'I Vow to Thee My Country', Blake's 'Jerusalem' or the national songs of 'Scotland, Ireland, Wales and England'; readings from the Bible; and patriotic speeches by a lord mayor 'counselling' his listeners 'to be wise rulers of men in [the] far-flung Empire'.[6] While children in Britain were wearing red, white and blue, marching around their respective playgrounds, singing anthems and saluting the Union Jack, my dad in Jamaica, like children all over the British West Indies, was also marching, singing the same songs and pledging allegiance on the exact same day.

P. D. James, my mother and Bill Woods were addressed, despite their different class and gender locations, not only as a 'people of the world', but as 'wise rulers of men'. Jamaican, Barbadian or Trinidadian children marched around their school playground, if their school had one, and 'to the main town to be lectured by some prominent person about their civic duties'.[7] In *Growing Up Stupid under the Union Jack*, Austin Clarke describes how, as a child in Barbados, he was schooled to be the 'English of Little England. Little Black Englishmen'. Scrubbed clean with bars of Pears soap wrapped in labels bearing the history of Lord Nelson, the hero of Trafalgar, Clarke remembers, 'Nelson had been dead for hundreds of years, but every small boy in Barbados giggled in the suds of his memory and history.'[8]

Some years ago, on a visit to my parent's house, I found my dad reading a collection of nineteenth-century English poetry. He had been rummaging around in the books I had acquired during my years as an undergraduate, books abandoned by me when I left to live in the United States, books my parents had carefully transported to the city of York when they moved from London twelve years ago. My dad told me that he was reading two of his favourite poems, 'Elegy Written in a Country Graveyard' by Thomas Gray and Oliver Goldsmith's 'The Deserted Village'. I didn't know that these were his favourite poems; I had never even had a conversation with my father about English poetry, not even during the years I was reading English at university. From the US I was always mailing my dad books about 'race' and biographies of black lives and we would talk about them. Through gifts I was persistently dragging him into my world of racialized subjects and subjectivities and here was my dad reading and rereading Thomas Gray. I noticed that this poetry was always next to his chair. Now it is next to his bed. I didn't ask him why this poetry was important to him, why he loved it so, or what connections he was making through this rereading. I don't know why I didn't ask.

Those born in Jamaica in the 1920s, like my dad, are at the tail end of the second generation of freemen.[9] Not granted the vote until 1944, they nevertheless volunteered to fight in two world wars, before they had the right to vote, to fight not just for the British but *as* British. My dad was among the first of those in Jamaica to volunteer to join the RAF and, in 1943, he was transported from Kingston to New York by sea and then across land to a Commonwealth air training base in Moncton, New Brunswick, Canada. If you look up histories of the Commonwealth air training plans you will find stories of the brave white Canadians, New Zealanders, Australians and South Africans who willingly risked their lives to rally to Britain's aid in her darkest hour. I have been unable to find any reference to anyone from the Caribbean. Nevertheless, my father and other West Indian volunteers, schooled as British subjects, were in Moncton training as the pilots, navigators and wireless operators who eventually flew bombers and fighter planes from the UK into the heart of Europe. The erasure of the presence of my dad and other West Indians in New Brunswick lies layered upon other erasures from the same soil. The erasure of the broken promises made to the 3,500 black loyalists in 1783 and 2,000 black refugees from the war of 1812, 'who came with nothing to nowhere, were landed with indifference' in the Maritime Provinces without money or provisions, 'plunked on rocky, thorny land (soon laced with infant's skeletons) . . . so poor, they supposedly didn't even have history'.[10]

As my father's mind fragments from dementia, much of his sixty-five years of living in the UK since the war and all sense of the present dissolves, while the years of his youth in Jamaica and service in the RAF return for us both. He can still recite his RAF number. One day I was deep into research, trying to locate copies of the books my father read in his Kingston classrooms. I found copies of the Royal Readers he clearly remembers, texts which were used to school imperial subjects all over the empire. In Royal Reader No. 5 is 'Elegy Written in a Country Churchyard' by Thomas Gray and 'The Deserted Village' by Oliver Goldsmith.

> *Every story is, by definition, unfaithful. Reality . . . can't be told or repeated.*
> *The only thing that can be done with reality is to invent it again.*
>
> Tomás Eloy Martínez, *Santa Evita*

My education is and isn't a product of the 'disorderly year' of 1968, a year fissured by contradictions that have long since been paved under a seamless cultural mythology of student rebellion.[11] I was an undergraduate between 1967 and 1970, reading for a degree in English and history, steeped in Marxist theory, from a talented, progressive faculty at what was then Portsmouth Polytechnic and is now Portsmouth University. I was an eager student in 1967, a successful student, if exam results are the measure of success, but my schooling so far had 'filled me with questions that were not answered'.[12] I was remarkably unaware that most of what I thought I already knew, information I could regurgitate at a moment's notice, I was going to have to unlearn if I was going to know anything.

The city of Portsmouth was not a university town, it suffered from neglect, it was decaying. In the late 1960s bomb damage from the Second World War was still evident and unexploded ordinance was frequently uncovered whenever repairs to buildings or roads was undertaken. Portsmouth could not survive on the paltry commerce produced by the seasonal cycle of poverty-stricken renters and tourists: students who arrived each October were replaced each July by coachloads of octogenarians in floral prints hoping for an inexpensive holiday by the sea. During the last three weeks of each spring term our landladies would be eager for us to be gone, willing us away with uncharacteristic impatience because the senior citizens paid twice as much for each room as we did.

Portsmouth was dependent for its economic health and the employment of its residents upon the Portsmouth naval base, which had been an integral part of city since 1194. The Royal Navy eventually occupied three miles of its waterfront and more than 296 acres of the city centre. From the windows of our lecture halls, we could cast our minds adrift and gaze across the acres of destroyers, frigates and minesweepers of Her Majesty's Royal Navy. I saw the ships, I saw the city, but I did not see anything. As Jamaica Kincaid puts it, 'I did not yet know the history of events, I did not know their antecedents'.[13]

I had been schooled in the history of the heroes of the Royal Navy. I knew that Sir Francis Drake, *c.*1540–96, born, as I was, in the county of Devon, was a revered British hero, a 'founding father' of British naval might, the most famous vice admiral of the British fleet who led the attack on the Spanish Armada in 1588. I knew nothing about the Francis Drake who, along with Sir John Hawkins, led the first slave-trading expeditions and then later supplemented his wealth through acts of piracy, plundering throughout the West Indies and South America. Both were knighted for their exploits. I did not know that at least eight slave ships left Portsmouth between 1699 and 1711.[14]

While I studied literature and history in a city whose history I could not access, my education took place on streets that became very familiar to me. I learnt about the power of the state, not in my college classrooms, but in confrontation with the British riot police sent to guard 24 Grosvenor Square, London. I was the first in my family to go to college, or to regard the United States as anything other than the saviours of the 'free' world. However, what I was learning during the protests against the Vietnam War had little, if anything, to do with American power and everything to do with confronting the friendly British 'bobby' whose mission was smiling and helping lost children, dogs and the elderly, or so I had been taught.

My brother and I were very young when we learnt that bobbies did not help 'nigger kids', 'black bastards' or 'half-caste scum'. But my parents did not know this; my parents could not imagine that anyone, leave alone 'bobbies', saw my brother and me as 'half-caste scum'. My respectable parents believed in teaching their respectable children, 'If you are ever lost, or in trouble, find a policeman.' Anyone who was afraid of the police, in their eyes, was not respectable and must have a reason to fear authority, presumably because they misbehaved. My parents had never witnessed a riot squad of 'bobbies' on horseback unleashed on people taking part in a peaceful protest. But if they had witnessed this, if they had seen the swinging batons breaking heads, I do not know that they would have thought the police action wrong. My parents regarded what they called my 'antics' outside the American embassy as more than foolish. My mother felt that I was being disloyal and that I was disloyal because my education was sorely lacking. I did not know, she said, what the British nation (and, by implication, I as an individual) owed to the people of the United States of America. 'The Americans didn't have to come all the way over here and put their lives at risk to help us during the war,' she repeated, endlessly. These words were more than a reminder; they were issued as a warning, as if to say that when 'we' needed the Americans again they might not come next time because of the behaviour of ungrateful people like me. When I was in college, I actually worried about this.

During the Second World War my mother was a civil servant in the Air Ministry and my dad was a flight sergeant and navigator in the RAF. Persecuted and ostracized as a 'multiracial' couple and having only meagre financial resources, education was their primary investment as a material legacy for their two children. Education was not just a path to financial security and social mobility; it was armour for their children. 'Sticks and stones will break your bones, but words will never harm you' and 'just be the best, be the first in your class and they will leave you alone' were the phrases that resonated in the background of our school years. Were these words offered in comfort? Were these words offered as a protection? Did these words originate from the depths of my parents' bewilderment and frustration, from a profound ignorance of what to do? Or do these words, offered as wisdom, signal denial, a denial of how deeply racism was shaping post-war Britain?

My brother and I knew from first-hand experience the limited value of these offerings, of course: words of hatred signalled imminent danger, often immediately preceding the sticks and stones that broke bones, or in my case teeth. But when we were hurt, we told our parents that we had had an 'accident', for admitting that we had been beaten meant that we were not trying hard enough, were not good enough and, thus, had let *them* down in some unfathomable way. My brother and I were always having 'accidents'.

Education, in my family, demanded endless sacrifice. We were removed from the local schools and sent to private schools. Was this move an unspoken recognition that we were suffering more than accidents? I do not know. My brother had a partial scholarship to his school, but my mother still had to work multiple jobs, day and night, for years to pay the fees. I am convinced that my parents' belief in the promise and transformative power of a British education was a measure of the depth of their faith in Britishness. My brother and I never witnessed the wavering of this faith, not even when my father had to go to the Tottenham Court Road police station to obtain the release of my Dulwich Prep– and Alleyn's School–educated brother who had been arrested and detained under the notorious SUS laws for walking along Oxford Street with a cheque book (assumed stolen but actually his own) in his hand.

You could say that I inherited an obsession with education, but I translated it into an entirely different political and intellectual agenda. Or did I? I certainly didn't have faith, but I retained my grasp of an endless list of questions. I registered for a postgraduate degree in education at the Institute of Education, London University, because I wanted to understand why the British educational system, instead of challenging inequalities, of class, gender and race, preserved, reproduced and promoted institutional racism alongside class and gender divisions. At the end of the year, in my final examination, instead of responding to the questions asked I wrote what I considered to be a devastating analysis of the institute's postgraduate programme as it completely ignored the issue of racism. I graduated with even more questions about the education system than when I had begun, but now I was certified as an integral part of it.

Who knows what happened to that paper after I literally stormed out of the exam room, but the next thing I knew I was contacted by the chief education officer of the London Borough of Newham and recruited to be part of an educational experiment in a newly formed high school in a sector of London with extremely low income and high unemployment. A single-sex school system was going co-ed for the first time, neo-Nazi gangs and the Kray brothers ruled the streets, and the area had a substantial Afro-Caribbean and black British population. As I prepared for my first teaching job in August 1972, Idi Amin expelled British Asians from Uganda. Shocked and stunned, many of them found themselves in Newham, and their traumatized teenage sons and daughters I met in my classroom.

My mother drove me to my first teaching job at Eastlea, a high school in the East End of London and she wept copious tears as she helped me move into what she regarded as the 'slums'. If this was the result of private schools, and college degrees, if the fruit of her sacrifice was depositing me in an area of even deeper poverty than the poverty she had struggled so hard to climb out of and move away from, then my mother wanted no part of it. I had accepted the position as an English teacher in Newham because I naively thought I could be part of fixing what was so obviously broken. I guess going to the Centre for Contemporary Cultural Studies (CCCS) at Birmingham University was another step in the same direction.

I arrived at the centre, an obnoxiously self-righteous, anti-racist activist, in my seventh year as a high school teacher of English on a fully paid sabbatical paid for by Newham. Into the corridors of CCCS I carried the baggage of those years: a politics of the classroom forged in defence of the tenets and practices of progressive education against the insidious incursions of the Department of Education under 'Maggie Thatcher the Milk Snatcher', and a politics of the street honed in anti-racist battles waged against fascist gangs and their racist cousins in police uniform who patrolled our neighbourhood.[15] While I learnt much from each of those struggles, they cost me little. However, I riffed upon them brazenly, elaborating them as 'street cred', to disguise how terrified and insecure I felt about being back and black in graduate school.

I had worked in the vibrant and turbulent multiracial, multi-ethnic, unstreamed classrooms of a comprehensive school where a handful of us worked collectively in the hope that our pupils could be equal partners in the learning process. I saw how young minds and bodies opened under progressive, creative and imaginative educational practices supported by generous resources. But, in the midst of possibility, I also saw my black and brown students terrorized by violence and the threat of violence: bricks were thrown through their windows as they slept; faeces and flaming bottles full of petrol were pushed through their letter boxes; and to get to and from school, or the shops, they were pushed and shoved, or punched and beaten as they passed by the racist slogans daubed all over the walls, doors and streets of our neighbourhood. At any hour of any day, they could be subject to physical and mental abuse, in or out of school, from their peers, from shopkeepers, from the police and from the social service workers appointed to assist them. To be of any use to these students my classroom had to be transformed into a safe place: a laboratory for the forensic examination of racist encounters and for the translation of analysis into practical strategies for countering and overcoming the effects of institutional racism.

When I applied to attend the centre I had a much-thumbed copy of Paolo Freire's *Pedagogy of the Oppressed* on my bedside table, a text which informed my practice in my high school and in the adult literacy programme that I ran two evenings a week in the same building.[16] I had also assembled a growing library of books and papers published by CCCS, including *Resistance through Rituals* and *On Ideology*.[17] Exhausted at the end of the day, in moments stolen from grading papers or working on lesson plans, or during a weekend when I wasn't taking my class on a camping trip, or to the theatre, I read with diligence and care what was being written at the centre. I was eager for an intellectual challenge, though I sometimes found the reading difficult and occasionally impenetrable. But I never doubted that the effort was worth it.

Even though I hadn't yet met any of the members of CCCS I regarded them as allies in the fight against the increasingly authoritarian and conservative forces being mobilized against the poor, the working class, the black and the immigrant, in short, against everyone in my world. I devoured the insights that addressed our condition in an area with high levels of unemployment, imprisonment, immigration and racism, inadequate housing and very low levels of income. CCCS publications, I thought, contained analyses with which one could begin to develop defensive strategies and to imagine the construction of paths to a just and equitable world. The interview, which followed my application to the centre, terrified me, but the letter offering me a place terrified me even more. I was afraid that I would be unable to translate the knowledge I carried with me into what I regarded as the theoretically sophisticated world of CCCS.

Before I left Newham, I carefully explained to my students that I was going to the Centre for Contemporary Cultural Studies for a year to study and get a master's degree, and they all seemed to understand and applaud my reasons and motives. When I met five or six of them outside the butcher's shop around the corner from my flat in Forest Gate, after my first term in Birmingham, they were very pleased to see me and we chatted for ages. But gradually they revealed some doubts about my rate of progress, were curious as to exactly how hard I had been studying and asked if I was sure that I could pass my exams at the end of the year. Eventually it dawned on me that the cause of their concern derived from the fact that my manner of speaking had not 'improved' in their eyes, despite the months that had been spent studying culture. Only gradually did I understand the terms of their equation: for my students, 'cultural studies' translated into becoming 'cultured', and being 'cultured' meant sounding like a BBC broadcaster. Culture, then, was the means by which I was to acquire class mobility, class position in Britain being recognized and confirmed through accent. My failure to make 'progress' was registered in my voice and much was at stake in my evident lack of success. If I hadn't learnt to speak 'properly' how on earth was I going to be able to return to teach them, or their children, how to be cultured and thus upwardly mobile. If I didn't make it, they didn't either.

The year before this conversation, during my last year as their teacher, we had taken a class trip, not one of our major expeditions, just a walk down the road to the office of the London Docklands Development Corporation in the last class period of the day. There we walked around and between tables on which lay detailed models of the future of the area in which we lived. Gone were the familiar shabby streets, decaying high-rises and council flats. The voices of my pupils, usually loud, energetic and buoyant, were hushed, their almost whispers a measure of a certain awe and respect, if not of comprehension. I stood apart from them, leaning against the wall, strictly an observer, for I had visited this office before, I had seen the display, and I was aware of what the development plans meant for the residents of the area. I didn't have the heart to translate it for them; I wanted them to see and understand for themselves what was coming. One conversation will stay with me always: 'Its beautiful,' I heard one say, followed by,

'Which of these houses do you want?'

'I want this one right on this canal.'

'I don't, its too close to the water.'

Pause . . .

'Why does the water go right under the side of these houses?'

'So you can keep your boat in there, stupid.'

'But my mum doesn't have a boat.'

Silence was followed by gradual realization. First, they understood that these houses were not for people who didn't have boats, especially not for people who couldn't even imagine owning a boat. Then they saw that redevelopment was not for them, that people like them were not to be included in the rosy images of the future docklands. How many of them knew that people like them were expendable and would, inevitably, be displaced, I don't know. The volume of their voices rose to their normal levels; they glanced out of the corner of their eyes, trying to not to read in my face explanations they didn't want to hear. Without being prompted they collectively turned their backs on the tables, gathered their jackets and bags and moved to the door ready to leave. In a discordant chorus of voices each of them announced other places they had to be. A year later, outside the butchers, as my students searched my face, another hope, the one they had eagerly placed in their teacher, bit the dust.

The years from 1978 to 1984, when I was associated with CCCS, completing first an MA and then the PhD which produced the study *Reconstructing Womanhood*, were years of seemingly inexhaustible intellectual energy, passionate commitment and political vision. Pessimism of the intellect, a response to a rapidly increasing state authoritarianism, the brutal effects of everyday racism and gender inequality and what appeared to be the continual defeat of left and progressive agendas, was countered by an optimism of the will exercised in intellectual activity in the service of social, political and economic transformation. But I am to this day haunted by the loss of the students I left behind.[18]

> *Memory ... often strikes me as a kind of dumbness. It makes one's head heavy and giddy, as if one were not looking back down the receding perspectives of time but rather down on the earth from a great height, from one of those towers whose tops are lost to view in the clouds.*
>
> W. G. Sebald, *The Emigrants*

In the process of writing *Child of Empire*, I have read parts of it to audiences in Britain and the US. This may have been a mistake because I have become increasingly aware that as I write I am predicting and addressing responses in advance. It is the response of many Americans to the story of my parents' interracial wartime liaison that has surprised and dismayed me. In the United States, audiences seem to expect, if not demand, that I deliver a fully fledged romance with all the trimmings, a tale of a love that triumphed against tremendous odds, starring a couple who resemble a youthful Sidney Poitier and starry-eyed Veronica Lake. Americans who have never actually met my parents interpret and project a romance evolving in a time of war, a romance triumphal despite British governmental and military attempts to impose segregation and stop black men from fraternizing with white women, a romance that blossomed into a marriage in the face of national anxiety about the consequences of the birth of half-caste citizens.

A project originally conceived as a confrontation and reckoning with the long tradition of racist thought and practice in Britain has evolved into an act of translation. I now write also to repudiate romance – the romance US audiences have with the British Isles and the romance that the story of race has become in the United States. I write in defiance of both *Masterpiece Theatre* and the Hallmark hug of comfort that seems necessary to cushion a US readership against the shock of discovering that the British are racist. Romance not only comforts and cushions; it disguises and represses. Black and white sex, while it can still shock and horrify Americans in the street, also serves as a metonym for the history of the unresolved struggle for racial justice in the United States.

I ask myself if the desires and whims of current times are evident in the need for the relationship between a Jamaican airman and a Welsh civil servant to stand as a racial romance. The popular cultural script of romance and its academic theoretical counterpart, postcolonial theories of hybridity, promise progress through creolization, a fluid utopia of possibility flying in the face of pastness, fixture and regression. But, for me, a large part of what it meant to be a child of empire was watching two people confront the stomach-churning, acidic, corrosive effects of racism every day and being destroyed by it. Perhaps, if my parents had been middle-class and wealthy, the blows of ignorance and prejudice would have less affected them. Perhaps. Growing up in south London in the racial tensions and anxieties of a post–Second World War Britain was nothing like *Guess Who's Coming to Dinner*. It was an acid rain that fell on my parent's parade and eroded all possibility of affection.

From the moment they met, during the Second World War, they must have realized they were courting danger. Rebelling against racialized codes of behaviour and flaunting that rebellion in the face of friends and family must have stimulated the passion of their sexual attraction into a heady measure of frisson impossible for them to rationalize or for me to dissect and analyse into discrete segments of affect. The marriage of my parents was not a romantic union but a step into purgatory. Crossing the lines of acceptable British conduct, breaking racial and sexual taboos did not fuse them into a couple but drew them apart, and eventually bound them into mutual emotional isolation. The question of how life could and should be lived in the face of the external antagonism outside our four walls was never discussed but turned the house into a pressure cooker. The racialized and gendered beliefs, practices and prejudices of the British social and political order made the social, economic and political circumstances of our lives very difficult, but within those circumstances my parents failed, or did not care, to listen, to know or to understand one another. They were strangers then and strangers they remained throughout the years of marriage and parenting.

My younger brother and I had to navigate our way around, through and over currents of violence, the magma flow that hardened into the core of their relationship. We came to fear the night when one or the other of us tumbled or were pulled (often out of bed) into the maelstrom of their wrath. When they were spent, we were left to drag ourselves out of the ashes and glowing embers of their fury to lick our wounds alone: wounds of childhood, scabbed over, toughened but unhealed.

If much of the pleasure of research lies in the process of detection, identifying clues and tracking down leads, if not suspects, then delving into the lives of my parents I have become less like a detective, assembling details into a recognizable pattern of events with discernible causes and effects, and more like a moth flying towards the open flame of their seething resentments. The rewriting of the past is fuelled by temptation, the lure of revelation, the possibility of creating reason out of unreason, the hope of harvesting knowledge from the bleak years of the British post-war world. My career is my flameproof body suit, the retardant, skills sharpened in research, sprayed on a surface toughened with feminist theory. All moths are convinced of their invulnerability; they do not deviate when they feel heat, and they do not hesitate as they head into the flame.

15

Becoming Modern Racialized Subjects: Detours through Our Pasts to Produce Ourselves Anew

I.

Identity is not in the past to be found, but in the future to be constructed.

Stuart Hall, 'Negotiating Caribbean Identities'

[C]ulture is not just a voyage of rediscovery, a return journey. It is not an 'archeology.' Culture is a production. It has its raw materials, its resources, its 'work of production.' It depends on a knowledge of tradition as 'the changing same' and an effective set of genealogies. But what this 'detour through its pasts' does is to enable us, through culture, to produce ourselves anew, as new kinds of subjects. It is therefore not a question of what our traditions make of us so much as what we make of our traditions. Paradoxically, our cultural identities, in any finished form, lie ahead of us. We are always in the process of cultural formation. Culture is not a matter of ontology, of being, but of becoming.

Stuart Hall, 'Thinking Diaspora: Home Thoughts from Abroad'

In this essay I will meditate upon the narration of encounters within which and through which we are brought into being as racialized subjects. Stuart Hall has argued that 'identity is always in part a narrative', that identity exists 'always within representation'.[1] I want to consider the creative, contested, contradictory and laborious work of constructing racial identities in narrative acts. My examples are drawn from varied historical moments but what each narrative has in common is that the racialized self is invented in the process of an encounter, produced, in other words, as a subject dialogically constituted in and through its relation to an other or others. While not attempting to create a genealogy that could, in any way, be considered complete or sufficient, I have turned to narratives which work to produce racialized subjects in a variety of different ways. Each encounter is 'structured in dominance', and while thinking about how 'relations of subjugation manufacture subjects', I will translate my consideration of subjugation from Michel Foucault's frame into an investigation of the production and reproduction of unequal power relations and the 'manufacture of subjects' through narration.[2]

We live with and in the midst of the consequences of the multiple histories of the formation and re-formation of a 'highly exclusive and exclusivist [English] cultural identity', though the multiple ways in which its creation and re-creation are haunted by and dependent upon the invention of the black other has been forgotten, repressed and denied.[3] What is at stake is what we will make of our cultural identities in the future but, because I believe that in order to be able to 'make ourselves anew' we need to undertake critical 'detours' into the past, I begin by returning to *The Interesting Narrative of the Life of Olaudah Equiano*, and then quickly traverse a variety of narrative places, spaces and times in each of which I find a particular form of 'creative friction' in the representation of unequal encounters.[4] The multiple histories and consequences of struggles over the production of English or British cultural identity remain as 'stone age traces' in the modern racialized state which Britain becomes during the Second World War and its immediate aftermath, which is where this essay concludes.[5]

'Theory', Hall has argued, 'is always a detour on the way to something more important'.[6] 'Becoming Modern' is in close dialogue with many of Hall's essays, but in particular 'Negotiating Caribbean Identities (1995), 'When Was "the Post-colonial"? Thinking at the Limit' (1996), 'The Local and the Global: Globalization and Ethnicity' (1997), 'Old and New Identities, Old and New Ethnicities' (1997) and 'Thinking the Diaspora: Home Thoughts from Abroad' (2005).[7] The ways in which I think about issues of 'race', and ethnicity in general, however, have been shaped by the entire corpus of Hall's work, not only those essays which directly address processes of racialization. The extraordinarily rich proliferation of ideas, political insights and historical paradigms, developed in the long engagement with Marxist theory to be found in Stuart Hall's publications and lectures, signpost the 'detour' I have travelled for my entire academic and activist career. Hall's political commitment and vision and, above all, his political and intellectual integrity are the bass line in the rhythm of my walk.

My current project, tentatively titled *Child of Empire*, interweaves memory and history in its narrative of racial encounters. I want to avoid the pitfalls of the binary thinking, the polarities of opposition and difference, that have dominated historical narratives of the workings of empire and its subjects, polarities which have not only maintained but also reproduced inequities of knowledge and power. Instead, I have been thinking about both the particularities and the commonalities in experience and history across and within the colonial boundaries of empire that Manichaean divisions and hierarchies of supposed racial difference cannot acknowledge. I turn to Hall's work to help me unravel the knotty complexities of difference, divisions in history, consciousness and humanity, that are intertwined in the geopolitical oppositions of colonial centre and colonized margin, home and abroad, and metropole and periphery. Imperial and racist calculations based on these divisions have determined which subjects and societies will be regarded as modern and which societies and subjects should be relegated to the status of in need of modernization.

In 'When Was "the Post-colonial"?', Hall seeks 'to explore the interrogation marks which have begun to cluster thick and fast around the question of "the post-colonial" and the notion of post-colonial times'. It opens with a series of questions that I have been pondering since it was published. Hall asks,

> If post-colonial time is the time *after* colonialism, and colonialism is defined in terms of the binary division between the colonisers and colonised, why is post-colonial time *also* a time of difference? What sort of 'difference' is this and what are its implications for the forms of politics and for subject formation in this late-modern moment?[8]

As Hall has warned, the postcolonial is a concept which 'could take us on a detour through a conceptual labyrinth from which few travellers return' – What follows in this essay is a response to the temporal enigma that haunts these questions and an exploration of the sources of tension, contention and anxiety in the process of constituting subjects through difference.

As I see it, Hall's questions are asking us to reconsider not only issues of difference but also, implicitly, how we conceive of time (and consequently history) in relation to difference. In 'Gramsci's Relevance for the Study of Race and Ethnicity', Hall pointed to 'the novel and radical ways' in which Gramsci conceptualizes 'the *subjects* of ideology'. Hall argues that Gramsci

> altogether refuses an idea of a pregiven unified ideological subject – for example, the proletarian with its 'correct' revolutionary thoughts or blacks with their already guaranteed current anti-racist consciousness. He recognizes the plurality of selves or identities of which the so-called 'subject of thoughts and ideas is composed.' He argues that this multifaceted nature of

> consciousness is not an individual but a collective phenomenon, a consequence of the relationship between 'the self' and the ideological discourses which compose the cultural terrain of a society. 'The personality is strangely composite,' he observes. It contains 'Stone Age elements and principles of a more advanced science, prejudices from all past phases of history . . . and intuitions of a future philosophy . . .'[9]

It is the composite nature of the creation of the subject in narrative that I wish to capture, looking for the simultaneous imagining of past, present and possible future triggered in my examples by movement or migration, forced or voluntary. We need to be alert to the occasions when racialized subjects not only step into the recognitions given to them by others but provide intuitions of a future in which relations of subjugation will (could) be transformed, even if the present of the narrative is dislocated in time from decolonization and postcolonial movements and formations. Don't we attempt to 'emancipate ourselves from mental slavery' in incomplete or uneven fits and starts out of synch with the formation of emancipatory social and political movements?[10] How do these intuitions of human possibility and complexity erupt into narrative acts? What status do we give to attempts to surmount our racialization when we write ourselves into an imaginative liberty of sorts?

Obviously, I am shifting and displacing Hall's arguments and Gramsci's analysis onto a creative and imaginative terrain, an invented or reimagined landscape, temporality and space of relations brought into being through storytelling. But, then, I teach literature rather than sociology. I am rewording Hall's questions to consider what sort of 'difference' exists in the creative articulation of the racialization of a subject and to tease out the political implications of the type of narrative subject being invented. Understanding 'race as a relationship and not a thing' applies equally to the difference adhering to the colonial and the postcolonial.[11] If the temporal and spatial terms of the colonial relation between oppressor and oppressed are significantly defied, challenged or reconfigured in imaginative acts, is this evidence of the emergence or intuition of a postcolonial consciousness even if this defiance, challenge or reconfiguration takes place in the eighteenth century?

I always argue that it is important to think historically, to be historically grounded, but I don't think that the proliferation of posts that embroider our contemporary critical and theoretical vocabulary necessarily signals historical thinking, in fact I don't think that a simple before and after adequately captures what these rapidly multiplying posts signal. (To the terms I have already cited we could add post-feminist and post-race to see that it is a political turn that is being referenced, not periodicity.) I want to suggest that an exclusive concentration on the linearity of temporality pushes other possible modes of interpretation and definition to the side. What could we gain by focusing on the geopolitics of encounters, the where in addition to the when of subject formation? Is it possible to use terms like 'modern', or 'postcolonial', to denote actions, activities and actors in the context of forced or voluntary migrations in very different historical circumstances?

We have invented or imagined temporal, spatial and geopolitical boundaries between the multiple conceptual terrains of the colonial, the postcolonial, modernity and the late modern (the late modern being, as I see it, a temporal frame within which we can still talk about the formation of subjects, a process that the postmodern has abandoned or rejected). But I want to reimagine these boundaries as liminal, fluid and porous and I find that Hall's work enables me to think of these conceptual terrains as mutually constitutive rather than mutually exclusive. Do linear or progressive notions of temporality have to determine or frame how we think about postcoloniality or can we think in terms that presuppose that formations of the modern racialized subject erupt into, interrupt and disrupt the binary nature and supposed linearity of discursive articulations of the colonial and postcolonial?

At which moments and in which texts can we see a modern black subject narrated onto the stage of a global history? How is that figure brought into being through narration and what are the terms and conditions that shaped or determined its modernity? Is what we conceive of as the modern subject produced out of the encounter between Africans and Europeans in search of profit? Is what we understand as a modern subject *de facto* a racial or racialized subject and is this racialization the sign or marker of its modernity? Are the categories of black and white, African and European, brought into being through this commerce? If so, which of these subjects is made modern in the economics of the transaction: the African, or the European, or both? Does it matter where encounters between Africans and Europeans, between those constructed as 'black' and 'white', take place: in an African or English village, town or city; if they occur in the impenetrable and claustrophobic darkness of the dungeon of a coastal fort or hold of a slave ship, or take place, face to face, in the glaring light reflected from the Atlantic Ocean; if they are confrontations on the shores of a Caribbean island or on the streets of a metropolitan imperial city? Perhaps it is not, in fact, only the place that is significant but also the manner of the journey and arrival, the eager walking or manacled stumble, the panicked flight, or forced or voluntary sailing towards and away from each other. How do we take political account of the biomechanics of movement between and among places, spaces and peoples, the scattering that results in the racialized modern encounter? Is it, then, finally, the geopolitics or the biopolitics of these violent transactions that produces modernity and its subjects?

II.

> [I]dentity is not only a story, a narrative which we tell ourselves about ourselves, it is stories which change with historical circumstances. And identity shifts with the way in which we think and hear them and experience them. Far from only coming from the still small point of truth inside us, identities actually come from

> outside, they are the way in which we are recognized and then come to step into the place of the recognitions which others give us. Without the others there is no self, there is no self-recognition.[12]

In 1789, the publication of *The Interesting Narrative of the Life of Olaudah Equiano*, and its many reprints, made its author 'the first successful professional writer of African descent in the English-speaking world'.[13] In the first two chapters readers are told of Equiano's forced abduction from his home, his journey to the African coast and transportation in chains across the Atlantic Ocean. Stating that he was born in what is now southern Nigeria in 1745, Equiano records that he had 'never heard of white men or Europeans, nor of the sea' in his village.[14] In the second chapter of the *The Interesting Narrative* Equiano is kidnapped along with his sister (who remains nameless) and both are enslaved.

While the overwhelming majority of *The Interesting Narrative* is 'remarkably consistent with the historical record', Vincent Caretta, author of the most recent biography of Equiano, states that Equiano's baptism certificate of February 1759 and his naval records of 1773 reveal that he was, in fact, born in South Carolina.[15] If 'the available evidence suggests that [its] author . . . may have invented rather than reclaimed an African identity', how do we respond to the first two chapters of *The Interesting Narrative*, which are, along with his account of the Middle Passage, 'the most frequently excerpted sections'? Do we label them 'historical fiction', as Caretta does,[16] and leave it at that? Werner Sollers has argued that if Equiano turned out to be 'one of the very first black American expatriates in Europe . . . [it would] require a new interpretation of the *Narrative*'.[17]

Perhaps we will never know, for sure, on which side of the Atlantic Equiano was born, but would the information definitively determine how the narrative is to be read? Even if he was born on the African continent, isn't Equiano still turning to 'invention' to create an African identity? And, if he was born in the New World, can't we also argue that Equiano is 'reclaiming' an African identity? Shouldn't our interpretation of the first chapters of *The Interesting Narrative* be asking what meaning is produced in these processes of invention *and* reclamation? While the debate about the status of the first two chapters rages, whether they are autobiographical, an 'identity in the past to be found', or fiction, I would rather avoid the either–or of these questions and ask, instead, what these chapters produce, examining them as providing the raw materials and resources out of which Equiano creates a 'return journey' and 'genealogy' in order to write 'a history of the present'.[18] I will argue that Equiano's 'detour through the past' enables him to produce himself anew, as a new kind of subject.

What does Equiano make out of the tradition he constructs? First, Equiano is writing into a present that is increasingly interested in accounts of travellers to the continent [of Africa], most of whom were associated with the slave trade. Much of this interest, however, was prurient, a fascination with stories of a savage land without culture or history. Equiano dispels such mythologies as he creates a travelogue of his own and enters the debate about the slave trade. I would argue that these are not separate enterprises for, the aspects of *The Interesting Narrative* that most resemble the genre of the travelogue, and which are enriched by Equiano's wide reading of accounts of Africa, are completely integrated with the anti-slavery politics of the text. For, unlike the authors he read, in Equiano's account the subject undertakes his long and perilous journey towards the African coast *as property*: a journey punctuated by his being sold numerous times to, and working for, various masters. During this journey Equiano is separated from, briefly reunited with and then again separated from his sister, a figure who remains nameless and is never brought into being as a conscious subject through narration. Standing only as a severed last link with family and the place from which Equiano came, the figure of 'sister' is not a subject in her own right but merely register of, or signifier for, Equiano's condition as a singular, abducted male, an orphan who will be reborn in the course of the narrative.

Equiano travels through what are described as various 'nations and people' with whom he feels comfortable and who have 'manners, customs, and language' that resemble his own. He acquires fluency in a range of dialects. If the first stage of estrangement is the loss of the signifier, sister, the second stage begins when Equiano

> came at length to a country, the inhabitants of which *differed* from us in all those particulars [of manners, customs, and language]. I was very much struck with this difference, especially when I came among a people who did not circumcise, and ate without washing their hands. They cooked also in iron pots, and had European cutlasses and cross bows, which were unknown to us, and fought with their fists among themselves.[19]

Difference enters the text at this moment and is marked not only as difference in culture, 'manners, customs, and language', but as a difference inscribed on the body. This somatic difference is narrated in conjunction with the appearance of European influence, a presence marked not by its people but through the technology of war, and this influence is associated with the first evidence in the narrative of contentious human relations.

Can we read this account of an encounter with somatic and cultural difference, the presence of technology, and evidence of conflict, as the register of modernity in the narrative? It is an intuition of what is to follow, but although Equiano is disturbed by these strangers and their practices, they are still, to him, people. Difference, at this point in the narrative, is presented as a variation within the familiar, if a somewhat dramatic variation. While Equiano refuses the invitation to be inducted into this community through the ritual scarification of his body, the offer to make and mark his body in their likeness is recognized as a gesture of inclusion from strangers, an explicit recognition of shared peoplehood. At this point *The Interesting Narrative* reads as a travelogue educating Equiano's readers in the positive aspect of the diversity of the continent.[20]

Six or seven months after his abduction from his home, Equiano reaches the coast, an area described as being devoted to colonial agricultural production and the arts of war. It is at this point in the *Narrative*, I would argue, that Equiano is forcibly inducted into modernity as a subject. He describes what he sees in the following words:

> The first object which saluted my eyes when I arrived on the coast was the sea, and a slave ship, which was then riding at anchor, and waiting for its cargo. These filled me with astonishment, which was soon converted into terror when I was carried on board. I was immediately handled and tossed up to see if I were sound by some of the crew; and I was now persuaded that I had gotten into a world of bad spirits, and that they were going to kill me. Their complexions too differing so much from ours, their long hair, and the language they spoke, (which was very different from any I had ever heard) united to confirm me in this belief. Indeed such were the horrors of my views and fears at the moment, that, if ten thousand worlds had been my own, I would have freely parted with them all to have exchanged my condition with that of the meanest slave in my own country. When I looked round the ship too and saw a large furnace or copper boiling, and a multitude of black people of every description chained together, every one of their countenances expressing dejection and sorrow, I no longer doubted of my fate; and, quite overpowered with horror and anguish, I fell motionless on the deck and fainted.[21]

The sections we have read up to this point in the text seem carefully crafted stages of preparation for this encounter, an encounter which I am calling modern and which initiates the stages of Equiano's transformation into a racialized subject. What are its characteristics?

Equiano steps into the place of the recognitions given to him by others. The narrative self is not recognized as a self by the beings Equiano confronts, a recognition and confirmation that the self is no longer human but is tossed about and categorized as 'cargo' by those who see and handle him. However, this process of dehumanization is represented by Equiano as being mutual: Equiano regards the beings he confronts, the beings that deny him his humanity, as non-human or unhuman; he visualizes them as 'bad spirits', as representing death in its undead form. Terror and anguish follow Equiano's realization of the fragility, vulnerability and possible annihilation of the self, and movement, speech and consciousness cease, registering his symbolic death.

The moment of this mutual non-recognition of the other as fully human is precisely and simultaneously the first moment in the *Narrative* when bodies become 'ours' and 'theirs', not merely differentiated but racialized, a racialization which seems, on the surface, to become the yardstick of affiliation and allegiance. This is the first time in his account that Equiano divides people into a binary structure of two opposing groups: the crew and the multitude, the former referred to as 'white' and the latter as 'black'. 'When I recovered a little', Equiano states when he returns to consciousness, 'I found some *black* people about me, who I believed were some of those who brought me on board, and had been receiving their pay . . . I asked them if we were not to be eaten by those *white* men with horrible looks, red faces, and loose hair'.[22] But, of course, this categorization of peoples is being imagined and recreated by Equiano within the terms of 1789 Britain.

Equiano's affiliations will not always be based on a politics of the body as *The Interesting Narrative* runs its course.[23] Roxanne Wheeler has shown how variable and fluid Equiano's use of skin colour is throughout the text, which 'underscores that black complexion is a way of experiencing the world rather than a way of statically *being* in the world determined by climate, customs or physical features'.[24] Yet it is in Equiano's reconstruction of one particular space, the deck of a slave ship at anchor on the Atlantic coast of the African continent, that bodily difference is established as the signature of a break in the process of recognizing the other as human. I want to argue that it is the recognition of this break which is a mark of the conscious entry of the subject into modern Western racialized discourse: the point at which Equiano steps into the place of recognition which others have given him.

In *The Interesting Narrative* Equiano was not black in the place in which he grew up. Nor did he see himself as African. Although enslaved, Equiano was not black or African at any point on his journey towards the Atlantic coast, but he is represented as becoming black *in the encounter* with the crew of the slave ship, who, simultaneously with their refusal to recognize a shared humanity with Equiano, become white. The African, or black subject, and the European, or white subject, are produced in mutual relations of affiliation/disaffiliation and, at this moment, Equiano turns to those he gauges as being *like* himself for knowledge and assurance. However, it is this absolute division that the entire *Interesting Narrative* is written against. Even at this moment, on the deck of a slave ship, however, the absolute break represented as a binary of opposition between African and European subjects cannot hold; difference remains between and among those constituted as African or black, even though they are produced as a unity in relation to the crew. This difference produces meaning at multiple levels of the narrative.

The yardstick that Equiano uses as a measure of alikeness is recognized by him as being produced by the same body politics that operate to deny him his humanity. Held in tension, or creative friction, are both the potential of affiliation through a racialized body politics and a realization that, in the relations of subjugation and exploitation that constitute the colonial encounter, the politics of the body simultaneously produces racialization as the technology or mechanism of differentiation *and* exceeds its boundaries. Equiano is well aware that those he turns to are *not* like him in every respect, for when he wakes and sees 'black people' around him, among them are some he recognizes as 'those who brought me on board', people who not only are responsible for his predicament but profit from his transformation into cargo. Those Africans that Equiano refers to as 'a *multitude* of black people of every description chained together', are not an undifferentiated unity but of 'every description'. Following his account of his induction into modernity as a racialized subject, Equiano situates such racialization as the history of the present, a body politics which he immediately rejects. The multitude is presented as 'a set of singularities', a social collectivity that cannot be reduced to sameness.[25]

In this encounter Equiano is not only recognized by others and by himself as black; he is also, and simultaneously, inducted into capitalist relations as cargo. His double inscription thrusts him into the violence and brutality which characterize this forced scattering of peoples, the formation of the black diaspora. Are these the conditions of the entry into modernity? This dialectical creation of an identity marks a significant moment in the 'becoming' of modern racialized subjects. I would argue that Equiano's entire narrative is being written back to the moment of his own recognition of the meaning of his symbolic death as enslaved being, as property, as raced. *The Interesting Narrative* is being created out of what could be called a postcolonial consciousness/subjectivity, a consciousness which does not turn its back on or renounce the subject of the moment prior to the encounter with modernity, nor is the subject prior to the encounter dismissed as subject which is premodern and in need of modernization. Rather, Equiano reinscribes, indeed reinvents, the subject as it exists prior to the encounter with Europeans, as the bearer of a valuable and valued perspective and knowledge for his contemporary readership. This narrative move is even more significant if these chapters are the political imaginings of an author of New World origin.

In these first chapters of his *Interesting Narrative* Equiano establishes for his readers the composite nature of his subject, a constantly shifting plurality of selves that prepare them for how they should read the rest of the narrative. The account of becoming a 'black' and abject subject, the history of the past, is superseded by the history of the present narration, the author writing not only as a 'free' person but as a 'black' and British citizen. As Wheeler characterizes it, 'Equiano's narrative continually spotlights this dilemma of the difference his skin colour makes in the colonial world, and yet he maintains the similarity of his mind, feelings and aspirations to his readers.'[26] Equiano is, self-consciously, 'stepping into the recognitions that others give us' and manipulating these recognitions for his own purposes. While acknowledging that he exists within the limitations of the body politics of modernity, Equiano's constant urge to move beyond them is the ground of his intuition of a future cultural identity broader and more enlightened than the narrow and exclusionary national cultural identity of his English readership. If that readership would only step into the place of recognitions Equiano offers them, they could participate in a future in which the racialization of subjects has been transcended. Equiano speaks as a composite subject, a subject inhabiting multiple differences, as African, as black, as British, as Christian, as a diasporic and transnational citizen of the world, and in the process offers his readers the possibility of imagining a more complex cultural and national identity for themselves. *The Interesting Narrative*, then, is powerful far beyond what has been acknowledged either in its political effect, as anti-slavery text, or with regard to what may be recognized in the future as the political work of a 'black American expatriate'. For Equiano, in 1789, offered the reading public an articulation of a way of being in the world that embodied an intuition, a possibility, of broadening and internationalizing what it could mean to be English and British.

Taking a 'voyage of rediscovery', a 'return journey' ourselves to the fluid, multiple and complex modern subjectivities produced in the course of *The Interesting Narrative* we can reconsider the cultural identities we have inherited stepping into the recognition of our double inscription and its consequences with the hope of building ourselves anew. If we follow the incisive analysis of Hall's essay, 'When Was "the Post-colonial"?', we can locate examples of the narration into being of the racialized modern subject as a process of double inscription, narratives that attempt to transcend the binary oppositions of black/white, and/or colonizer/colonized, in the creation of subjectivities that are mutually constitutive, coming into being in modernity simultaneously in relation to and through each other. But what do we make of these traditions?

Almost two hundred years after the publication of *The Interesting Narrative*, in a postcolonial moment, Caribbean writer George Lamming takes up Equiano's challenge to acknowledge the double inscription of the modern transatlantic racialized encounter.[27] In the extraordinarily powerful novel *Natives of My Person*, Lamming examines how the modern British national subject emerged out of the voyage to purchase, transport and sell enslaved humans. The process of becoming this type of modern subject is recorded by the commandant of the slave ship *Reconnaissance* in his diary:

> Under my grave command, and by the loyal direction of my officers, Steward, Boatswain, Priest, and Surgeon, I had determined to cause this crew of former strangers to break free and loose from the ancient restrictions of the Kingdom of Lime Stone; and I declare it was my pride and no less to build from this battalion of vandals and honest men alike such an order as might be the pride and example of excellence to Lime Stone herself; that I would plant some portion of the Kingdom in a soil that is new and freely chosen, namely the Isles of the Black Rock, more recently known as San Cristobal. For I have seen men of the basest natures erect themselves into gentlemen of honour the moment they were given orders to seize command over the savage tribes of the Indies. Here is a perfect school in the arts of conquest and command.[28]

Lime Stone is a thinly disguised reference to a Britain that is portrayed as a factionalized land of 'former strangers' who are wedded to 'ancient restrictions', strangers to each other but beings who find themselves belonging to a country that needs a colonial project to modernize and nationalize itself. Out of these 'raw materials' Lamming builds a 'voyage of rediscovery' through which to articulate the other side of the double inscription of the modern racialized encounter.

Natives of My Person narrates the emergence of Lime Stone as a modern nation through a voyage of enslavement and colonization. In a reversal of the narrative perspective of Equiano, Lamming allows his readers to access the consciousness of the *Reconnaissance* crew on the deck of the slave ship as their national subjectivity is formed in a mutual and simultaneous double inscription with the African as its property and source of future wealth. As the crew make the preparations for and receive their human cargo a national cultural identity and community gradually emerge from the encounter. During the transatlantic crossing the 'battalion of vandals and honest men alike' form, break and re-form alliances and allegiances, making themselves modern men and freeing themselves from 'ancient restrictions' in order to become modern British national subjects who are liberated from the burden of their pastness. But this liberated subject is realized through, and utterly dependent upon, the creation of the unfree modern subject.

We are all familiar with Marlow's description of the 'city that always makes [him] think of "a whited sepulchre" ' in Joseph Conrad's *Heart of Darkness*. The reference, of course, comes from the condemnation of the scribes and Pharisees in Matthew (23:27–8): 'Woe unto you . . . for ye are like unto whited sepulchres, which indeed appear beautiful outward, but within are full of dead men's bones, and of all uncleanliness.' Marlow visits the Company in Brussels seeking employment in the colonies. In the waiting room he sees

> a large, shining map, marked with all the colours of a rainbow. There was a vast amount of red . . . a deuce lot of blue, a little green, smears of orange, and . . . a purple patch . . . However, I wasn't going into any of these. I was going into the yellow. Dead in the centre'.[29]

The yellow, of course, marks Belgium's colonial possessions, the site of Marlow's future journey from Kinshasa to Stanley Falls. Far from being marginal or peripheral to Belgium, then, Conrad situates the site of the colonial as being 'dead in the centre', not just of the wall but in the heart of the European city. *Heart of Darkness* is a modernist text which performs a double inscription of the colonial periphery into the metropole, a double inscription which transcends notions of centre and margins, over here and over there, as separate histories with separate subjects.

In the face of Britain's contemporary amnesia about and nostalgia for its colonial past, Pauline Melville, in her contemporary collection of short stories, *The Migration of Ghosts*, accomplishes a similar double inscription as she demonstrates that colonization and neocolonialism are never external to the societies of the imperial metropolis but always deeply embedded within them. In one of these stories, 'The President's Exile', the ghost of a deposed president of an unnamed Caribbean nation, Baldwin Hercules, haunts the corridors, and rooms of the buildings in London in which he studied law, institutions into which he was subsequently welcomed as the president of a Commonwealth nation. A dictator who had his opponents tortured and assassinated, a president who constantly rigged his own re-election, Hercules is presented as a creature created by and granted his power within the walls of the London School of Economics, the Inns of Court, the Royal Commonwealth Society and the Colonial Office. The institutions in which we teach and work, while apparently invested in producing free, independent-thinking modern subjects, are deeply implicated in the production, maintenance and reproduction of imperial power during and after colonialism. But they are wrapped in the architectural and ideological facades that hide the 'dead men's bones and uncleanliness' of continued neocolonial exploitation.[30]

These examples imaginatively read colonization as part of an essentially transnational and transcultural global process, renarrativizing it as a double inscription, a breaking down of the inside/outside, here-and-there, them-and-us, home-and-abroad perspective.[31] This breaking down of these binaries, particularly those of home and abroad, structure both Conrad's and Melville's narratives even though one is a modernist text and the other a product of late modern Britain. In Conrad's description of Marlow signing his contract, Marlow describes the process as being 'let into a conspiracy'. The company's 'door of Darkness' in the heart of the metropolitan city of Brussels is the portal through which Marlow passes into the colony.[32]

Instances of reworking and rewriting the emergence of the racialized subject become even more complex when engaged with a feminist politics. Maryse Condé returns to the transatlantic terrain of Equiano and Lamming in a historical fiction to counter and rewrite the lack of voice of the enslaved female and to position her as product of the same movement and diasporic becoming as the masculine subject which became the normative voice of the modern racialized subject.[33] In contrast to Equiano's failure to imagine his sister as a complex consciousness in his gradual journey towards modernity and beyond, Maryse Condé initiates the passage of a black female subject of the seventeenth century into modernity in the three short and abrupt sentences that constitute the opening lines of her novel *I, Tituba*:

> Abena, my mother, was raped by an English sailor on the deck of *Christ the King* one day in the year 16** while the ship was sailing for Barbados. I was born from this act of aggression. From this act of hatred and contempt.[34]

There is a quality of the routine and quotidian in the manner of the recitation of this rape, and in the unspecified year and the casual insertion of 'one day'. In *The Interesting Narrative*, Equiano's unnamed sister is the repeating sign of his loss and abject status at the local level during the multiple stages of his passage into the diasporic estrangement of a global order. The loss of 'sister' also establishes the autonomous existence of the masculine subject as merely a metaphor and sign; Equiano's sister is fixed not only in the local but also irrevocably in the past.

To transcend the local particularities of the representation of the female in modern becomings, Condé creates a modern female racialized subject who is conceived through an act of violence:

> Questions of cultural identity in diasporas ... have proved so troubling and perplexing for Caribbean people precisely because, with us, identity is irredeemably a historical question. Our societies are composed, not of one, but of many peoples. Their origins are not singular but diverse. Those to whom the land originally belonged have long since largely perished – decimated by hard labour and disease. The land cannot be sacred because it was 'violated' – not empty but emptied. Everyone who is here originally belonged somewhere else. Far from being continuous with our pasts, our relation to that history is marked by the most horrendous, violent, abrupt, ruptural breaks. Ahead of the slowly evolving pact of civil association so central to the liberal discourse of Western modernity, our 'civil association' was inaugurated by an act of imperial will. What we now call the Caribbean was reborn in and through violence.[35]

The violent sexual violation of an African female captive in Condé's novel is, indeed, a horrendous act of imperial will, but here the emergence of the Caribbean subject in modernity is given many particularities. Tituba is conceived in the transitional and transnational space of the forced transportation of African labour from the African continent to the New World but, for the female subject, being property and being labour take on the additional characteristics of being sexual property and being violently inducted into sexual labour. In addition to the bio-political economy of sexual transaction and transgression, the conception of Condé's Caribbean protagonist is also carefully situated geographically. Tituba is a figure whose becoming is not only rooted in the violence of the encounter between Europe and Africa as the literal and metaphoric offspring of 'hatred and contempt', she is also a modern female racialized subject who emerges from and is located in the geopolitics of the encounter: Tituba is brought into being at the centre of a triangulated Atlantic. In Condé's use of sexual subjugation, rape and sexual labour, as an originary moment of the entry of the black female subject into modernity, she joins other black female intellectuals who have challenged dominant paradigms of the lone black male as the representative subject for understanding enslavement, oppression and the forced scattering of peoples.

But is the modern subject produced at the moment of consciousness of their selves as modern, as a subject, as a modern subject, only when they govern the terms of their own narration? And is this narration always, simultaneously, a renarrativization of the relations of dominance and subordination inscribed in the encounter with colonial power or imperial will? In Austin Clarke's *The Polished Hoe*, the tool of back-breaking labour of the title is transformed by its black female protagonist into a weapon, a weapon which she wields against those who have colonized and enslaved her body. This act of physical violence and rebellion, however, is not the subject matter of *The Polished Hoe*; what we assume to be a violent murder takes place before the novel opens. Rather, what is the concern of Austin's novel is an act of narrative and discursive violence and rebellion through which the modern subject emerges in its refusal to be bound by the terms and conventions of Western modernity. The protagonist denies absolutely the terms and conditions of an Enlightenment legal discourse, a discourse within which she is supposed to confine an account of her actions. The rejection of this discourse is a powerful act of narrative deconstruction and destruction both of which presage the creation of an alternative complex and multifaceted narrative created by the subaltern herself. *The Polished Hoe* becomes a renarrativization through which the black female produces herself as a modern subject who can contest the terms and conditions of knowledge, power and subordination which have produced her as merely a colonized body.

III.

> Nineteen forty-eight was ... the year of the arrival at Tilbury Docks in the UK of the SS *Empire Windrush*, the troopship, with its cargo of West Indian volunteers, returning from home leave in the Caribbean, together with a small company of civilian migrants. This event signalled the start of post-war Caribbean migration to Britain and stands symbolically as the birthdate of the Afro-Caribbean black diaspora ...
>
> Migration has been a constant motif of the Caribbean story. But the *Windrush* initiated a new phase of diaspora formation whose legacy is the black Caribbean settlements in the UK ... The fate of Caribbean people living in the US or Canada is no more 'external' to Caribbean history than the Empire was 'external' to the so-called domestic history of Britain, though that is indeed how contemporary historiography constructs them.[36]

> There is, it seems to me, an overwhelming tendency to abstract questions of race from what one might call their *internal* social and political basis and contexts in British society – that is to say, to deal with 'race' as if it has nothing intrinsically to do with the present 'condition of England'. It's viewed rather as an 'external' problem, which has been foisted to some extent on English society from the outside: it's been visited on us, as it were, from the skies. To hear problems of race discussed in England today, you would sometimes believe that relations between British people and the peoples of the Caribbean or the Indian sub-continent began with the wave of black immigrants in the late forties and fifties ...
>
> [Neither right nor left] can nowadays bring themselves to refer to Britain's imperial and colonial past, even as a contributory factor to the present situation. The slate has been wiped

> clean. Racism is not endemic to the British social formation. It has nothing intrinsically to do with the dynamic of British politics ... It is not part of English culture ... it does not belong to the 'English ideology'.[37]

When I began my current project, *Child of Empire*, I intended that it would begin in 1948, when I was born into the bleak, scrupulously rationed world of post–Second World War Britain, and became the daughter of a Welsh mother and a Jamaican father. *Child of Empire* was going to be the story of the post-war years in which I saw a new racial formation being established and new racialized British subjects coming into being. But the longer I have worked on it the further back I have pushed my narrative, realizing that I should not ignore, or take for granted, the history out of and into which a subject emerges as a historical subject. For Hall's insistence that 'the fate of Caribbean people living in the US or Canada is no more "external" to Caribbean history than the Empire was "external" to the so-called domestic history of Britain' has structural and conceptual consequences for how we shape our narratives, for how we write our histories of the emergence of Britain as a modern racialized state, and for how we tell our stories of becoming racialized subjects.

In the wake of the fiftieth anniversary of the end of the Second World War there has been a flurry of re-discoveries of the history of contemporary black Britain, a past which is being narrated as having its symbolic roots in the arrival of the SS *Empire Windrush* in 1948. This paradigm of migration has now become the dominant convention for understanding the racialization of subjects in modern Britain.[38] Each of these narrative inventions/reinventions has created specific kinds of racialized subjects that constitute the modern, black British subject and community, but they all tell the story of the emergence of a modern British 'blackness' which has its origins in post-war migration. I have decided to begin in a different moment, to tell a story that has its roots in a place that makes the historical paradigm of the

Windrush more complicated.[39] I argue that it is not the *Windrush* alone which initiated a new phase of the formation of a Caribbean diaspora in the UK and ushered in a new racial state, but the presence of black civilian and military personnel during the Second World War.[40]

The mobilization of women in the homeland and of colonial troops and civilians in the Caribbean resulted in racialized encounters between young women from the colonial heartland and young men from its colonized periphery. The racialization of subjects during the Second World War occurred in the context of the expression of fears and anxieties which had developed about 'race' in the colonies and in British cities. These fears and anxieties circulated around these two sets of bodies: the racialization of black men was articulated in relation to white women and the subjecthood of white females was, in turn, articulated in relation to the black men. Many of these encounters flourished into sexual relationships and, despite overwhelming opposition from friends, family, strangers and society at large, some culminated in marriage and increased the number of what officials regarded as the 'problem' of 'half-caste children'. I see, then, an alternative genealogy for post-war settlement, a genealogy that grows out of the struggles over English/British national and cultural identity during the war. There is much at stake in the sort of narrative decisions we make. I do not intend to write 'a mere romantic recreation of the past, not a looking backward in nostalgia.' For I agree with Hall that 'the problem of living and writing more fully now is related to the full, critical experience we have of the past'.[41]

The many roles that Caribbean men and women played in the Second World War have not been documented in comprehensive histories of the period.[42] Of those based in the UK there were approximately twelve and a half thousand volunteers in the armed services, the vast majority from Jamaica and serving in the RAF. Of the civilians recruited by the Ministry of Labour there were a thousand technicians and trainees working in Merseyside and Lancashire munitions factories and twelve hundred British Hondurans working as foresters in Scotland.[43]

Beginning in 1942 upwards of 3 million American troops began to arrive, 130,000 of whom were black.[44] British politicians were alarmed at the possible consequences of the presence of black colonial *and* US personnel on British soil. In the reactions of these politicians to these black bodies and in the policies that were instituted to control and discipline them we can trace the emergence of the UK as a modern racialized state, as a modern racial formation, years before the *Windrush* docked. Most accounts of American troops stationed in Britain during the war and of Britain's wartime relations with its colonies are written as separate and discrete histories. However, the response of British politicians to the presence in Britain of black troops and civilians, from the US and the colonies, was influenced by an interrelated and interdependent series of ideological and political beliefs: by ideas of race that circulated throughout and about the British Empire, by actual and imaginative relations to Britain's colonial subjects, and by a desire to appease Britain's most powerful ally, the USA.

My own introduction to British history began in the 1950s, in my elementary school, when my whole class was asked to describe the contribution of our fathers to the war effort. When it was my turn I stood and said that my father was in the RAF. At home we had a photograph of my dad in his uniform, RAF cap at the correct jaunty angle, wearing an airforce moustache and holding a pipe in his hand, the epitome of heroic British manhood, I thought. The teacher interrupted me before I could describe the photograph to my classmates, telling me, abruptly, to sit down and listen carefully to what she had to say. First, I was issued a very stern warning about the dire consequences of lying, then I was assured that there were no 'coloured' people in Britain during the war, or serving in its armed services, leave alone in the RAF, the crème de la crème of the military. Finally, our teacher addressed us all, 'coloured' people, we must remember, were not British but came as immigrants arriving after the war was over. I guessed that this meant that I wasn't British either because I had absorbed a previous lesson that I was 'coloured'. In spite of the fact that the wartime activities of black peoples in Britain was quickly and effectively erased from cultural memory, I would argue that reactions to their presence were significant factors in the formation of modern, British/English national culture.

I am always amused by the accounts of the American servicemen who characterized their British hosts as the opposite of how they would define a modern people. One early American volunteer for the RAF liked English people but also viewed them in a fashion similar to that of George Lamming's character, the Commandant, as being tied to 'ancient restrictions'. He described his frustration at what he saw as the inertia produced by Britain's 'old-school-tie' class consciousness, a society governed by the forces of 'tradition and precedent', forces which he found so strong that, in his words, 'thinking in politics, business and religion seems to have congealed'. He viewed the British as 'the most economically backward people' he had met, a people who heartily resisted 'labor-saving devices and short-cut direct business methods'.[45] Others describe the presence in Britain of up to 3 million American service personnel causing a 'social revolution'. If, in some ways, Britain resisted the modern world as represented by America, it conceded to the USA's dominant discourse through which racialized subjects were produced as the absolute other. The policies and practices of the British government during the war manufactured racialized subjects in accord with segregated relations of subjugation.

The recruitment of civilian workers from the Caribbean into Britain began in February 1941 and they were sent to areas of previous black settlement in the North West because that is where officials thought they would be 'most easily *absorbed*'.[46] These schemes for industrial workers were deliberately designed to prevent any further black settlement and were linked to programmes for post-war colonial development: limited terms of employment followed by immediate repatriation. Some bright sparks in the Colonial Office even imagined that segments of the already settled black population in British ports could be removed when the war ended: ' "the great coloured social problem" in Liverpool and other port towns would be "greatly eased by the resettlement of African peoples in West Africa where they could obtain proper and adequate employment" '.[47] As early as January 1942 there was official dismay at the prospect of black servicemen being based in Britain. The Foreign Office consulted with other departments and then issued a memo expressing anxiety about the possible consequences: 'the recruitment to the United Kingdom of Coloured British subjects, whose remaining in the United Kingdom after the war might create a social problem, was not considered desirable'.[48]

Although the British government was already worried about its homegrown black residents and the increasing presence of black colonial subjects, histories of the response to the presence of black American soldiers in Britain have been written as though an American 'racial problem' was imported into the UK with US troops and that the UK had no experience of how to deal with it.[49] Winston Churchill had been urging President Roosevelt to send American troops to Britain since the autumn of 1941, but when Roosevelt announced to Congress on 6 January 1942 that US forces were to be stationed in the UK the British government did all it could to dissuade the Americans from sending black GIs and the British chiefs of staff asked for the maximum number of *white* engineering regiments.[50] Throughout that spring and summer, British officials pressured the government of the United States to 'reduce as far as possible the number of coloured troops . . . sent to this country'. In what has to be considered a pathetic attempt to represent this exclusionary British policy as altruistic, Foreign Secretary Anthony Eden told American ambassador Winant, 'our climate was badly suited to negroes'.[51]

But black GIs arrived and kept on arriving. The US military command insisted that they were needed to service and supply their European theatre of operations (ETO); the occupants of

Whitehall, along with ETO, resolved that these black troops would have to be managed, and being managed meant segregating them. On a visit to Britain, Arthur Sulzberger, the publisher of the *New York Times*, actually recognized that Britain already had a resident black population when he made what he thought was 'a gesture of sympathy' for Whitehall's dilemma, and suggested that black American troops 'be moved out of rural areas and concentrated in ports like Liverpool' because it was in places like these that the British were 'used to all kinds of foreigners, including negroes'.[52]

What evolved were government, military, national and local practices that produced racialized subjects as external to ideologies of what constituted acceptable conventions of British/English subjecthood and citizenship. These practices were intended to police encounters of very specific kinds, sexual encounters between black men and white women: 'Politicians reasoned . . . that if sexual contacts with indigenous women were to cause the least anxiety, methods of controlling them would have to be found.'[53] Specific meanings adhered to these black male and white female bodies and to the geopolitics of their encounters, to the spatial relation they inhabited on the cultural terrain of British society.

Commanders in the US military were worried about the antagonism that would arise between their black and white troops if the black troops were seen with white women. General Eisenhower suggested that a rotation of leave passes, which would guarantee that white and coloured troops were never in the same town on the same day, would solve the 'problem'.[54] And, indeed, the British government decided that managing the issue meant instituting practices of racial segregation. The War Office and the Home Office were more than happy to oblige their white American 'cousins'; black Americans have never been embraced by this familial term, because racial segregation relieved their own fears and anxieties about the consequences of sexual relations between white and black. The Colonial Office did not want the British role in instituting American-style racial segregation to be revealed to the general public because of a concern that such revelations would cause anger and frustration in British colonies.[55]

> The National Association for the Advancement of Coloured People (NAACP) complained to the A[merican] R[ed] C[ross] on several occasions about 'segregated recreational centers in London and other English cities for Negro soldiers' and its executive secretary, Walter White, cabled Churchill in November about reports that the British government had asked Washington to send no more black troops to Britain. (After long consultation the Foreign Office decided discretely to ignore the telegram because it was doubted 'whether we could honestly give a categorical denial.')[56]

However, it would have been difficult for the British government to institute segregation without the cooperation of its regional commissioners, many of whom were ex-colonial officials, and without the participation of local police forces and local government officials.

Covert racial segregation became the practice in the West Country from July 1942.[57] In Somerset, the county in which my mother grew up and not far from where I, eventually, would be born:

> Wherever possible a new black unit in SOS [services of supply] was 'quarantined on base' to allow time to 'indoctrinate' it about British conditions and to coordinate arrangements with local officials ... liaison officers working with British Southern Command made arrangements in towns like Yeovil and Chard for separate blocks of cinema seats or separate rooms in pubs for black troops. The aim ... was to prevent 'white and coloured soldiers from attending the same activities simultaneously', while giving each race 'an equal opportunity of attending the same [kind of] functions as the other.' But, to avoid imputations of racial discrimination, everything was to be done 'on an

> organizational basis' – in other words, a dance would be held for a company of the '98th Engineer Regiment' (which happened to be black) or for a company of the 16th Infantry Regiment (which happened to be white). As [Gen. J. C. H.] Lee himself put it: 'While colour lines are not to be announced or even mentioned, entertainments such as dances should be "by organization." The reason, if any, given for such an arrangement should be "limitation of space and personnel." '[58]

My mother worked in the Air Ministry, a government department which had been moved out of London to Worcester, but she says she did not realize, until I told her, that black and white American troops were segregated in the area where she lived and worked. For soldiers stationed in the general depot at Ashchurch three miles outside Tewkesbury, white troops had passes on Tuesday, Thursday and Saturday; black troops on Monday, Wednesday and Friday; and white and black on alternate Sundays. A day club was established for black troops at Tewkesbury and clubs at Worcester and Cheltenham for white troops.[59] But the warning from the Colonial Office was heeded, and practices of racialization were always denied; instead it was 'organizational' justifications that were provided for the existence of such segregation. While officially 'the British government distanced itself from' the US Army's practices of racial segregation, the US Army could not have instituted and maintained racial segregation 'without cooperation or at least acquiescence from British authorities'.[60]

Nor were the leaders of the British Armed forces opposed to segregation. It was agreed at the War Office that 'British officers should lecture their troops, including women soldiers of the Auxiliary Territorial Service (ATS), on the need to minimise contact with black GIs.' Even though at the War Office they 'were reluctant to put anything on paper, because of the delicacy of the subject', 'General Arthur Dowler, the senior administrative officer in Southern Command, went ahead and issued his "Notes on Relations with Coloured Troops" ' on 7 August 1942.

In this document Dowler stated that the '"generality" of blacks "were of simple mental outlook" and lacked "the white man's ability to think and act to a plan" . . . British soldiers', he continued ' "should not make intimate friends with them, taking them to cinemas and bars" ';

> 'white women should not associate with coloured men' at all: they 'should not walk out, dance or drink with them'. Dowler wanted 'the British, both men and women, to realize the problem and adjust their attitude so that it conforms to that of the white American citizen'.

There was no objection, not even from the Colonial Office, 'to the double standard policy of covertly supporting US Army segregation as long as the British authorities were not implicated in its enforcement.'[61] Nancy Cunard and George Padmore wrote a pamphlet, *The White Man's Duty* (1942), to publicize how

> the coloured soldier of the USA over here in very large numbers . . . may be the same as a white American soldier in democracy, when democracy is a battlefield, [but] he is not the same in daily relations with the people of Great Britain, because some of his chiefs have requested that this be not so.

And as Cunard and Padmore went on to stress, 'the colour issue in Britain was part of the wider question of racial discrimination within the empire as a whole.'[62]

The anxieties and fears, the frantic exchange of covert memos and circulation of not so covert 'notes', the endless wrangling and manoeuvring among the ministries, the Foreign Office and the Colonial Office about the spatial management and control of white and black bodies, the 'what-on-earth-to-do' nature of it all, swirl and coalesce around the figures of my parents. The mechanisms of racialization policed and attempted to prevent what they are doing, what they might have done and what they might be thinking of doing in a 'capillary functioning of power'.[63] These bodies were the fulcrum, 'the point where power reaches into their actions and attitudes, their discourses, learning processes and everyday lives'.[64] Cabinet discussions drew upon racist ideologies articulated in relation to the past and present of subject peoples in the colonies and black settlements in Britain in order to predict what it would face in the future. The Home Secretary, Herbert Morrison, stated that he was 'fully conscious that a difficult sex problem might be created . . . if there were a substantial number of cases of sex relations between white women and coloured troops and the procreation of half-caste children.'[65]

Morrison's articulation of what he called a 'sex problem' did not arise from the recognition of 'an "external" problem', which had been 'foisted to some extent on English society from the outside',[66] or imported into Britain with the arrival of the bodies of black GIs. On the contrary, it was 'homegrown' composite racialized consciousness, drawing upon official responses in the past to the existence of black communities in Britain and racialized bodies in colonial territories, a consciousness that gave English national culture its character, meaning, substance and resonance. Before the war this consciousness had been nurtured, given form and realized in the policing and disciplining of colonial subjects and black residents of Bristol, Cardiff, London and Liverpool.[67]

West Indians who served in the RAF during the war have recently begun to tell their own stories of their humiliation. They have recounted memories of British women groping their rectums in order locate their tails, tails that they imagined West Indian men hid in their trousers, and of children running from them in fear.[68] They tell stories about the Paramount dance hall on Tottenham Court Road and the brutality they suffered at the hands of those British and American white men who resented West Indians dancing with English women. Antagonism to this 'intimate socializing' was also expressed in the newspapers who had a 'field day talking about "ill-timed and unwanted fraternizing" and that blacks and whites should never be allowed to mix in such a way.' One West Indian remembers reading an article entitled 'Don't Let this Go On' which suggested that the Paramount should be bombed. It was 'a concerted attempt', he concluded, 'to besmirch the name of the Paramount who dared to permit black servicemen to pass through its doors'.[69]

Photograph of the author's parents *c.* 1945

Another Jamaican ex-serviceman tells the story of being refused service in a pub after a game of cricket and says that in the more than fifty years since, he has never forgotten how he felt:

> I had to take myself, my little case containing my cricket kit, my unquenched thirst and walk slowly home . . . I was taking stock of myself and, for the first time in my life, I was asking myself: Why have I travelled thousands of miles to be on the receiving end of such treatment? I was as British, nay I considered myself more British than the British . . . and more patriotic than the most fanatic Anglophile.

He walked back to his base in floods of tears, he told his interviewer, remembering how Jamaica had presented the UK with a squadron of Spitfires at the beginning of the war.[70]

My father wrote to me to describe his arrival in the UK as a Jamaican airman recently flown in from training in Canada. When he and the other Jamaican volunteers arrived in RAF Padgate, Bridgenorth, early in 1943, before they were even taken to their billets the sergeant receiving them 'took us to the ablutions where we received instructions in meticulous detail on how to use the shower, the wash basins and the toilets, as if to say we had never seen or used a bathroom before'.[71]

It was not only black subjects that were policed and disciplined. Black servicemen were dialogically constituted in their blackness in and through their potential and actual encounters with white women, who were also to be 'managed'. Reynolds records the 'intensive efforts [that] were made to guide the conduct of British women'. For women who were in the armed service, 'military discipline was invoked' to discourage them from fraternizing with black soldiers, and by January 1944 these policies had hardened when 'the Women's Territorial Auxiliary issued an order "forbidding its members to speak to coloured American soldiers except in the presence of a white [person]" '.

These systems of surveillance were not only instituted and regulated by the military; they were also enabled and maintained by members of local constabularies, who 'routinely reported women soldiers found in the company of black GIs to their superiors'. Even civilian women were prosecuted by their local police, who evoked 'a variety of laws' to take them into custody when they were found 'in company of black soldiers'.[72]

White women were counselled by families, friends and authorities alike against marriage with black men; black American soldiers who wished to marry British women were refused permission to do so by their commanding officers and quickly transferred. Black journalist Ormus Davenport, 'himself a wartime GI, claimed that there had been a "gentleman's agreement" to prevent mixed marriages'. But 'in the 8th Air Force Service Command where most of the American Air Force blacks were concentrated, a total ban on such marriages was quite explicit'.[73] The result was disastrous for their offspring.

If 'loose lips sank ships', women with 'loose' morals were regarded as a direct threat to the health and safety of the nation. White women who became the escorts of, or married, black servicemen were placed beyond the pale of acceptable behaviour. One Jamaican ex-serviceman recalls,

> Women who befriended the Westindian servicemen were a much maligned body of people, being objects of derision, jibes and taunts. Yet most never wavered in the allegiance and loyalty when the going was toughest and no amount of praise could be too high for them. In the very early days they remained a tower of strength and were among the few to extend a hand of welcome to the lads.[74]

Sonya Rose has provided us with a comprehensive account of the moral panic 'about the declining morals of girls and young women in British cities and towns' during the Second World War.[75] She argues that definitions of the nation during the Second World War 'could not incorporate within it pleasure-seeking, fun-loving, and sexually expressive women and girls. The women and girls who could not or would not put aside their "foolish world" to rescue the nation were constructed as anti-citizens – in contrast to those who were self-sacrificing'. Women who crossed the boundaries of conventional behaviour, particularly in wartime, were labelled 'good-time girls' and became associated within official discourses with venereal disease, thus becoming a threat to the health of the nation.[76] But women who openly expressed their sexual selves and sexual desires in encounters with black servicemen were particularly vilified and seen as a particular threat to the nation's future.

Graham Smith discovered, in the records of the Colonial Office, minutes from a Bolero committee meeting about black GIs in August of 1942 in which someone wondered 'whether "an open statement on the danger of venereal disease" would deter British women from associating with the blacks', and someone else suggested initiating a 'whispering campaign' along those lines. Despite objections from others in attendance at the meeting, Smith thinks it 'likely that a programme of rumour-spreading' about black GIs and VD '*was* started' and that it was facilitated through the vehicles of the Women's Voluntary Service (WVS) and, possibly, the BBC.[77] In this manner, both black male bodies and white female bodies were designated vectors of disease, carriers of a threat which could literally and metaphorically infect the nation. But the greatest fear was reserved for the future of the nation. If white women became the bearers of half-caste children, a post-war era of peace and stability, for which so many hoped, would be irrevocably disrupted.

Whereas George Lamming in *Natives of My Person* represented the formation of the modern European national subject, a subject liberated from the burden of its pastness, as being realized through and dependent upon its enslavement of others, during the Second World War the British made themselves modern and began the process of liberating themselves from their ancient restrictions, from the pastness that was the colonization of others, through new processes of racialization and racist practices in their encounter with black people on their own soil. These encounters between a parochial British population and both black Americans and black volunteers from the Caribbean prefigured the formation of post-war black British subjects.

'The Babies They Left behind Them', *Life Magazine*, August 1948

I used to imagine that being born a brown baby in a tiny village outside Okehampton in the county of Devon, in January 1948, was being born into a homogeneously white social and cultural landscape, but, only three years before, thousands of US black troops has been based in Devon and the adjacent county of Somerset. Not far from where I was born, twenty brown British babies were wards of Somerset County Council and the British Home Office. They were housed in Holnicote House, which the Somerset Council ran as an orphanage.[78] *Life* magazine published a photograph of seven of the children under the headline 'The Babies They Left behind Them'. The article which accompanies the photograph describes the children as the offspring of US black soldiers and English women: 'Their fathers have returned to the US. Their mothers have given them up, in most cases reluctantly, because of ostracism by village neighbours.' These children were not imagined as present and future citizens but as 'problems' that should be exported. The British government, the article states, 'are now considering offers of adoption received from US negro families'.[79] The double inscription of racialized encounters in modernity was resolved, not only in the dialectics of the encounter between black and white, but through the rejection of the transgressive bodies of their offspring, the 'absolute pathology which underwrote the half-caste category justifying the subordinate positions of Africans, Afro-Caribbeans, the white women married to them, and their children within society'.[80]

Recently, I have been writing about the visual representation of brown bodies and thinking about visual narratives of spectacle and cultural memory. I am particularly interested in the complex narratives of gendering, racialization, and sexual and class affiliations at work in the representation of British racialized subjects in the 1940s and 1950s. *Picture Post* is a particularly rich source of these images because within its pages is enacted a claim to its being considered a global magazine, not in so far as it represented or attracted a global readership, but in so far as it functioned as a mechanism which translated the global into the local site of Britishness/Englishness. In a dialectical process of translation, Britishness/Englishness is both imagined and produced as a belonging that existed in multiple dimensions, local and global. In the immediate post-war years, when it is clear that the United States has emerged as the dominant political and economic force in the world, there is deep anxiety about empire, about what constitutes Britishness/Englishness within the terms of empire, about what values it does or could or should embody. It is in the production of definitions of Britishness/Englishness that *Picture Post* reveals the cracks, fissures and contradictions in modern British subjecthood.

The author, two years old

Picture Post, 3 April 1948

It is within this context of a crisis and anxiety about national subjecthood that images of Britain's post-war 'coloured' citizens appear. Black citizens were represented as being as external to the history of the nation. *Picture Post* articulated a national voice, a sense of national belonging that depended on exclusion. Black Britons were citizens who were located within discourses of outsiderness, colonialism, subject peoples, empire and migration, but never within discourses of belonging. With the juxtaposition of these two images, a family photograph and a photograph from *Picture Post*, two different narratives appear.

In the photograph here I am two years old, a black British subject standing in the back garden of our house in Streatham in south London. There is nothing unusual about this photograph; in fact it is in many ways a typical family photograph in a typical British backyard, small, with a fence, flowers, weeds and a path. My dress is handmade with smocking and gathered sleeves, typical of 1950; the socks and shoes are clean and bright. I was obviously dressed for the camera, not for play, and clearly located in a time and a place. The other photograph is *Picture Post's* 1948 image of 'The Lonely Piccaninny', with the caption 'So small and defenceless, so waiting to be comforted'.

What is so interesting about the *Picture Post* image is that this young child is located precisely nowhere – the blank white space emphasizes a total lack of affiliation and erases from imagination any possibility of belonging. Erwin Blumenfeld, the photographer, delighted in contrivance, according to the art critic Vicki Goldberg. His 'photographic setups were composed with infinite care . . . In the arrangements and then again in the darkroom, he went to such lengths that it can be almost impossible to tell how the picture was made, and the contrivance occasionally overshadows the subject.'[81] Looking at 'The Lonely Piccaninny' I am prompted to ask, what was the contrivance that caused the child such misery? Was the photograph taken against a blank studio wall, or was it taken in a location (that related to the misery), a location that was subsequently erased? Was the misery caused by the photographer?

Whatever the conditions of its production, we must also consider the historical conditions at work in the production of meaning that the editors of *Picture Post* imagined it would have in their reproduction of the photograph in the context of Britain in April 1948. The pain, the way the figure is totally turned in on herself, and the total lack of external referents situates this figure as completely isolated and dislocated, coming from nowhere, belonging nowhere, except perhaps within the discourse of empire as a 'defenceless' subject awaiting an act of British magnanimity. Frozen in time and completely dislocated spatially, this black child has no past, present or future: its condition is alien – outside the temporality and place of the nation. Of course a 'piccaninny' would be miserable, and alone the figure was by definition an aberration in the racial politic of the time. But in the very absence of a sign or referent that could place this figure as belonging to the nation, a discourse of who is actually included in the national community is being produced in the form of a 'highly exclusive and exclusivist [English] cultural identity'. A British subject is what this 'piccaninny' is not, but through this act of negation is brought into activity a biopolitics which not only defines belonging and citizenship in post-war Britain, but also constitutes a refusal 'to produce ourselves anew'.

16

Imperial Intimacies: Further Thoughts

When she was invited to formulate a response to essays responding to *Imperial Intimacies: A Tale of Two Islands*, she hesitated.[1] Then she vacillated. Each morning, day after day, she wrote hundreds of words, only to delete them in the afternoon. Paule Marshall told her once that if she managed to compose a perfect paragraph in a morning, she was satisfied. It seemed impossible to attain that goal.

She had no idea why she was so confounded by, and felt estranged from, a task that most academics would find conventional and unremarkable. As an author she had already been allotted the most economically viable amount of space, just under 123,000 words and more than fifty images bound into four hundred pages. The result was affordable, and surely enough could be said within those parameters. She may have been deluded (she often was), but she did not imagine herself to belong among satirical portraits of professors who never tire of hearing their own voice. On second thought, she had to modify this claim and admit that three years before this response to respondents would be read, the manuscript she had submitted to the publishers as the final version was much longer. There were plenty of out-takes lying on the cutting room floor – or, more accurately, deposited in the 'Extraneous' folders of Scrivener.

Subject to the intense scrutiny of an extraordinarily talented and perspicacious editor who wrangled with it – untangling knotted prose, clearing the underbrush of obscure argumentation and a scattershot assortment of punctuation marks – the manuscript became a book that readers could enter and find their way through. Extraneous? At the time she had written what was now discarded, she had thought the words worthy of utterance – was it *time* that made the ideas irrelevant or the economics of publishing? As she wrote *extraneous*, she could not help but wonder if there was anything to be resurrected from those files. But that was then, and this is now, a very different moment. How to speak into it?

When people encounter her primarily as an author/writer, they want to know why she wanted to write the book. Again, she is often indecisive. She had originally considered writing about the racist social and political ordering of the United Kingdom after the Second World War but quickly realized that in order to dispel the historical amnesia that shrouded British colonialism and imperialism she must push beyond the arrival of the *Empire Windrush* in June 1948, an event that profoundly dissatisfied her as a historical marker and common sense reference point for the Caribbean presence in the metropole. Trying to explain why *Imperial Intimacies* moves constantly across the Atlantic in a historical arc of three hundred years is more complicated. As a professor she had to justify the length of time the project took to complete. There was no singular response to this, for it depends on an interpretation of how and when her ideas began to germinate. It has been simplest to state that the research and writing that preceded the editing process took a decade. The academy exercises a variety of modes and methods of surveillance instituted through accounting practices, one of which is a requirement to make an annual declaration of 'productivity', as measured by the number of publications listed. 'Child of Empire', her initial title, and then 'Imperial Intimacies' appeared as a 'work in progress' on at least ten of the faculty activity reports used by the university to gauge her general worthiness and determine her value to the institution: a value affirmed by awarding, or denied by withholding, a small rise in salary. No one was going to give her credit for spending a year within the horrors of slave registers or another trying to track a foot soldier who would become a slave owner through the ledgers of regiments of the British Army sent to the West Indies in the late eighteenth century.

From the submission of the fifth report onward, when she pressed the send button she flinched in anticipation of sighs of disbelief and impatience seeping from under the door of the office of her departmental chair and murmurings of dissatisfaction and dismissal floating through the corridors of the offices of the provost and dean of the faculty. She felt – well, she was – diminished in the pages of university ledgers. It would have been more profitable, in institutional terms, to spend those years becoming a public intellectual, writing topical essays for the *New Yorker* or *The Atlantic* and accumulating an impressive number of citations to be entered in the profit column of the university ledger rather than disappearing into the bowels of the colonial archives in Jamaica and London, which could only be counted as a numerical loss or absence. A senior administrator in the graduate school severely criticized her for helping her students obtain funds to support international travel to archives, travel that the graduate school regarded as educationally unnecessary and a detriment to their policies requiring a 'timely' completion of dissertations under threat of severing financial support after six years. As many black, Chicana/o, indigenous and Latinx faculty have discovered, the extraordinary labour of unsilencing history can imperil a career. To spend ten years writing one book may raise eyebrows in many quarters of the academy; it raises disbelief and mirth in other professions. A decade has been the simplest response, but it disguises the fact that she lies because she does not know the answer.

In 'Zippin' Up My Boots, Going Back to My Routes', Eddie Chambers engages the *longue durée* of various cultural evocations of black roots and genealogies, from Gunnar Myrdal through Alex Haley to Ancestry.com.[2] Before taking up the mantle of a university professor she was a teacher of English at a comprehensive secondary school in the East End of London. The genealogy of *Imperial Intimacies* is rooted there, beginning with an exercise that she set before her multiracial classes in the 1970s. She introduced her pupils to historical amnesia, both the practice and the consequences of silencing the past, by asking them to comb the indexes of the history books in the school library looking for references to enslavement. Year after year they reported the same listing – 'Britain, slavery, abolition of', the sole entry. This is the point at which she encouraged them to question the content and nature of the accounts of pastness they received. The legacy of the historical erasure of colonialism and empire was evident in the transnational racialized composition of her classroom and the racist character of the neighbourhood and the Metropolitan Police force.

The experience of teaching in a state school was where she began to understand how educational institutions are tethered to rigorously bounded formations of knowledge that obscure the relations of power and inequality they maintain. Dismantling these bonds, she learnt from Paolo Freire, was not merely a question of methodology but of transformative, radical, critical thought and praxis.[3] Teaching became the political commitment artfully articulated by Robert Nesta Marley in 1980, when he wove Marcus Garvey's words into 'Redemption Song', a song that would inform her pedagogy for the rest of her life: 'Emancipate yourself from mental slavery / None but ourselves can free our minds.'[4] Her critical thought and practice amplified and developed in the intellectual ferment of the Centre for Contemporary Cultural Studies and was shaped by the teaching and writing of its director, Stuart Hall. For the first time she found a voice as a writer in the intense collaborative work of the Race and Politics Group that produced *The Empire Strikes Back: Race and Racism in Seventies Britain*.[5]

Here, in the now, Eddie Chambers, Marisa J. Fuentes and Marc Matera raise a number of important questions about ongoing, if unresolved, conversations about archives, methodologies and narrative form. In the pages of *Imperial Intimacies*, the reader is witness to a writer not only immersed in but in a constant struggle with and against the colonial archive. Archives are not silent and static but, on the contrary, subject to processes and practices of *silencing* and *being silenced*.[6] Can these processes be brought to account while exploring and enacting the possibilities and limits of developing alternative ways to narrate racialized lives into being? In 'Genres of History and the Practice of Loss: Attending to Silence in Hazel Carby's *Imperial Intimacies*', Marisa J. Fuentes goes to the heart of the dilemma of black feminist critique, practice and methodology – an archival struggle that is enacted on the page.[7] Previously, in her *Dispossessed Lives: Enslaved Women, Violence, and the Archive*, she brilliantly showed how she stretches 'archival fragments by *reading along the bias grain* to eke out extinguished and invisible but no less historically important lives'.[8]

The process of disentangling the fragments of the lives of racialized subjects in diaspora from the colonial archives and reassembling them into *Imperial Intimacies* fractured this writer's sense of being as narrator. For Édouard Glissant, 'every diaspora is the passage from unity to multiplicity.' He describes departure as 'the moment when one consents not to be a single being and attempts to be many beings at the same time' and arrival as 'the moment where all the components of humanity – not just the African ones – consent to the idea that it is possible to be one and multiple at the same time; that you can be yourself and the other; that you can be the same and different'.[9] The tension between the multiple forms of narration in *Imperial Intimacies* and its multivocality reproduce the conceptual, practical and theoretical difficulties of an immersive struggle to create a counterhistory in spite of the fictions and limitations of the archives.

To research and teach the black diaspora is an exercise in radical critical thought and practice which unsettles modes and methods of dominant knowledge formations and divisions. As Fuentes argues persuasively, this is not merely a question of genre, for what is at stake in bringing counterhistories into being through writing and publishing runs counter to the interests of furthering an academic career. The former contests the power of disciplinary genres, boundaries and methodologies; the latter requires acceding to the reproduction of conventional disciplinary structures, forms, tropes and canons.

In 'An Intimate History of Empire', an intellectually generous close reading of *Imperial Intimacies*, Marc Matera points to the importance of form, of finding 'more intimate and contingent modes of storytelling than academic history writing', forms of writing that can reach into 'those intimate spaces and practices of empire and racialization' inaccessible through the archives.[10]

Writing into the complex entanglements of diaspora that have arisen from its circuits of movement appeared to her at some moments to be a project of immense possibility, at others an insurmountable, impossible task. She had so many questions about the many departures and arrivals:

> Is it possible to produce a reckoning of movement between and among places, spaces and peoples, the scattering that results in racialized encounters and the violent transactions that produce racialized subjects? Pitting memory, history and poetics against each other in a narrative of racial encounters is intended to undermine the binary thinking that opposes colonial centre to colonized margin, home to abroad, and metropole to periphery. Does it matter *where* encounters between Africans and Europeans, between those constructed as 'black' and as 'white' take place: in an African or English village, town, or city; if they occur in the impenetrable darkness of the dungeon of a coastal fort, or in the claustrophobic hold of a slave ship, or take place, face to face, in the glaring light reflected from the Atlantic Ocean; if they are confrontations on the shores of a Caribbean island or on the streets of a metropolitan imperial city? Perhaps it is not,

in fact, only the place that is significant but also the manner of the journey and arrival, the eager walking, or manacled stumble, the panicked flight, or forced or voluntary sailing toward and away from each other.[11]

Unearthing racialized existence from the complex layering of the colonial archives became a geological exercise, the labour of research a form of stratigraphy, a slow gradual revelation of the remains of lives lived on a scale of history vastly different to the temporal organization of the archive itself. She had no expectation that the labour of excavation through the imperial layering of historical knowledge would forge a direct path to liberation from the material conditions of oppression and she knew there was no social justice to be mined.

From the moment of her entry into the archives as a researcher, she was compromised by its system of classification and language of dissimulation.[12] To locate the registers of enslaved people, she had to search for 'property' within the financial records of Her Majesty's Treasury and the Office of Registry of Colonial Slaves and Slave Compensation Commission, which had been charged with reimbursing those designated as owners of human beings for loss of their 'property' on emancipation. Even if she had to follow this system of classification, it could not be allowed to dictate the shape of her narrative. Her work, her storytelling, had to enact her refusal to validate the terms and conditions of the world in which those records were created and refute the world that maintained and authenticated them. She tentatively began her own search for a language of disruption and contradiction.

Rejecting the easy assurance of the singular self, the apparently simple 'I' used to mark subjectivity, she embraced instability, probing the conflicting motives of the researcher, the writer, the daughter and the black woman descended from those she was to locate in the archives. The process of research and writing required becoming aware of and struggling against the indecision and immobility rooted in the tension between intentions and desires. She seized ambivalence as an opportunity, a critical awareness, the possibility of grasping historical consciousness, an important recognition of the fictional nature of a unified self.

17

The National Archives

I dressed conservatively; I did not appear to be a disruptive or unruly researcher. I was indistinguishable from the others who arrived at the National Archives early in the morning and who stood, patiently, waiting for the doors to open while swans, graceful in their every movement, nuzzled the weeds underwater. As they raised their long necks and droplets of water rolled on the surface of feather, I become aware of my own poor posture and straightened my spine. We who left late in the evening passed through doors that rapidly closed behind us, and did not notice swans. We marched together to and from the Kew Gardens Tube station everyday carrying computers and clutching umbrellas, too intent on our work to acknowledge each other with more than a brief incline of the head and half-smile. After leaving the locker room and climbing the stairs, all similarity with my fellow travellers ceased: they seem to parse the same historical manuscripts day after day, while I sought to undermine the edifice of knowledge to which I was granted generous access.

I was exposed but felt completely in the dark. Florescent light was diffused across the room from large grey rectangles embedded in the ceiling. Behind me was a wall of glass through which, if I wanted to turn, I could have seen the sky, swans, geese, ducks swimming on a pond, and the Royal Botanic Gardens at Kew. The wings of jumbo jets landing at Heathrow Airport skimmed the roofs of the neighbourhood but, inside the room, the roar of their Rolls Royce engines was muted. Like everyone else at work in The National Archives of the UK, I was hermetically sealed away from bird song, from the smell of wet soil, from the fragrance of shrubs and flowers, from the drone of London traffic, from the sounds and rhythms of everyday life.

The building precludes distraction, natural and artificial light illuminate inconspicuous interiors. This room is designed to promise transparency in all transactions: a promise that nothing will be withheld or concealed, that everything can be known. In this vacuum of light, no shadows would dare fall to obscure, disguise or blunt the edges of documented truths bound in files and books and papers tied together with ribbon. Uniform exposure to the light offers assurance that what is past can be recovered, made easily accessible and available to all who have the time to sit and stare.[1] Revelation, however, does not ensure accountability.

That morning, in early summer, I sat at a computer workstation searching the catalogue, *Discovery*. What eventually surfaced on the screen sent a jolt through my spine; the sudden movement caused the four wheels on my chair to roll across the surface of the industrial-strength floor covering. A nondescript weave of rectangles in multiple shades of soft grays, the carpet duplicated the shapes on the ceiling. There was nothing in either pattern to catch the eye and distract attention from the serious business of research.

A room full of people thinking is quiet but it is not silent. There was a low-frequency hum of constant activity, pages were turned, documents were scanned and delivered, but all motion was circumspect – coughs, sneezes and ahems were stifled. My urge to exclaim was strangled in my throat and, when I glanced over my shoulder, I was relieved to see that the abrupt movement of my chair had not attracted attention or disrupted the gentle flow of hush that washed across the room. I had found what I set out to discover but I was staring at the carpet instead of the catalogue entries. I was reluctant to submit the call numbers that would trigger the delivery of materials to 14B, the number of my bright orange cubby and dull green desk.

My search was for financial matters, for 'property'. Methodically I had found 'Records created or inherited by Her Majesty's Treasury', and within them the 'Records of Commissions and Committees . . . [which] reflect core Treasury functions such as financial and establishment matters'. I felt compromised by the language of the system of classification, the language of dissimulation I was forced to follow. I refuse the terms and conditions that shaped the world in which these records were created. I need different language, a different map, different truths.[2]

I temporarily avoided the object of my search, what I had at some point to confront, by thinking instead about the structure of the classification system that determined my path. The catalogue consisted of a hierarchy of terms which organized knowledge. The intention is to provide a gradual progression, a descent into the 'matters' for which any researcher seeks. However, when I found the 'matter' I was looking for I was not sure that I wanted to see it. Persistence, being determined to find out, to know, to interrogate, kept me in my chair, but I was also cautious, hesitant, weighing and calculating the costs of finding out.

I considered the source of my hesitation, my fractured sense of being, my loss of a singular I who knew what she wanted. I probed my conflicting motivations as a researcher, as a daughter, as a black woman descended from those I was about to find; I weighed opposing outcomes and fought the indecision and immobility rooted in the tension between intentions and desires. I wanted to seize my ambivalence as an opportunity, a moment of historical consciousness, an important recognition of the fictional nature of a unified self. There is no simple 'I', marking subjectivity here. Having fallen down the equivalent of Charles L. Dodgson's rabbit hole, I needed to take stock, to reassemble my multiple selves and motives, to pull myself together and catch my breath. The organization of knowledge in the classification system appeared, on its surface, perfectly logical, in accord with established pathways to enlightenment, but I landed not in the light of knowledge but beneath its surface, in the soil where it began to take shape, in the blackness where the roots of enlightenment become entangled with the rhizomes of unreason.

The architecture and pathways of the chamber of knowing in which I found myself are the product of a history I have spent a career contesting and challenging. In 'Commissions and Committees', I tunnelled through 'various bodies dealing with compensation and other issues relating to slavery, land and war', until I encountered the records of the 'Office of Registry of Colonial Slaves and Slave Compensation Commission', which took the form of a Cheshire Cat curled up in the darkest corner of its burrow, in wait for me. Its grin widened, its maw opened and its body dissolved, leaving the words 'Slave Compensation Commission' behind, hovering in the atmosphere of fetid breath.

I was unsure of my footing, balanced precariously on the terrain of treachery as well as dissimulation. In an alternative world, a world that was just and equitable, the title 'slave compensation' would mean that the brief of this commission was to compensate the enslaved for the theft of their selves, of their labour, of their offspring and of their future: compensation for the wealth wrung from their agony; wealth generated from lives of unremitting toil; wealth welling up from an inundation of tears, of pain, of frustration and of fury, flooding the hold of slave ships, watering the unforgiving soil of plantations, nurturing the seeds of rebellion. Immense wealth, produced by the labour of generations of enslaved human beings, enriched and consumed within the colonial heart of empire; generations of labourers were rewarded with immiseration and ineffable physical and psychological violence.

The language of the archives is specious; duplicity burdens research with a terrible weight. I forced myself to pause; I closed my eyes and indulged in the comfort of fantasy. It seemed important to dwell, just for a moment, on the possibility that compensation might actually have been granted *to* the enslaved instead of enriching those who, on paper, and in the eyes of Her Majesty's Treasury, were designated owners of their bodies. I held my breath.

There should be space for alternative realities, alternative ways of knowing, in the archive. There should be room for imagining a world in which justice, not injustice, triumphed, a world where wealth had been returned to those who had produced it, but I knew that I was wasting time, that no one should look to the colonial archives for social justice. To complete the task at hand I forced breath back into my lungs, opened my eyes, lifted my chin, clenched my jaw and continued to search. Committees and commissions are not the only bodies buried here in boxes and files and tied with ribbon and string; truths, by any measure or definition, are difficult, if not impossible, to excavate, to expose to the light. Over the course of ten years I followed the White Rabbit, confronting and interrogating colonial archives in London and in Kingston, Jamaica, in search of records.

In 1816, the British government instituted a process to register all of the enslaved in every territory of its empire. Human beings who lived and breathed were confined within the straitjackets of columns and bound within ledgers: 'REGISTRATION', 'SLAVE REGISTERS'. By 1817, the first year of registration was complete and henceforth, until emancipation, records of 'increase' and 'decrease' were updated every three years. 'Increase' covered birth and purchase. 'Decrease' covered sale, escape, being sent to the workhouse and death, but did not distinguish between death from torture, from punishment, from disease or from a broken heart. The language of these documents confirms that the only interest in keeping these registers of bodies was as accounts of profit and/or loss.

What life raft of reason is within reach of descendants of those listed in these account books of enslavement, of empire? Is there hope, comfort or escape to be found in remembering only those who survived? I grieved for lives maimed, destroyed, cut short. If someone I found disappeared without explanation from a subsequent record, I hoped they ran, ran fast and far, and renamed themselves so as to be forever hidden from capture by former owners and the archives. Records of those condemned, viciously punished and murdered stilled me.

As each person in the register was recorded they were categorized not as a human being but as property by HM Treasury. This practice of dehumanization is preserved and reproduced, without end, in the language and structure of classification: the headings, subheadings and definitions. No one should imagine that entering this archive is journeying back in time to a history that is past, that is over. Travelling through the archive imposes an experience of time that is not linear, but circuitous. A passage through the living language of humans as property is an ever-present entrapment in, and assertion of, the *right to own*; it is a continual imposition of subjection and endless possession. To enter this archive is to become conscripted into an ongoing process of trading in flesh.

In Portland, Jamaica, in 1817,[3]

> John Carby Negro 6 years old Creole

is listed as:

> son of Nancy 30 years old African

I followed broken threads of information written into ledgers by the hands of clerks who cared about tallying numbers, detailing property and establishing ownership, but had no care for the accuracy of the names of this 'property', for they did not regard 'it' as human. I found precious but inconsistent traces of more than one Rose Munro: in Hanover, an enslaved Rose Munro, African, 'said' to be twenty-six years old in 1817, was 'registered' as thirty-eight years old in 1829; in Kingston in 1820, a Rose Munro, free black, eight months old, was baptized (a daughter, I wondered?); in 1822, the manumission of a Rose Munro for ten shillings is recorded.[4]

I have utilized the tension between my working self as scholar and as a descendant, a daughter, a granddaughter and a great-granddaughter. I created connections between disparate threads of ancestry, followed the name Rose as it passed through generations until bestowed, as if a gift, upon my grandmother, Millicent Rose Munro, who, known simply as Rose, gave birth to my father in Kingston, Jamaica in 1921. I knew that I would be able to assemble only fragments of histories and traces of ancestors, that I could not recreate the lives of all of those from plantations even though I found this conclusion unacceptable. As a daughter and granddaughter, I was left bereft, dissatisfied and unsettled that lives silenced in and by the archives and by enslavement are irretrievable.

In the large document room, I walked to and from the reserve desk carrying large grey boxes. They were bulky and heavy. Inside each box was a single volume of triennial returns for the parishes of Portland and St Georges, Jamaica, beginning in 1817, and continuing through 1820, 1823, 1829 and 1832. I clutched each box tightly to my chest, using my body as a brace, afraid that one would slip from my arms, fall and burst apart, spilling its contents over the floor. As I reached a table, I lowered each box, gently, and removed a white cotton ribbon.

The passage of time was marked not by the measure of seconds, minutes and hours but by the repetitious nature of my movements, which assumed the character of ritual. I stood with bent back, lifted a lid, set it aside, and stared down at the contents of a box while the first of many clouds of particles I disturbed rose and settled. Squeezing my fingers between the interior edges of each box and a register I gripped each tome and lifted. When these ledgers were created, copied, bound, transported across the Atlantic and stored, did officials of the British Treasury imagine that, like their empire, these records would last forever?

Tropical environments, humidity, insects, ocean journeys, human neglect, defeated the aims of clerks to preserve records in the form they intended: book boards, with marbled covers separated from their spine and signatures, bindings have partially disintegrated, rag paper pages have been attacked by mould, but most of the stitching has held. As I searched through the registers and turned page after page, it was as if the particles of hemp, linen, cotton and board that constituted these ledgers of the long dead had a consciousness, were seeking to attach themselves to me, refusing to be neglected or left behind: reddish orange, brown and cream fragments drifted around me, covered my clothes and worked their way inside, stuck to my skin, settled in my hair.

I was unable to leave the dead, who cleaved to me. When I walked from the archive to the tube station I left a trail of fragments in my wake; on the train I stood in a pall of residue. In the shower I watched as particles flushed down the drain, when I woke they were on my pillow; I left remains in the house of my closest friends. When I passed through customs and border control on the other side of the Atlantic, I wondered, should I declare that I carried this residue on my person and in my heart?

Acknowledgements

The essays in this volume previously appeared in the following publications:

'We must burn them', *London Review of Books*, vol. 44, no. 10, 26 May 2022.

'Peine forte et dure', *London Review of Books*, vol. 42 no. 15, 30 July 2020.

'Safe? At Home?', Feminist Review blog, 07 June 2020.

'US/UK's Special Relationship: The Culture of Torture in Abu Ghraib and Lynching Photographs' (draft), final version published in *NKA*, vol. 61 (Fall 2006).

'Aftermath' (draft), final version published in *Souls: A Critical Journal of Black Politics, Culture, and Society*, vol. 4, no. 1 (30 November 2010).

'What Is This "Black" in Irish Popular Culture?' (draft), final version published in *European Journal of Cultural Studies*, vol. 4, no. 3 (2001).

'Promoting Blackness', unpublished lecture delivered Center for Culture and History of Black Diaspora, DePaul University, 23 May 2001.

'Figuring the Future in Los(t) Angeles' (draft), final version published in *Comparative American Studies*, vol. 1, no. 1, 23 May 2001.

'The Work of Claudia Tate', lecture published in 'African American Intellectuals Symposium', *Journal of African American History*, vol. 88, no. 1 (Winter 2003).

'The New Auction Block: Blackness and the Marketplace' (draft), final version published in Lewis Gordon (ed.), *Companion to African American Studies* (London: Blackwell, 2005).

'Black Feminism' (conference paper), Feminism in the World panel, Arab Feminism: A Critical Perspective, American University of Beirut, 2009, published in Jean Said Makdisi, Noha Bayoumi and Rafif Sidawi (eds), *Arab Feminisms: A Critical Perspective* (Beirut: Center for Arab Unity Studies, 2013).

'Between Black and White', *London Review of Books*, vol. 43, no. 2 (7 January 2021).

'Making Race Matter', (draft) final version published as 'Foreword', in Claire Alexander and Caroline Knowles (eds), *Making Race Matter: Bodies, Space and Identity* (Basingstoke and New York: Palgrave Macmillan, 2005).

'Lost (and Found?) in Translation' (lecture), Reconstructing Womanhood: A Future Beyond Empire, a Symposium, Columbia University, 2007, revised version published in *Small Axe*, vol. 28 (March 2009).

'Becoming Modern Racialized Subjects: "detours through our pasts to produce ourselves anew"', (draft) final version published in *Cultural Studies*, vol. 23 (4 July 2009).

'*Imperial Intimacies*: Further Thoughts', *Small Axe,* vol. 64 (March 2021).

'The National Archives', *Invisible Culture*, vol. 31 (15 November 2020).

Notes

Preface

1 For a recent example see Hazel V. Carby, 'The Limits of Caste', *London Review of Books*, 43, 2 (21 January 2020), at lrb.co.uk.

2 See Hazel V. Carby, 'Imagining Otherwise', in Michael W. Hartman and Jami C. Powell (eds.), *Reenvisioning Histories of American Art: Transforming Museum Practice* (Seattle: The Hood Museum of Art, Dartmouth, in association with the University of Washington Press, 2025), pp. 168–90.

3 All figures of wealth inequalities are drawn from 'Income Inequality', at Inequality.org (accessed 23 November 2024); and 'Global Inequality', at Inequality.org (accessed 23 November 2024).

4 Lonnie Bunch III, 'Why Is America Afraid of Black History?', *Atlantic*, 13 November 2023.

4. US/UK's Special Relationship

1 Quoted in Robert J. C. Young, *Postcolonialism: A Very Short Introduction* (Oxford: Oxford University Press, 2003), pp. 34–5.

2 Douglas Little, *American Orientalism: The United States and the Middles East since 1945* (Chapel Hill: University of North Carolina Press, 2002), p. 5.

3 Tania Branigan, 'Analysis: The Known Unknowns,' *Guardian*, 15 June 2004, p. 17.

4 Seymour Hersh, 'Torture at Abu Ghraib', *New Yorker*, 10 May 2004, p. 42.

5 See Neil A. Lewis, 'Documents Build a Case for Working Outside the Laws on Interrogating Prisoners', *New York Times*, 9 June 2004, p. A8; and *NPR Morning Edition*, 2 July 2004, at npr.org.
6 MG Antonio M. Taguba, 'Article 15-6 Investigation of the 800th Military Police Brigade' (the Taguba report), pp. 16–17.
7 Susan Sontag, 'Regarding the Torture of Others', *New York Times Magazine*, 23 May 2004, pp. 24–9, 42.
8 See James Allen (ed.), *Without Sanctuary: Lynching Photography in America* (Santa Fe, NM: Twin Palms Publishers, 2000).
9 Taguba report, p. 17.
10 Taguba report, p. 19.
11 See Sven Lindqvist, *Exterminate All the Brutes* (New York: The New Press, 1996), p. 157.

5. Aftermath

1 Arundhati Roy, 'The Algebra of Infinite Justice', at guardian.co.uk.
2 As reported on NPR, 3 October 2001, there were thirteen days of bad air in the year 2000. There have already been twenty-five days of air designated as bad as of 1 October 2001.

6. What Is This 'Black' in Irish Popular Culture?

1 Stuart Hall, 'What Is This "Black" in Black Popular Culture', in Gina Dent (ed.), *Black Popular Culture* (Seattle: Bay Press, 1992), p. 21.
2 William T. Lhamon Jr, *Raising Cain: Blackface Performance from Jim Crow to Hip Hop* (Cambridge, MA: Harvard University Press, 1998), p. 68.
3 Paul Gilroy, *The Black Atlantic* (Cambridge, MA: Harvard University Press, 1997).
4 Eric Lott, *Love and Theft: Blackface Minstrelsy and the American Working Class* (New York: Oxford University Press, 1995), p. 53.
5 Stuart Hall, 'Race, Articulation and Societies Structured In Dominance', in *Sociological Theories: Race and Colonialism* (Paris: UNESCO, 1980), pp. 305–45.

6 Terry Eagleton, *Crazy John and the Bishop and Other Essays on Irish Culture* (Cork: Cork University Press, 1988), pp. 312–13.
7 Elaine Dutka, 'Lord of the Dance Inc.', *Los Angeles Times*, 26 August 1998, p. F1.
8 See Jann Parry and Gary Parks, 'The Irish Dance Phenomenon: Celtic Crossover', *Dance Magazine* vol 71, no. 10 (October 1997), p. 70.
9 For the purposes of this essay I will be referring to filmed performances available on video as follows: *Riverdance: The Show*, directed by John McColgan, Tyrone/RTE Video, Columbia Tristar, 1995; *Riverdance: Live from New York City*, directed by John McColgan, Tyrone Productions, Columbia Tristar, 1997; *Michael Flatley: Lord of the Dance*, directed by David Mallet, PolyGram 1997; and 'The Making of' *Michael Flatley: Lord of the Dance*, directed by David Mallet, PolyGram 1997.
10 Parry and Parks, 'The Irish Dance Phenomenon', p. 70.
11 Ibid.
12 See Hazel V. Carby, 'Lethal Weapons and City Games', in Hazel V. Carby, *Race Men* (Cambridge, MA: Harvard University Press, 1998), pp. 167–91.
13 Carby, *Race Men*, 1998.
14 Frederick Douglass (1855), *My Bondage and My Freedom*, rpt (Chicago: Johnson Publishing Company, 1970), p. 76; Frederick Douglass, 'Letter to William Lloyd Garrison', 26 February 1846, in *The Life and Writings of Frederick Douglass: Early Years, 1817–1849* (ed. Phillip S. Foner) (New York: International Publishers, 1950), pp. 138–41. Douglass had to struggle to understand the causes behind the conditions which so appalled him. At first, he blamed this poverty on drunkenness but later came to understand that English imperialism was the common factor in the exploitation of Irish and African American peoples. See Frederick Douglass, 'The Position of the British Government Toward Liberty', in *The Life and Writings of Frederick Douglass: Reconstruction and After* (ed. Phillip S. Foner) (New York: International Publishers, 1955), pp. 266–9.
15 Frederick Douglass, 'Letter to William Lloyd Garrison', 28 October 1845, in *The Life and Writings of Frederick Douglass: Supplementary Volume, 1844–1860* (ed. Philip S. Foner) (New York: International Publishers, 1975), p. 7, emphasis in original.
16 Matthew Frye Jacobson, *Whiteness of a Different Colour: European Immigrants and the Alchemy of Race* (Cambridge, MA: Harvard University Press, 1998), pp. 15, 48–9.

17 See Brenda Dixon Gottschild, *Digging the Africanist Presence in American Performance* (Westport, CT: Greenwood Press, 1996).
18 Jacqui Malone, *Steppin' on the Blues: The Visible Rhythms of African American Dance* (Urbana: University of Illinois Press, 1996), p. 32.
19 Marshal Stearns and Jean Stearns, *Jazz Dance* (New York: Macmillan, 1968), pp. 146–7, 157, 201–3.
20 Michael Flatley in *The Making of Michael Flatley: Lord of the Dance.*
21 'Brace Yourself: A Kaleidoscope of Michael Jackson HIStory', *Michael Jackson Video Greatest Hits – HIStory*, Epic Music Video, MJJ Ventures, 1995.
22 Charles Dickens, *American Notes for General Circulation* (London: Chapman and Hall, 1842), pp. 215–16, 218.
23 See 'Black or White', on *Michael Jackson Video Greatest Hits.*
24 Lhamon, *Raising Cain*, p. 151.
25 George G. Foster, *New York by Gas-Light and Other Urban Sketches* (Berkely: University of California Press, 1990), p. 142–3.
26 See Stearns and Stearns, *Jazz Dance*, p. 173.
27 See Sidney Kaplan, 'The Miscegenation Issue in the Election of 1864', *Journal of Negro History*, vol. 34. no. 3 (1949), pp. 274–343.
28 Ibid., p. 281–2.
29 Roddy Doyle, *The Commitments* (New York: Vintage Books, 1989), p. 113

7. Promoting Blackness

1 These are reflections that would later appear in Hazel V. Carby, *Imperial Intimacies: A Tale of Two Islands* (London: Verso, 2021).
2 See, for example, Rinaldo Walcott, *Black Like Who?* (Toronto: Insomniac Press, 1997).
3 See, for example, Kim D. Butler, *Freedoms Given, Freedoms Won: Afro-Brazilians in Post-abolition São Paulo and Salvador* (New Brunswick, NJ: Rutgers University Press, 1998); and Michael Hanchard (ed.), *Racial Politics in Contemporary Brazil* (Durham, NC: Duke University Press, 1999).
4 See, for example, Orlando Patterson, *The Ordeal of Integration: Progress and Resentment in American's 'Racial' Crisis* (Washington, DC: Civitas/Counterpoint, 1997); and Orlando Patterson, *Rituals of Blood: Consequences of Slavery in Two*

American Centuries (Washington, DC: Civitas/Counterpoint, 1998), where he proposes that 'Euro-American' should be substituted for the term 'white'. In suggesting such a substitution Patterson is drawing upon a common sense understanding that, indeed, Europe is, simply and completely, white.

5 Paul Gilroy also makes this point very forcefully in *Against Race* (Cambridge, MA: Harvard University Press, 2000).

6 Stuart Hall, 'Racism and Reaction', in Stuart Hall, *Five Views of Multi-racial Britain* (London: Commission on Racial Equality), 1978.

7 Gilroy, *Against Race*.

8 The theory of double consciousness is a concept similar to Lacan's work on the mirror phase but it pre-dates it by thirty years. It is a sign of the field's parochial tendencies that instead of comparing these two concepts, double consciousness is taken as a sign of blackness only.

9 Henry Louis Gates Jr and Cornel West, *The Future of the Race* (New York: Knopf, 1996).

10 See Angela Davis, 'Masked Racism: Reflections on the Prison Industrial Complex', *Colour Lines: Race, Culture, Action*, vol. 1, no. 2 (Fall 1998), pp. 11–17; Eric Sclosser, 'The Prison–Industrial Complex', *Atlantic Monthly*, December 1998, pp. 51–77. See also the publications on the websites of Human Rights Watch at hrw.org and the Sentencing Project at sentencingproject.org.

11 See Hazel V. Carby, 'What Is This Black in Irish Popular Culture?', *European Journal of Cultural Studies*, vol. 4 (2001), pp. 325–49 and earlier in this volume.

12 I urged that these connections be made in a paper titled 'ETHNY2K: From Black Souls to Immigrant Acts', delivered at the Asian American Studies Conference held in Philadelphia, 1 April 1999. I draw upon my remarks there in what follows.

13 Lisa Lowe, *Immigrant Acts: On Asian American Cultural Politics* (Durham, NC: Duke University Press, 1996), particularly chapter one.

14 See Tera W. Hunter, *To 'Joy My Freedom: Southern Black Women's Lives and Labors After the Civil War Cambridge* (Cambridge, MA: Harvard University Press, 1997).

15 See Immanual Wallerstein, 'The Bourgeois(ie) as Concept and Reality', chapter nine of Etienne Balibar and Immanuel Wallerstein, *Race, Nation, Class: Ambiguous Identities* (London: Verso, 1991), pp. 135–52.

16 Antonio Gramsci, *Selections from the Prison Notebooks* (London: Lawrence and Wishart, 1971), pp. 8–9.

17 See Hazel V. Carby, 'The New Auction Block: Blackness and the Marketplace', in Lewis Gordon (ed.), *Companion to African American Studies* (London: Blackwell 2005), pp. 119–35.

8. Figuring the Future in Los(t) Angeles

1 Todd S. Purdum, 'A 200 Million School That May Never Open', *New York Times*, 28 July 1999, p. A12.
2 It was announced that the project had been abandoned on *Morning Edition*, National Public Radio, 26 January 2000.
3 Helen Gao, 'Belmont's New Woes: Earthquake Fault Found under Trouble-Plagued School', *Daily News of Los Angeles*, 14 September 2002, p. N1.
4 Mike Davis, *Ecology of Fear* (New York: Metropolitan Books, 1998), p. 354.
5 Ibid., p. 278.
6 Ibid., p. 355.
7 Ibid., p. 276.
8 Edward Soja, "Seeking Spatial Justice in Los Angeles," *My Los Angeles: From Urban Restructuring to Regional Urbanization* (Berkeley: University of California Press, 2014), pp. 219–46.
9 Karina Vernon, 'The Black Arctic: Literature and Subjectivity in Black British Columbia', paper presented at the Black Atlantic Graduate Symposium, Purdue University, 21–3 March 2002, p. 3; Wayde Compton, *Bluesprint: Black British Columbian Literature and Orature* (Vancouver: Arsenal Pulp, 2001).
10 James Holston and Arjun Appadurai, 'Introduction: Cities and Citizenship', in James Holston (ed.), *Cities and Citizenship* (Durham, NC: Duke University Press, 1999), p. 3.
11 Chester Himes, *The Quality of Hurt: The Early Years* (New York: Paragon House, 1971), p. 73.
12 Chester Himes, *If He Hollers Let Him Go* (New York: Signet, 1971; first published 1945), pp. 23–4.
13 Ibid., pp. 7–8, emphasis in original.
14 David Harvey, *Justice, Nature, and the Geography of Difference* (Cambridge, MA: Blackwell, 1996).
15 Holston and Appadurai, p. 3.
16 I would agree with David Harvey that a socialist politics needs to come to terms with issues of geographic scale – as he puts it, 'to negotiate between and link across different spatial scales of social

theorizing and political action'. Harvey, *Justice, Nature, and the Geography of Difference*, pp. 41–2.

17 Himes, *The Quality of Hurt*, p. 76.

18 David Harvey has argued that 'theory is never a matter of pure abstraction. *Theoretical practice* must be constructed as a continuous dialectic between the militant particularism of lived lives and a struggle to achieve sufficient critical distance and detachment to formulate global ambitions' (emphasis in original). Harvey demonstrates how we can utilize fiction in the crucial task of 'building a critical, materialist, and thoroughly grounded ... understanding of places, space and social theory'. Harvey, *Justice, Nature, and the Geography of Difference*, p. 44. Novels, he feels, are 'not subject to closure in the same way that more analytic forms of thinking are. There are always differences, subtle shifts in structures of feeling,' he concludes, 'all of which stand to alter the terms of debate and political action even under the most difficult and dire of conditions'. Ibid., p. 28.

19 Donna Haraway (*Simians, Cyborgs, and Women: The Reinvention of Nature* [New York: Routledge, 1991], quoted in Harvey, *Justice, Nature, and the Geography of Difference*, p. 284) argues that

> the topography of subjectivity is multi-dimensional; so, therefore, is vision. The knowing self is partial in all its guises, never finished, whole, simply there and original; it is always constructed and stitched together imperfectly, and therefore able to join with another, to see together without claiming to be another. Here is the promise of objectivity; a scientific knower seeks the subject position not of identity but of objectivity; that is of partial connection.

20 Octavia Butler, *Clay's Ark* (New York: Warner Books, 1984), p. 34. *Clay's Ark* concerns the transmission of disease organisms brought back to Earth by a lone survivor of a space mission. The processes of transmission and spread of these organisms provide Butler with literary opportunities to discuss the complex relations of self and other and the struggles for power and control that are similar to her use of the pattern.

21 Octavia Butler, *Parable of the Talents* (New York: Seven Stories Press, 1998).

22 Octavia Butler, *Parable of the Sower* (New York: Four Walls Eight Windows, 1993), p. 11.

23 Ibid., p. 18.

24 Ibid., pp. 47–8.

25 Harvey, *Justice, Nature, and the Geography of Difference*, p. 245.
26 Ibid., p. 44.
27 Butler, *Parable of the Sower*, p. 9.
28 Ibid., p. 72.
29 Ibid., p. 77.
30 Ibid., p. 18.
31 Davis, *Ecology of Fear*, pp. 93–148.
32 Walter Mosley, *Always Outnumbered, Always Outgunned* (New York: Simon & Schuster, 1998), p. 181.
33 Ibid.
34 The Easy Rawlins series includes *Devil in a Blue Dress, A Red Death, Black Betty*, and most recently *Bad Boy Brawley Brown*. Paris Minton is the protagonist in *Fearless Jones*.
35 I would like to thank Rachel Rodewald for her astute reading and careful editing of this chapter.

10. The New Auction Block

1 Fredric Jameson, 'Reification and Utopia in Mass Culture', in *The Jameson Reader* (ed. Michael Hardt and Kathi Weeks) (Oxford: Basil Blackwell, Inc., 2000), p. 140.
2 Pierre Bourdieu, *Acts of Resistance: Against the Tyranny of the Market* (New York: The New Press, 1998), pp. 94–105; Salman Rushdie, *Fury* (New York: Random House, Inc., 2001).
3 'Black Women Image Makers', *Black World*, Vol. 23, no. 10 (August 1974), cover. *Black World*, published by the Johnson Publishing Company, began in 1942 as *Negro Digest*.
4 Barbara Christian, 'But What Do We Think We're Doing Anyway: The State of Black Feminist Criticism(s) or My Version of a Little Bit of History', in Cheryl A. Wall (ed.), *Changing Our Own Words* (New Brunswick, NJ: Rutgers University Press, 1989), p. 59.
5 Wall, *Changing Our Own Words*.
6 Hortense Spillers, 'Cross-currents, Discontinuities: Black Women's Fiction', in Marjorie Pryse and Hortense Spillers (eds.), *Conjuring: Black Women's Fiction, and Literary Tradition* (Bloomington: Indiana University Press, 1985), p. 245.
7 Wall, *Changing Our Own Words*, p. 1.
8 Ibid., 2.
9 Nancy Armstrong, 'Feminism and the Utopian Promise of Fiction', paper presented at The Future of Utopia: An Interdisciplinary

Conference in Honor of Fredric Jameson, Duke University, 24–7 April 2003.

10 Deborah E. McDowell, 'Reading Family Matters', in Wall, *Changing Our Own Words*, p. 75.

11 Mel Watkins, 'Sexism, Racism, and Black Women Writers', *New York Times Book Review*, 15 June 1986, pp. 1, 35.

12 McDowell, 'Reading Family Matters', pp. 76–7.

13 Ibid., p. 83.

14 For the purposes of this essay, by 'public' I mean publications outside academic journals and presses.

15 C. Wright Mills, 'The Cultural Apparatus', in *Power, Politics and People: The Collected Essays of C. Wright Mills* (ed. Irving Louis Horowitz) (New York: Ballantine Books, 1963), 406, emphasis in original.

16 Ibid.

17 Ann duCille, *Skin Trade* (Cambridge, MA: Harvard University Press, 1996), p. 81.

18 Ibid., p. 87.

19 Ibid.

20 Adam Begley, 'Henry Louis Gates Jr.: Black Studies New Star', *New York Times Magazine*, 1 April 1990, pp. 24–7, 48–50.

21 DuCille, *Skin Trade*, 92.

22 Begley, 'Henry Louis Gates Jr.', p. 26.

23 Ibid., p. 25.

24 Seventeen men and eight women contributed to the issue but there was a vast disparity in the substance of their contributions. Most of the female contributions were one page or less.

25 Wright Mills, 'The Cultural Apparatus', p. 409.

26 Russell Jacoby, *The Last Intellectuals* (New York: Basic, 1987), cited in Robert S. Boynton, 'The New Intellectuals', *Atlantic Monthly*, March 1995, pp. 53–6, 60, 62, 64–8, 70.

27 Michael Bérubé, 'Public Academy', *New Yorker*, vol. 70, no. 43 (9 January 1995), p. 74.

28 Ibid., p. 1.

29 Bérubé, 'Public Academy', p. 75.

30 Boynton, 'The New Intellectuals', p. 54.

31 Ibid., p. 53.

32 Bérubé, 'Public Academy', p. 74.

33 Boynton, 'The New Intellectuals', p. 56.

34 Bérubé, 'Public Academy'. p. 75.

35 Ibid., p. 73.

36 Boynton, 'The New Intellectuals', 56.

37 Ibid., pp. 60, 56.

38 Ibid., p. 70.
39 Eugene Rivers, 'On the Responsibility of Intellectuals in the Age of Crack', *Boston Review*, vol. 17 (September–October 1992), at bostonreview.mit.edu.
40 Ibid.
41 See *Boston Review*, vol. 18, no. 1 (January–February 1993) and vol. 19, no. 1 (February–March 1994).
42 See Eugene F. Rivers III, 'A New Black Nationalism', *Boston Review*, vol. 20, no. 3 (Summer 1995): n.p.
43 Robin D. G. Kelley, 'A Response to Eugene Rivers', *Boston Review*, vol. 20, no. 4 (October–November 1995): n.p.
44 Ibid.
45 Don Terry, 'Waters Are Roiled in the Civil Rights Mainstream', *New York Times*, 10 July 1994, p. E6.
46 Harold Cruse, *The Crisis of the Negro Intellectual: From Its Origins to the Present* (New York: William Morrow and Company, Inc., 1967).
47 Hortense J. Spillers, 'The Crisis of the Negro Intellectual: A Post-date', *Boundary* 2, vol. 21, no. 3 (Fall 1994), p. 73.
48 Salman Rushdie, *Fury* (New York: Random House, Inc., 2001), p. 3.
49 Ibid.
50 Ibid., p. 14.
51 Ibid., pp. 14–15.
52 Ibid., pp. 68–9, emphasis in original.
53 Ibid., pp. 193–4.
54 Ibid., pp. 87, 67.
55 Ibid., pp. 57–8.
56 Antonio Gramsci, 'The Intellectuals', in *Selections from the Prison Notebooks*, Q. Hoare and G. N. Smith (ed. and trans.), (New York: International Publishers,1971), pp. 3–23.
57 Slavoj Žižek, 'Multiculturalism, Or, the Cultural Logic of Multinational Capitalism', *New Left Review*, no. 225 (September–October 1997), p. 46, emphasis in original.
58 Roland Barthes, *Mythologies* (New York: Hill and Wang, 1972), p. 116.
59 IBM, 'In the Past, Resurrecting Texts That the World Forgot', *New Yorker*, 11 November 2002, pp. 22–3.
60 Barthes, *Mythologies*, p. 117.

11. Black Feminism

1 See Hazel V. Carby, *Reconstructing Womanhood* (New York: Oxford University Press, 1987).
2 'Black Feminism in the United Kingdom', at encyclopedia.jrank.org.
3 'Southall Black Sisters: Home', at southallblacksisters.org.uk.
4 Alliances have existed like that between African American and Latina lesbians in Salsa Soul Sisters and Third World Wimmin Inc. Collective, but the organization now exists as African Ancestral Lesbians United for Societal Change, the oldest black lesbian organization in the United States. 'Salsa Soul Sisters' at en.wikipedia.org.
5 See the INCITE! website at incite-national.org.
6 See 'World Social Forum', at Wikipedia.

13. Making Race Matter

1 Simon Schama, *Landscape and Memory* (New York: A.A. Knopf, 1995); W. E. B. Du Bois, *The Souls of Black Folk: Essays and Sketches*. Chicago: A. C. McClurg & Co., 1903.
2 Schama, *Landscape*, pp. 3–4.
3 Henry David Thoreau, journal, 30 August 1856, quoted in Schama, *Landscape*, p. 3.
4 Ibid., p. 15.
5 Ibid., p. 312.
6 Linda Colley, *Britons: Forging the Nation, 1707–1837* (New Haven, Conn.: Yale University Press, 2005), p. 9.
7 Ibid., p. 5.
8 Kathleen Paul, *Whitewashing Britain: Race and Citizenship in the Postwar Era* (Ithaca, NY: Cornell University Press, 1997), p. 9.
9 Ibid., p.26.
10 Niall Ferguson, *Empire: How Britain Made the Modern World* (London: Allen Lane, 2003), pp. xiii–xiv.
11 Claire E. Alexander and Caroline Knowles (eds), *Making Race Matter: Bodies, Space, and Identity* (Basingstoke, Hampshire: Palgrave Macmillan, 2005), p. 1.

14. Lost (and Found?) in Translation

1 The last Prince of Wales to be recognized as such by the English Crown was Llywelyn ap Gruffydd, who was overthrown by Edward I of England in 1282. The title fell into disuse until Glyndwr rebelled and made his claim to it.

2 I was taught to spell this as Caernarvon, the Anglicized version of the name of this town in Gwynedd and the version which Microsoft Word insists is the 'correct' spelling. Edward I of England built the castle when he defeated Llywelyn, since which point it has been a very visible sign and symbol of English domination. The choice of this site for the investiture therefore resonated with a history of contestation, of Welsh insurgency on the one hand and the maintenance and reinforcement of English claims to the territory and its people on the other. This contestation remains in the choice of spelling, in the selection of place for such a ceremony and in the coding of software.

3 Paul Richard Thompson, *The Edwardians: The Remaking of British Society* (Bloomington: Indiana University Press, 1975), p. 181.

4 Quoted in ibid., p. 181.

5 P. D. James, *Time to Be in Earnest: A Fragment of Autobiography* (London: Faber, 1999), p. 24.

6 Jane Madders and Grace Horseman, *Growing Up in the Twenties* (Bovey Tracey: Cottage Publishing, 1993), pp. 50, 55–6, 70.

7 James Carnegie, *Some Aspects of Jamaica's Politics, 1918–1938* (Kingston: Institute of Jamaica, 1973), p. 40, quoted in Erna Brodber, *The Second Generation of Freemen, 1907–1944* (Gainesville: University Press of Florida, 2004), p. 125.

8 Austin Clarke, *Growing Up Stupid under the Union Jack* (Toronto: Thomas Allen, 2005), pp. 56, 55.

9 This phrase is taken from the title of the study of Jamaica by Erna Brodber. As Brodber states. 'With the enactment of this legislation the exercise of the vote was no longer tied to a property ownership clause which had kept most African Jamaicans outside the formal political process.' Brodber, *The Second Generation of Freemen in Jamaica*, p. 2.

10 George Elliot Clarke, *George and Rue* (Toronto: HarperCollins), p. 14. See also the 'Author's Note' to the US edition.

11 Ruth Wilson Gilmore, *Golden Gulag: Prisons, Surplus, Crisis, and Opposition in Globalizing California* (Berkeley: University of California Press, 2007), p. 24.

12 Jamaica Kincaid, *The Autobiography of My Mother* (New York: Penguin, 1997), p. 79.

13 Ibid., p. 15.

14 Dr John Oldfield, University of Southampton, 'Hampshire's Slavery Links: The South and Transatlantic Slavery', at bbc.co.uk, accessed 19 October 2007.

15 Margaret Thatcher held the office of minister of education in the Conservative government led by Edward Heath from 1970 to 1974. In June 1971 this phrase was screamed in the streets by striking teachers, of which I was one, protesting the abolition of the programme which supplied free school milk, one of the earliest of Thatcher's attacks on the welfare state. Thatcher became leader of the opposition 1975 and prime minister in 1979.

16 Paulo Freire, *Pedagogy of the Oppressed* (New York: Seabury Press, 1970).

17 Stuart Hall and Tony Jefferson (eds.), *Resistance through Rituals: Youth Subcultures in Post-war Britain* (London: Hutchinson, 1976); Centre for Contemporary Cultural Studies, University of Birmingham, *On Ideology* (London: Hutchinson, 1978).

18 An earlier version of this narrative appears in the introduction to the 'Race' section of Ann Gray, Jan Campbell, Mark Erickson, Stuart Hanson and Helen Wood (eds.), *CCCS Selected Working Papers*, vol. 2 (London: Routledge, 2007).

15. Becoming Modern Racialized Subjects

1 Stuart Hall, 'Old and New Identities, Old and New Ethnicities', in Anthony D. King (ed.), *Culture, Globalization and the World System: Contemporary Conditions for the Representation of Identity* (Minneapolis: University of Minnesota Press), p. 49.

2 Stuart Hall, 'Race, Articulation and Societies Structured in Dominance', in *Sociological Theories: Race and Colonialism* (Paris: UNESCO), p. 305; Michel Foucault, *'Society Must Be Defended': Lectures at the Collège de France 1975–1976* (New York: Picador, 2003), p. 45.

3 Stuart Hall, 'The Local and the Global: Globalization and Ethnicity', in King, *Culture, Globalization and the World System*, p. 20.

4 Anna Lowenhaupt Tsing, *Friction: An Ethnography of Global Connection* (Princeton, NJ: Princeton UniversityPress, 2005), pp. 4–5.

5 Antonio Gramsci, *Selections from the Prison Notebooks* (London: Lawrence and Wishart, 1971), p. 323. This emerging racial state provides the context for my current work in progress, *Child of Empire*.

6 Hall, 'Old and New Identities, Old and New Ethnicities', p. 42.

7 Hall, 'Negotiating Caribbean Identities'; Stuart Hall, 'When Was "the Post-colonial"? Thinking at the Limit', in Iain Chambers and Lidia Curti (eds.), *The Post-colonial Question: Common Skies, Divided Horizons* (London: Routledge, 1996), pp. 242–60; Hall, 'The Local and the Global'; Hall, 'Old and New Identities, Old and New Ethnicities'; Hall, 'Thinking the Diaspora'.

8 Hall, 'When Was "the Post-colonial"?', p. 242, emphasis in original.

9 Stuart Hall, 'Gramsci's Relevance for the Study of Race and Ethnicity', *Journal of Communication Inquiry*, vol. 10, no. 2 (Summer 1986), p. 22.

10 Bob Marley, 'Redemption Song', on Bob Marley, *Uprising* (Tuff Gong/Island Records, 1980).

11 Laura Tabili, *'We Ask for British Justice': Workers and Racial Difference in Late Imperial Britain* (Ithaca, NY: Cornell University Press, 1994), p. 4.

12 Hall, 'Negotiating Caribbean Identities', p. 8.

13 Vincent Caretta, *Equiano the African: Biography of a Self-Made Man* (Athens: University of Georgia Press, 2005), p. 366.

14 Olaudah Equiano, *The Interesting Narrative of the Life of Olaudah Equiano, Or, Gustavus Vassa, The African, Written by Himself* (ed. Werner Sollers) (New York: W.W. Norton & Company, 2001; first published 1794), p. 20. All references will be to this edition.

15 Caretta, *Equiano the African*, pp. xvi, 2. Caretta points out that in Equiano's first years of life he is in a non-literate society and it is these years of life that are in doubt. Once he is in a literate society, and by that Caretta means a society with institutions that keep written records, like that of the Royal Navy, *The Interesting Narrative*, he declares, is 'remarkably consistent with the historical record'. Ibid., p. xvi.

16 Ibid., pp. xiv, xii.

17 Werner Sollers, 'Introduction' to *The Interesting Narrative of the Life of Olaudah Equiano, Or, Gustavus Vassa, The African, Written by Himself* (ed. Werner Sollers) (New York: W.W. Norton & Company, 2001), p. xxi.

18 Hall, 'Thinking Diaspora', p. 556; Michel Foucault, *The Foucault Reader* (ed. Paul Rabinow) (New York: Pantheon, 1984), p. 178.

19 Equiano, *The Interesting Narrative*, p. 37, my emphasis.

20 Roxanne Wheeler, *The Complexion of Race: Categories of Difference in Eighteenth-Century British Culture* (Philadelphia: University of Pennsylvania Press, 2000), p. 275.

21 Equiano, *The Interesting Narrative*, pp. 38–9.

22 Ibid., p. 39, emphasis added.

23 See the very rich and interesting account of the complex, contradictory and multiple nature of Equiano's affiliations in relation to his own slave trading and political involvement in the scheme to export the poverty-stricken black residents of London to Sierra Leone in Srinivas Aravamundan, *Tropicopolitans: Colonialism and Agency, 1688–1804* (Durham, NC: Duke University Press, 1999), pp. 233–88.

24 Wheeler, *The Complexion of Race*, p. 274, emphasis added.

25 'The multitude is composed of a set of *singularities* – and by singularity here we mean a social subject whose difference cannot be reduced to sameness, a difference that remains different.' Michael Hardt and Antonio Negri, *Multitude: War and Democracy in the Age of Empire* (New York: The Penguin Press, 2004), p. 99.

26 Wheeler, *The Complexion of Race*, p. 274.

27 George Lamming, *Natives of My Person* (London: Longman, 1974).

28 Ibid., pp. 16–17.

29 Joseph Conrad, *Heart of Darkness and Selections from The Congo Diary*, (New York: Modern Library, 1999), pp. 24, 25.

30 Pauline Melville, 'The President's Exile,' in *The Migration of Ghosts* (London: Bloomsbury, 2014).

31 Hall, 'When Was "the Post-colonial"?', pp. 246–7.

32 Conrad, *Heart of* Darkness, p. 26.

33 Maryse Condé, *I, Tituba, Black Witch of Salem* (New York: Ballantine Books, 1994).

34 Ibid., p. 3.

35 Hall, 'Thinking Diaspora', pp. 546–7.

36 Ibid., p. 543.

37 Stuart Hall, 'Racism and Reaction', in *Five Views of Multi-racial Britain* (London: Commission for Racial Equality), pp. 23–4, emphasis in original.

38 See Mary Chamberlain, *Narratives of Exile and Return* (London: Macmillan, 1997); Vivienne Francis, *With Hope in Their Eyes: The Compelling Stories of the Windrush Generation* (London: Nia, 1998); and Mike Phillips and Trevor Phillips, *Windrush: The Irresistible Rise of Multi-racial Britain* (London: HarperCollins, 1998). These are some of the most obvious choices but there are

many, many more, among them: Wendy Webster, *Imagining Home: Gender, 'Race' and National Identity, 1945–1964* (London: Routledge, 1998); Kwesi Owusu, *Black British Culture and Society* (London: Routledge, 2000); James Procter, *Writing Black Britain 1948–1998: An Interdisciplinary Anthology* (Manchester: Manchester University Press, 2000); and Yasmin Alibhai-Brown, *Imagining the New Britain* (New York: Routledge, 2001). See also the BBC 2 television production *Windrush*.

39 *Child of Empire* returns to the interwar years in order to juxtapose the stories of growing up in the colonial periphery and the imperial heartland, a story I will not go into here.

40 Tabili, *'We Ask for British Justice'*, argues, 'In the 1920s and 1930s racial categories and racial subordination were reconstituted on British soil.'

41 Stuart Hall, 'Inside the Whale Again', *Universities and Left Review*, vol. 4 (Summer 1958), 14.

42 Ian Spencer, 'World War Two and the Making of Multiracial Britain', in Pat Kirkham and David Thoms (eds.), *War Culture: Social Change and Changing Experience in World War Two* (London: Lawrence and Wishart, 1995), p. 212.

43 Marika Sherwood, *Many Struggles: West Indian Workers and Service Personnel in Britain (1939–1945)* (London: Karia Press, 1985); Spencer, 'World War Two and the Making of Multiracial Britain', p. 212.

44 David Reynolds, *Rich Relations: The American Occupation of Britain 1942–1945* (London: HarperCollins, 1996); Graham Smith, *When Jim Crow Met John Bull: Black American Soldiers in World War Two Britain* (London: I.B, Tauris & Co. Ltd, 1987).

45 Reynolds, *Rich Relations*, p. xxv.

46 Sherwood, *Many Struggles*, p. 58, emphasis in original.

47 Paul B. Rich, *Race and Empire in British Politics* (Cambridge: Cambridge University Press, 1990), p. 162.

48 Reynolds, *Rich Relations*, 1996 p. 217.

49 Ibid., *Rich Relations*, Smith, *When Jim Crow Met John Bull.*

50 Smith, *When Jim Crow Met John Bull*, pp. 37–8, 50–1; Reynolds, *Rich Relations*, p. 217.

51 Reynolds, *Rich Relations*, p. 217.

52 Ibid., p. 218, Smith, *When Jim Crow Met John Bull*, pp. 190–1.

53 Smith, *When Jim Crow Met John Bull*, p. 190.

54 Reynolds, *Rich Relations*, p. 220.

55 Rich, *Race and Empire in British Politics*, pp. 150–3. See also the reproduction of documents containing these discussions in Thomas Hachey, 'Jim Crow with a British Accent: Attitudes of

London Government Officials toward American Negro Soldiers in England during World War II', *Journal of Negro History*, vol. 59, no. 1 (January), pp. 65–77.

56 Reynolds, *Rich Relations*, pp. 218–19; see also Smith, *When Jim Crow Met John Bull*, pp. 52–3.

57 Smith, *When Jim Crow Met John Bull*, pp. 54–5.

58 Reynolds, *Rich Relations*, 1996 p. 222.

59 Ibid., pp. 222–3.

60 Ibid., pp. 223, 224.

61 Ibid., pp. 224–335.

62 Quoted in Rich, *Race and Empire in British Politics*, pp. 154–5. This is one of the few sources I have found to discuss how attitudes toward 'race' during the war are shaped in relation to both the Americans' and Britain's colonial policy. When Viscount Cranborne for the Colonial Office opposed the dissemination of the War Office's 'Notes on Relations with Coloured Troops' and resisted attempts 'to bend to American pressure', Rich argues, 'Policy on racial discrimination and the preservation of British colonial policy . . . were . . . for Cranborne, crucially linked, and for the first time in British government policy there was exhibited a far-reaching understanding of the inter-relationship between race and wider public policy in both Britain and the colonial empire'. Ibid., pp. 151, 153.

63 Michel Foucault, *Discipline and Punish* (New York: Vintage, 1995), p. 198.

64 Michel Foucault, *Power/Knowledge: Selected Interviews and Other Writings, 1972–1977* (ed. Colin Gordon) (New York: Pantheon, 1980), p. 39.

65 Rich, *Race and Empire in British Politics*, p. 152.

66 Hall, 'Racism and Reaction', p. 23.

67 M. E. Fletcher, *Report on an Investigation into the Colour Problem in Liverpool and other Ports* (Liverpool Association for the Welfare of Half-Caste Children, 1930); Tabili, *'We Ask for British Justice'*; Jacqueline Nassy Brown, *Dropping Anchor, Setting Sail: Geographies of Race in Black Liverpool* (Princeton, NJ: Princeton University Press, 2005).

68 Robert N. Murray, *Lest We Forget: The Experiences of World War II Westindian Ex-Service Personnel* (Nottingham: Nottingham WestIndian Combined Ex-Services Association, 1996), p. 101–3.

69 Ibid., pp. 110–12.

70 Ibid., pp. 160–1.

71 Personal correspondence.

72 Reynolds, *Rich Relations*, p. 229.
73 Ibid., p. 231.
74 Murray, *Lest We Forget*, p. 111.
75 Sonya O. Rose, 'Sex, Citizenship, and the Nation in World War Two Britain', *American Historical Review,* October 1998, p. 1147.
76 Ibid., p. 1164.
77 Smith, *When Jim Crow Met John Bull*, p. 195, emphasis in original.
78 This long and complex story forms a substantial section of my current work-in-progress, *Child of Empire*.
79 'The Babies They Left behind Them', *Life* magazine, 23 August 1948, p. 41.
80 Brown, *Dropping Anchor, Setting Sail*, p. 196.
81 Erwin Blumenfeld, 'The Lonely Piccaninny', 'The Lonely Models', *Picture Post*, 3 April 1948, p. 16; Vicki Goldberg, 'Finding a Camera and a New Career', *New York Times*, 19 November 1999, E2, p. 42.

16. Imperial Intimacies

1 Hazel V. Carby, *Imperial Intimacies: A Tale of Two Islands* (London: Verso, 2019), hereafter cited in the text.
2 See Eddie Chambers, 'Zippin' Up My Boots, Going Back to My Routes', *Small Axe*, 64, March 2021: pp. 186–97.
3 See Paolo Freire and Myra Bergman Ramos, *Pedagogy of the Oppressed* (New York: Herder and Herder, 1970).
4 Bob Marley, 'Redemption Song', on Bob Marley, *Uprising* (Tuff Gong/Island Records, 1980).
5 Centre for Contemporary Cultural Studies, *The Empire Strikes Back: Race and Racism in Seventies Britain* (London: Hutchinson, 1982). The preface (pp. 5–6) is written by Paul Gilroy, a member of the Race and Politics Group, and gives the history of the collective at the Centre for Contemporary Cultural Studies, University of Birmingham.
6 See Michel-Rolph Trouillot, *Silencing the Past: Power and the Production of History*, with foreword by Hazel V. Carby, 20th anniversary edn, repr. (Boston, MA: Beacon, 2015; first published 1995).
7 Marisa J. Fuentes, 'Genres of History and the Practice of Loss: Attending to Silence in Hazel Carby's *Imperial Intimacies*', *Small Axe*, 64, March 2021: pp. 167–74.

8 Marisa J. Fuentes, *Dispossessed Lives: Enslaved Women, Violence, and the Archive* (Philadelphia: University of Pennsylvania Press, 2016), p. 7, emphasis in original.

9 Manthia Diawara, 'One World in Relation: Édouard Glissant in Conversation with Manthia Diawara', trans. Christopher Winks, *NKA*, no. 28 (Spring 2011), p. 5.

10 Marc Matera, 'An Intimate History of Empire', *Small Axe*, 64, March 2021: p. 178.

11 *Imperial Intimacies* (London: Verso, 2019), p. 3.

12 I have written about this experience in greater detail elsewhere. See Hazel V. Carby, 'The National Archives', *InVisible Culture*, no. 31 (November 2020), at ivc.lib.rochester.edu.

17. The National Archives

1 'A poor life this if, full of care, / We have no time to stand and stare.' W. H. Davies, 'Leisure,' *The Collected Poems of W. H. Davies* (London: J. Cape, 1929). Davies was a Welsh poet my mother was fond of quoting.

2 Kei Miller, *The Cartographer Tries to Map a Way to Zion* (Manchester: Carcanet Press Limited, 2014), pp. 18–19.

3 T71/151/37.

4 T171/190/578; T171/196; Baptisms in Kingston, 14 May 1820, p. 356, Jamaica, Church of England Parish Register Transcripts, 1664–1880, Kingston, Jamaica, Registrar General's Department, Spanish Town, FHL microfilm 1,291,763; CO/137/162.

Index